The Hatherleigh Guide

to

Child and Adolescent Therapy

The Hatherleigh Guides series

The Hatherleigh Guide

to

Child and Adolescent Therapy

▣ Hatherleigh Press • New York

The Hatherleigh Guide to Child and Adolescent Therapy

Project Editor: Joya Lonsdale
Assistant Editors: Stacy Powell, Lori Soloman
Indexer: Angela Washington-Blair, PhD
Cover Designer: Gary Szczecina
Cover photo: Christopher Flach, PhD

Compiled under the auspices of the editorial boards of *Directions in Mental Health Counseling*, *Directions in Clinical Psychology*, and *Directions in Rehabilitation Counseling*.

Library of Congress Cataloging-in-Publication Data

The Hatherleigh guide to child and adolescent therapy — 1st ed.
      p. cm. — (The Hatherleigh guides series ; 5)
      Includes bibliographical references and index.
      ISBN 1-886330-46-8 (alk. paper)
      1. Child psychotherapy. 2. Adolescent psychotherapy. I. Series: Hatherleigh
    guides to mental health practice series; v. 5.
RC456.H38 1995 vol. 5
[RJ504]
616.89 s—dc20
[618.92' 8914]   96-21525
                                                                                  CIP

First Edition: July 1996

10 9 8 7 6 5 4 3 2 1

About the photograph and the photographer

Malcolm, 1995
A little boy finds comfort under the safe harbor of towering bamboo.

Christopher Flach, PhD, is a psychologist in private practice in southern California. An avid photographer for more than 20 years, his favorite subjects include people and nature. He has studied photography with Ansel Adams, and his work has been on display in public galleries and in private collections.

Table of Contents

Illustrations

Introduction

With the profound changes that have occurred in the field of child and adolescent therapy in recent years, the task of keeping current has assumed epic proportions for most busy clinicians. Compounding this challenge is the fact that most mental health practitioners are "generalists," requiring that they stay abreast of a rapidly expanding literature across a wide spectrum of disorders and therapies. Today's practitioner does not have time to go meandering down every path suggested by the literature in the vague hope that something useful will be found along the way. Rather, the modern clinician needs to be able to hop onto an information superhighway, clear about the destination and assured at the beginning of the journey that it will be time well spent.

The Hatherleigh Guide to Child and Adolescent Therapy will be a valuable traveling companion for the practitioner. The contributing authors address some of the most critical concerns of the clinician in a broad range of topics encompassing various diagnostic groups, therapeutic approaches, and practical issues. The scope is broad, from work with preschoolers to adolescents, from disorders that are considered biopsychosocial in nature, such as attention-deficit/hyperactivity disorder, to conditions that are environmental, such as homelessness. The interventions presented are equally broad reaching, representing a number of theoretical orientations and including a variety of individual and group therapies. The chapters are practical; they present detailed case studies and concise guidelines for understanding different diagnostic groups and for providing therapy.

This book can be broadly divided into chapters discussing conditions or diagnoses and those dealing with interventions.

In all the chapters dealing with specific conditions or diagnostic groups, the importance of achieving diagnostic clarity is emphasized. Alayne Yates, in her presentation on anxiety, notes that anxiety disorders are among the most commonly occurring, yet underdiagnosed, disorders in children. The significance of appropriate diagnosis is magnified by the fact that the prognosis for most anxiety disorders, with the exception of separation anxiety disorder and social phobia, is good. One might *assume* that anxiety would be a common emotion in children without homes; however, in their timely chapter on homelessness, Janet Wagner and colleagues also underscore the importance of sound diagnosis. They describe the significant emotional difficulties often experienced by homeless children and discuss the pervasive impact that persistent depression may have on these children.

The need for critical thinking and solid clinical judgment in diagnostic decisions is also stressed by Barry Sarvet, in his discussion of depression, as well as by James Brown, in his work on adolescent suicide. The relationship between depression and suicide is complex, but despite an association, all depressed adolescents are not suicidal. The importance of immediate and appropriate intervention for both depressed and suicidal youth is stressed by both authors.

The chapters dealing with therapies present structured, directive, and brief approaches. Therapists must be aware of such time-limited interventions and use them when appropriate. Ann Hazzard's chapter on therapy and prevention activities for sexually abused children provides two excellent models for conceptualizing the psychological sequelae of sexual molestation on children. Dr. Hazzard and her colleagues have spearheaded the Recovery from Abuse Project, a clinical research project for sexually abused girls and nonoffending caretakers. The program presents a brief, psychoeducational intervention that includes therapy and prevention skills.

Sam Goldstein's chapter on attention-deficit/hyperactivity disorder (ADHD) includes a wealth of information about nonpharmacologic therapeutic interventions for this complex disorder. The mental health aspect relies heavily on a structured therapeutic protocol that includes a comprehensive psychoeducational component. So much has been written about the medical management of ADHD, it is useful to have a concise description of the full range of mental health services that can be used by this population.

My own work, which adapts cognitive-behavioral therapy and integrates it with more traditional play therapies, presents cognitive-behavioral play therapy as a directive, structured approach to treating preschool-age children. All three of these structured therapeutic approaches are also psychoeducational in focus, as is Seth Aronson and Saul Scheidlinger's work on group therapy for adolescents. Aronson and Scheidlinger note that adolescents function best with explicit limits and rules. They also discuss the cost effectiveness of group treatment with this population. The consideration of cost effectiveness of treatment is more informally considered in my own chapter, as well as in the chapters by Hazzard and Goldstein, respectively.

As therapists, we tend to focus on interventions for individuals who have already found their way to our offices. Yet, our expertise also should be geared toward helping at-risk children, including those from families unlikely to seek our services. As we strive for this broader understanding of what makes some children more resilient than others to forces that may cause psychological damage, our efforts to reach all children in need may, in turn, become more inclusive. Dr. Wagner and her colleagues highlight these concerns in their discussion of the protective factors that may help a homeless child be more resilient to the negative sequelae of being without a home. They note that one of the most important protective factors is the child's ability to process negative experiences cognitively. As we come to understand more clearly the factors that help a child adaptively process such difficult information, the significance of structuring thinking in a positive, adaptive way — one of the hallmarks of cognitive therapy — is highlighted.

Cognitive therapy, a unique system of psychotherapy, is supported by substantial empirical data. The chapters focusing on interventions exemplify the broad range of potential uses of this form of therapy. Its versatility is highlighted by its application to a wide range of ages (preschool to adolescent) and populations (sexually abused, aggressive, and suicidal youth).

This book challenges the reader to think about the practice of child and adolescent psychotherapy in the 1990s and beyond. For example, David Kirschner's discussion of adoption highlights the ways that issues, such as closed versus open adoptions, have been challenged over the past several decades. In fact, policies have been altered as a result of many of the changes in our understanding of advocacy for adopted children, and their birth and adoptive families.

Important resource materials are presented throughout the book. Many of these resources are in the form of bibliotherapy or videotapes, such as those suggested for sexually abused (Hazzard) and adopted (Kirschner) children. Many of the authors also provide structured treatment protocols to be used by clinicians. Examples include those on sexual abuse (Hazzard), ADHD (Goldstein), and aggressive youth (Glick).

In his chapter on protecting the confidentiality of children and adolescents, Edward Bartlett raises questions related to confidentiality that will challenge even the most cautious practitioner among us. Who has never pondered about what is appropriate to tell parents about their child's progress in therapy? Who can state with certainty that he or she has never worked in a setting where one patient might inadvertently see the name of another known patient on a desk or schedule book, or actually see an acquaintance or colleague in a waiting area? And if these relatively basic situations do not challenge us, Dr. Bartlett argues that the introduction of utilization review and case management potentially compromises the integrity of confidentiality for clients. Moreover, the use of computers in office management raises multiple questions about confidentiality.

Practitioners should be constantly in search of research-based findings as well as practical clinical applications. Many chapters describe innovative clinical research projects, such as the Recovery from Abuse Project (Hazzard); the Columbus, Ohio studies of homeless children (Wagner et al.); and the Youth Center projects, which implemented the Aggression Replacement Training (Glick).

The integration of clinical and research findings is stressed by James Brown in his discussion of the importance of empirically based indicators of suicide and the need for practitioners to stay current as new findings are disseminated. It is precisely such a dissemination of timely research and clinical expertise that *The Hatherleigh Guide to Child and Adolescent Therapy* accomplishes. A book with the most recent findings and critical syntheses of those findings will be an invaluable addition to the clinician's resource shelf.

In the rapidly changing world of mental health care, knowledge is critical, and keeping current a necessity. Staying abreast the latest research is challenging, but not impossible. From the graduate trainee to the seasoned therapist, this book will help the clinician at all levels of experience reduce that task to more manageable proportions.

Susan M. Knell, PhD
Cleveland, Ohio

Dr. Knell is Adjunct Assistant Professor, Cleveland State University; and Lecturer, Case Western Reserve University, Cleveland, OH.

1

Anxiety Disorders in Children and Adolescents

Alayne Yates, MD

Dr. Yates is Professor of Psychiatry at the University of Hawaii, Honolulu, HI.

KEY POINTS

- The anxiety disorders may be the most common—but least recognized—disorders in children and adolescents.

- In early life, anxiety disorders should only be diagnosed when the child is unable to function or is overwhelmed and experiencing extreme distress.

- Symptoms of anxiety disorders include excessive fear, worry, anticipatory dread, phobic avoidance, panic attacks, tachycardia, palpitations, headaches, nausea, dizziness, and fainting.

- In the DSM-IV, the only anxiety disorder listed under "disorders usually first diagnosed in infancy, childhood, or adolescence" is separation anxiety disorder. Adult anxiety disorder diagnoses also can be applied to younger clients.

- When making an assessment for anxiety in a child or adolescent client, it is essential to talk directly to the client as well as the parents to ascertain what biologic or environmental factors may be involved. Collaboration with babysitters, extended family members, and teachers may also be helpful.

- The characteristics of specific disorders are discussed, including prevalence rates, etiology, symptoms, and level of difficulty to treat.

- In most cases, anxiety disorders respond well to therapy, with or without medication.

BACKGROUND INFORMATION

Anxiety, which can be defined as an unrealistic sense of danger (Livingston, 1991), is common in childhood and adolescence and is usually not associated with psychopathology. In fact, teachers may try to increase the anxiety level of certain students so that they will learn more efficiently. Eventually, some children and adolescents discover they can study longer and harder if they make themselves anxious by anticipating failure. An anxiety *disorder* should only be diagnosed when the child is (a) overwhelmed and experiencing extreme distress or (b) unable to function. An example would be a child who refuses to attend school because he or she might be called on to answer a question in front of the class.

Symptoms of an anxiety disorder include excessive fear, worry, anticipatory dread, phobic avoidance, and panic attacks with autonomic diathesis. Autonomic symptoms include tachycardia, palpitations, blushing, perspiration, paresthesia (an abnormal sensation such as burning or tingling), blotchy rash, muscular tension, tremor, nausea, diarrhea, abdominal pain, headaches, chest pain, dizziness, and fainting (Livingston, 1991). Specific fears identified by anxious children involve kidnapping, strangers, being left alone, animals, drains, vacuums, being hurt, germs/illness, getting lost, blood, darkness, fire, heights, insects, snakes, and thunderstorms. A predominant fear of separation usually indicates a separation anxiety disorder; fear of strangers suggests avoidant disorder; and fear of social humiliation is indicative of social phobia. Other clearly delineated fears typically suggest simple phobia.

A clear developmental progression evolves in the symptoms of anxiety (Silver, 1979). Infants can express anxiety through restlessness and irritability. Indicators of separation anxiety emerge at about 9 months of age. In preschool, children begin to complain of specific fears (Rutter, Tizard, & Whitmore, 1970). Normal preschoolers can have separation anxiety and may be afraid of kidnapping, strangers, or being left alone. They may also fear animals, being sucked into a drain, or being sucked up by a vacuum cleaner. In early grade school, children worry about pain and physical injury. In the latter part of grade school, some children begin to fear failure in school or criticism from parents or peers. Normal adolescents often are anxious about being accepted by same-age mates and being able to become independent. However, true social phobia rarely develops before mid-to-late adolescence (Marshall, 1993).

The anxiety disorders are perhaps the most common (Bernstein & Borchardt, 1991) and least recognized (Costello, 1989) disorders of early life. Parents often underestimate children's anxiety because children rarely talk about their concerns, most likely because they often view their anxiety as a sign of weakness. Such children are apt to be compliant and cooperative. They do their best to please adults and, therefore, may carry unrealistically high self-expectations. Moreover, because children feel ashamed about being afraid, a discrepancy may develop between their ratings of their own anxiety and that of their parents. This creates a problem for researchers who assess anxiety by asking parents to complete checklists about their children. So far, almost all studies have been designed in this manner; as a consequence, they may grossly underestimate the prevalence of anxiety in children. Interview-based studies would be likely to identify more children who warrant a diagnosis of anxiety disorder than had been previously thought.

The best estimate of the prevalence of anxiety disorders in childhood and adolescence is 9% (Costello, 1989; Kashani & Orvaschel, 1990), with lifetime prevalence rates of 13% (Kessler et al., 1994). One third of these teenagers meet the criteria for two or more anxiety disorders. Nearly 69% of children and adolescents with an anxiety disorder also meet criteria for a major depressive disorder (Bernstein & Borchardt, 1991; Mitchell, McCauley, Burke, & Moss, 1988). Not surprisingly, anxiety and depressive disorders are closely related, and many of the symptoms overlap.

The anxiety disorders demonstrate significant comorbidity with major depression (Bernstein & Borchardt, 1991; de Misquita & Gillian, 1994). Approximately 17% of children (Anderson, Williams, McGee, & Silva, 1987) and 12% of adolescents (McGee et al., 1990) with anxiety disorder also qualify for major depressive disorder. Conversely, 40% of youngsters with major depression are diagnosed with an anxiety disorder, usually separation anxiety disorder (Kovacs, Gatsonis, Paulauskas, & Richards, 1989). Children and adolescents who present with both diagnoses are older and less healthy than those with only an anxiety disorder (Bernstein & Borchardt, 1989; Strauss, Last, Hersen, & Kazdin, 1988). A weaker association is evident with attention-deficit/hyperactivity disorder (ADHD) (Anderson et al., 1987; Last, Hersen, Kazdin, Finkelstein, & Strauss, 1987; McClellan, Rubert, Riechler, & Sylvester, 1990), and anxiety disordered girls are somewhat more likely than other girls to develop social phobia (Klein & Last, 1989).

The prognosis is fairly good in the anxiety disorders, with the exception of separation anxiety disorder and social phobia. Children often move in and out of these conditions. They are likely to continue to have problems with shyness and to be afraid of many things, but they usually develop into perfectly normal (albeit anxious) adults (Zeitlin, 1986). A few adolescents follow a pattern of many remissions and exacerbations into adulthood (Bernstein, 1991). In addition, a subgroup of youngsters continue to have significant problems with anxiety and depression (Keller et al., 1992); a greater-than-expected number develop an anxiety disorder in adulthood (Klein & Last, 1989). The existence of separation anxiety disorder seems to predict the emergence of multiple anxiety disorder diagnoses later on (Lipsitz et al., 1994).

The relationship between anxiety disorders in children and anxiety disorders in adults is hotly debated. Parents with an anxiety disorder do seem to be more likely than other parents to produce anxious children (Bernstein & Borchardt, 1991;

Bernstein & Garfinkel, 1988). Children of agoraphobic parents are seven times more likely to become afflicted with an anxiety disorder themselves (Turner, Beidel, & Costello, 1987), and the presence of anxiety disorders and major depression is correlated in certain families (Leckman, Weissman, Merikangas, Pauls, & Prusoff, 1983). However, with the exception of some simple phobias, most adults with an anxiety disorder indicate that they became anxious during adulthood (Robins, 1971).

DIAGNOSIS

In the *Diagnostic and Statistical Manual of Mental Disorders* (DSM-IV) (American Psychiatric Association, 1994), the only anxiety disorder listed under "disorders usually first diagnosed in infancy, childhood, or adolescence" is separation anxiety disorder. Other diagnoses are listed in the adult section with the understanding that they can be used for children and adolescents. Other adult diagnoses for which youngsters may qualify are panic attack, agoraphobia (extremely rare before adulthood), panic disorder without agoraphobia, specific phobia, social phobia, obsessive-compulsive disorder, posttraumatic stress disorder, acute stress disorder, generalized anxiety disorder, anxiety disorder due to a medical condition, substance-induced anxiety disorder, and anxiety disorder not otherwise specified.

The diagnostic categories reflect the strong biologic trend of the field. Neurobiologic factors are featured in the diagnostic criteria for panic disorder, obsessive-compulsive disorder, and posttraumatic stress disorder. Generalized anxiety disorder highlights autonomic hyperreactivity, vigilance, and muscular tension. The emphasis on the biologic may exclude certain children from these anxiety disorder diagnoses. However, they may be considered for anxiety disorder not otherwise specified or an adjustment disorder.

ETIOLOGY

The predisposition for developing an anxiety disorder is related to environmental and biologic factors. Children and adolescents with an anxiety disorder report a greater number of past stressors than do children and adolescents with other diagnoses (Costello, 1989; McGee et al., 1990). The manner in which parents and guardians respond to stress is important because they are role models. For example, they may be acutely sensitive to signs of anxiety in their child(ren); and when they notice anxiety in their child(ren), they may inadvertently reinforce the anxious response.

Kagan and colleagues (1984) described a group of behaviorally inhibited, timid 2-year-old children. They continued to be overly cautious; they withdrew when challenged and responded to minor stress with a marked, sustained increase in heart rate. By age 8, they were more likely to be afraid of crowds, strangers, and public speaking. Kagan suggested that these children were more likely to develop an anxiety disorder. Other researchers note that the parents of inhibited children are more likely than other parents to suffer from agoraphobia or panic disorder (Rosenbaum, Biederman, Hirshfeld, Bolduc, & Chaloff, 1991). Inhibited children do seem to be at greater risk for developing an anxiety disorder later on (Biederman et al., 1993). With this knowledge, it may be possible to devise early prevention programs to prevent the disorder from developing.

Biologic research in children is limited by ethical concerns. We know that in adults, anxiety seems to be generated in certain sites of the central nervous system. Panic attacks are associated with increased activity in the brainstem, especially the pons; anticipatory anxiety is associated with activity in the limbic system and cingulate gyrus; phobic avoidance is linked with activity in the prefrontal cortex (Gorman, Liebowitz, & Fyer, 1989). The central neurotransmitters most involved are γ-aminobutyric acid (GABA), serotonin, and norepinephrine. Peripheral mechanisms involve epinephrine release, increased cortisol concentration; and dysfunctional regulation of the autonomic nervous system.

ASSESSMENT

Assessment must include talking directly to the child as well as to the parent. Children with anxiety disorder often stay awake at night worrying about burglars, harm to parents, or their performance in school, *but they may not mention these fears to parents.* Ask children and adolescents about their experiences of separating from parents such as sleepovers or summer camp. Inquire about reactions to divorce, family illness, and changes in babysitters or other caretakers. Determine if a family history of anxiety, depression, or alcohol abuse exists. Note current closeness to, or dependence on, one parent. Note where children sleep and the presence of infantile behaviors. Assess the parents' achievement orientation and how strongly it is conveyed to the child(ren). Look for impending changes, such as a parent threatening divorce, a parent in danger of general medical hospitalization (e.g., because of asthma), or plans for a geographic move.

On the mental status examination, anxious children and adolescents may demonstrate shame, indecisiveness, performance anxiety, and perfectionistic tendencies. They may need continued reassurance from the examiner to complete the task. On the other hand, anxious youngsters who are also immature can be demanding, petulant, and controlling.

Clinicians may wish to use a self-report questionnaire to assess the child and track progress in therapy. The most common anxiety-specific scales are the Revised Children's Manifest Anxiety Scale (RCMAS) (Mattison & Bagnato, 1987) and the State-Trait Anxiety Inventory for Children (STAIC) (Spielberger, 1973). The RCMAS is a simple, useful scale, but it does not clearly differentiate anxiety from depression. The STAIC is effective in differentiating emotionally disturbed children from those who are considered normal but anxious.

COLLABORATION

Talking to babysitters, extended family members, and teachers can provide important information about how the child behaves away from home, how much the child experiences stress due to the need to achieve, and how much the child is (or is not) struggling to individuate from an enmeshed family. Forming an alliance with the teacher can be particularly helpful in the treatment of school refusal. In all cases, the therapist must have prior permission from the custodial parent(s) before speaking with the child's teacher or other informant.

Creative interventions at home, in school, and in the community are needed to treat anxiety-disordered children. An example can be seen in the case of a shy 14-year-old boy who stayed at home because he was terrified of being beaten up at school, although the worst that had happened in the past were taunts and a punch on the arm. By the time he was seen by a psychiatrist, he had already lost a semester and had been placed on home tutoring. The psychiatrist arranged for reentry into school, school counselor involvement, and a schedule change; a supervised community service activity to fill the after-school hours; and an increase in the boy's weekend activities with his father. More activities with his father became a reward for successful school attendance.

SPECIFIC DISORDERS

Separation Anxiety Disorder:

Separation anxiety disorder becomes evident sooner than the other anxiety disorders and is more likely to occur in white children of slightly lower socioeconomic status who are raised in single-parent homes (Last, Perrin, Hersen, & Kazdin, 1992; Strauss et al., 1988). The prevalence rate is 3.5%–5.4% (Costello, 1989), and the mean age of onset is 9.1 years (Bernstein & Borchardt, 1991). Separation anxiety disorder begins sooner than overanxious disorder (Last, Francis, Hersen, Kazdin, &

Strauss, 1987), and the number of children affected diminishes by adolescence (Kashani & Orvaschel, 1990). These children tend to worry about getting lost, getting sick, or being stung by a bee (Ollendick, Matson, & Helsel, 1985). They worry that their parents might be harmed and they often have trouble falling asleep. Three fourths of these children manifest school or camp refusal (Last et al., 1987). Because they are dependent on adults, they tend to have poor peer relationships. Although somatic complaints are present in many disorders, they are most consistently found in separation anxiety disorder. These children present an average of eight somatic complaints; abdominal pain and palpitations are the most frequent (Livingston, 1991).

Symptoms must be present at least 4 weeks for a child to qualify for a diagnosis of separation anxiety disorder. The child must exhibit three or more of the following criteria:

- Excessive distress when separated from parents

- Unrealistic worry about harm to parents

- Unrealistic worry about harm to self

- School refusal or preference to remain at home

- Reluctance to sleep alone or away from home

- Avoidance of being alone

- Recurrent nightmares about separation

- Somatic complaints

- Extreme distress at time of separation

Separation anxiety disorder must be differentiated from normal separation anxiety and overanxious disorder; in older children and adolescents, it must be differentiated from truancy and conduct disorder. Risk factors include small families, past illness with separation, illness or death in the family, divorce, moving to a different house, and the combination of ADHD and a learning disability. Separation anxiety disorders have far-reaching consequences for many children although the prognosis is better if the child is young and the symptoms are mild. These disorders can remit spontaneously, but half the patients continue to have significant problems in adulthood, such as chronic anxiety, constricted interests and activities, and persistent problems with school attendance (Herzov, 1985; Livingston, 1991). Many adults with agoraphobia report having had separation anxiety in childhood (Gittleman, 1986; Zitrin & Ross, 1988). Kagan and colleagues (1984) reported that 15% of children and adolescents with separation anxiety disorder have been hospitalized for a psychiatric disorder at least once before reaching maturity. Separation anxiety is often found as a basis for panic disorder and major depression in adults (Kagan et al., 1984).

Separation anxiety disorder is the most serious and difficult to treat of all the anxiety disorders during childhood. It demonstrates substantial comorbidity with depression (Kagan et al., 1984) and with other anxiety disorders (Klein & Last, 1989). Effective treatment often demands combination of parent counseling, behavior modification, individual therapy, pharmacotherapy, and school intervention (Bernstein & Shaw, 1993).

Occasionally, children with separation anxiety disorder must be hospitalized or placed in residential treatment to effect separation from the parents and the development of age-appropriate peer relationships. Although it may be necessary, separation is extraordinarily difficult for all concerned. Parents feel guilty, and children can become acutely depressed and angry. Parents may abruptly remove children from treatment at this stage; therefore, they need therapy and support during this difficult transition. Court involvement is an option of last resort when parents are unable or unwilling to insist that the child return to school.

Although tricyclic antidepressant pharmacotherapy was once thought to be efficacious in the treatment of separation anxiety disorder (Gittleman, 1986), recent studies have yielded equivocal results (Ambrosini, Bianchi, Rabinovich, & Elia, 1993; Klein, Koplewicz, & Kanner, 1992). Brief courses of benzodiazepines or antihistamines have also been used.

Generalized Anxiety Disorder:

Generalized anxiety disorder (GAD) which includes over-anxious disorder of childhood, usually develops when a child is in grades 3 to 6; its prevalence rate is 2.7%–4.6% (Costello, 1989). The gender distribution is approximately equal (Last, Hersen et al., 1987), but by adolescence, girls may predominate (Bowen, Offord, & Boyle, 1990). Less severe cases are linked to parental anxiety disorders (Last et al., 1987; Werry, 1991), but more severe cases are linked to parental depression and alcoholism (Livingston, 1991).

To warrant the diagnosis, the patient must exhibit four of the following six symptoms for a duration of more than 6 months:

- Restlessness or feeling on edge

- Easily fatigued

- Difficulty concentrating

- Irritability

- Muscle tension

- Difficulty falling or staying asleep, or restless sleep

Children and adolescents with GAD tend to be needy, self-conscious, and covertly controlling. They worry about past, present, and, especially, future disasters. They are often unable to relax and may present somatic complaints such as headache or abdominal pain (Livingston, 1991). Older children present more complaints than do younger children (McGee et al., 1990). They tend to be only children or first-born children in small, child-centered families.

Two family patterns are identified in GAD. In the first, the parents stress academic, sports, and other types of achievement (Adler, Bongar, & Katz, 1982). In the second, the parents are unable to set limits and the child becomes an angry, depressed, controlling "monster" (Barcai & Rosenthal, 1974). Treatment must be individualized accordingly.

The differential diagnosis includes hyperthyroidism and excessive use of caffeine or other stimulants (Bernstein & Shaw, 1993; Livingston, 1991). Approximately half the children and adolescents with GAD warrant an additional anxiety disorder diagnosis, most commonly simple phobia (Last, Hersen, et al., 1987). Children and adolescents with overanxious disorder are at risk for developing major depression (but not dysthymia) or bipolar disorder (Bernstein & Garfinkel, 1988; Last, Francis et al., 1987; Last, Hersen et al., 1987; Last et al., 1992; McGee et al., 1990). Those who exhibit extreme adverse or obnoxious behavior may qualify for oppositional-defiant disorder. GAD waxes and wanes; gradual improvement occurs in most instances.

Individual and family psychotherapy is the treatment of choice for GAD (Livingston, 1991). Depending on the situation, parents will need to decrease their expectations of the child's performance or set consistent, age-appropriate limits. The child will need to develop more reasonable self-expectations or gradually forfeit infantile omnipotence. Other therapeutic approaches include cognitive-behavioral therapy, relaxation training, activity group therapy, summer camp, role playing, and play therapy. Although psychopharmacologic research is sadly lacking, case studies suggest that administration of tricyclic antidepressants or short-term benzodiazepine can be useful when appropriate (Bernstein & Shaw, 1993).

Phobias:

Three phobias are described in DSM-IV: agoraphobia, specific phobia, and social phobia. (These have only recently been examined in children.) The prevalence rate of phobias in childhood is 2.3%–9.2% (Costello, 1989). Agoraphobia rarely, if ever, occurs in childhood. Specific phobia can begin in the preschool years, whereas social phobia does not develop until adolescence or young adulthood. Specific phobia is more common in girls, whereas social phobia occurs more frequently in boys. Fear of food or of becoming fat may indicate an eating disorder rather than a specific phobia.

True phobias are far less common in childhood than are the "normative" fears of animals, blood, darkness, fire, germs, heights, insects, strangers, snakes, and thunder (Ollendick et al., 1985). Specific phobias are irrational, extreme, but circumscribed fears. Examples include being hit by a car, being unable to breathe, getting bombed, being burned, falling from a high place, being burglarized, getting caught in an earthquake, or being killed. Exposure to the feared situation invariably provokes a panic response. Unless another psychopathologic disorder is present, simple phobia usually disappears whether or not the child receives treatment.

Social phobia is an intense, irrational, persistent fear of scrutiny or evaluation by others, with anticipation of humiliation or being made to appear ridiculous. Patients tend to focus on a specific social situation, such as public speaking, eating in public, attending parties, or competing in front of peers. The full syndrome rarely develops prior to adolescence (Marshall, 1993), yet the lifetime prevalence rate in the general population is 13%, with the onset usually occurring before age 18 (Judd, 1994). When most social circumstances are avoided, the diagnosis is more likely to be either avoidant personality disorder or schizotypal disorder. Social phobia follows a chronic, unrelenting course, often complicated by depression, substance abuse, or, less frequently, school dropout. Approximately 32% of persons with social phobia do not marry, 36% marry but later divorce, and 20% are reported to be on social welfare (Fishbein, Middlestadt, & Ottati, 1988).

Judd (1994) suggests that social phobia is a familial disease with a genetic basis, presenting in childhood as behavioral inhibition. Trower & Gilbert (1989) suggest that social phobias are formulated reactions that are "hard wired" in the brain. Patients are programmed to perceive social situations in terms of a dominance-submission hierarchy. In social gatherings, they immediately feel threatened with catastrophic loss of status, criticism, or humiliation. They may try to escape, avoid the situation completely, or become disorganized and make mistakes.

Specific phobias are best treated by cognitive-behavioral techniques such as relaxation training and systematic desensitization (Gelernter, Uhde, & Cimbolic, 1991) (Table 1.1). Tricyclic antidepressants and monoamine oxidase inhibitors (MAOIs) may be helpful, but research studies are lacking. In adults, social phobias are treated with β-blockers such as atenolol (Tenormin) and propranolol (Inderal) for a single major fear like performance anxiety. MAOIs such as phenelzine (Nardil) have the best demonstrated efficacy for generalized fear, but dietary restrictions to prevent hypertension and such adverse affects as weight gain, hypotension, and sedation must be considered carefully (Schneier, 1994). Other drugs that have demonstrated effectiveness in controlled studies are the benzodiazepines alprazolam (Xanax) and clonazepam (Klonopin) (Schneier, 1994). Selective serotonin reuptake inhibitors (SSRIs) (e.g., fluoxetine [Prozac], sertraline [Zoloft], and paroxetine [Paxil]), bupropion (Wellbutrin), buspirone (BuSpar), and clonidine (Catapres) are currently under intense study but have not proven effective (Ambrosini et al., 1993; Fishbein et al., 1988).

Panic Disorder:

No reports of panic disorder in children were published before 1987. Although there have been nearly 100 cases reported since 1987, the true prevalence of panic disorder in childhood remains a mystery. Panic disorder usually develops after the onset of puberty (Klein & Last, 1989); most cases are evaluated and treated by pediatricians who treat adolescents.

Table 1.1
COGNITIVE-BEHAVIORAL TREATMENT
FOR SOCIAL PHOBIA

1. Assess cognitive, behavioral, and physiologic components
2. Detail feared situations, modifying characteristics
3. Present model of anxiety
4. Use management techniques such as relaxation
5. Develop cognitive reframing strategies
6. Begin graded exposure

Panic disorder has a significant comorbidity with major depression, separation anxiety disorder, social phobia (Klein & Last, 1989), and borderline (Alessi, Robbins, & Dilsaver, 1987) or other personality disorders (Pollack, Otto, Rosenbaum, & Sachs, 1992). Panic attacks can be triggered by exposure to the feared stimuli, sleep deprivation, dieting, exercise, hyperventilation, caffeine, alcohol, cocaine, nicotine, and over-the-counter cold medication (Bradley & Hood, 1993).

Panic disorder can be distinguished from separation anxiety disorder by the nature of the fear (in separation anxiety disorder, the fear relates to separation, whereas in panic disorder it does not) and the nature of the complaint (patients with separation anxiety have somatic complaints, whereas patients with panic disorder display autonomic symptoms). Children with panic disorder complain about shortness of breath, palpitations, chest pain, choking, dizziness, sweating, trembling, and faintness—just as adult patients do.

In adults, a biologic basis for panic disorder has been established through family studies, infusion techniques, inhalation experiments, and drug responses. Possible biologic causes are respiratory center hypersensitivity, central noradrenergic hypersensitivity, and decreased serotonergic tone (Gorman et al., 1989). One study that attempted to isolate biologic markers in children at risk for panic disorder because their parents suffered with the disorder did not yield statistically significant results, although investigators found a trend toward higher catecholamine levels and greater monoamine oxidase activity in the at-risk youngsters (Reichler, Sylvester, & Hyde, 1988).

CONCLUSION

The anxiety disorders of childhood and adolescence are better recognized and treated than they were a decade ago. Clearly, these are common, serious disorders that have been underdiagnosed because children are reluctant to talk about their symptoms. Biologic and environmental factors both contribute to a young person's proclivity toward a given disorder. Some disorders, such as separation anxiety disorder and social phobia, are difficult to treat and can carry a poor prognosis. However, most anxiety disorders respond well to therapy, with or without medication.

REFERENCES

Adler, R., Bongar, B., & Katz, E. R. (1982). Psychogenic abdominal pain and parental pressure in childhood athletics. *Psychosomatics, 23,* 1185–1186.

Alessi, N. E., Robbins, D. R., & Dilsaver, S. C. (1987). Panic and depressive disorders among psychiatric hospitalized adolescents. *Psychiatry Research, 20,* 275–283.

Ambrosini, P. J., Bianchi, M. D., Rabinovich, H., & Elia, J. (1993). Antidepressant treatments in children and adolescents, II: Anxiety, physical, and behavioral disorders. *Journal of the American Academy of Child and Adolescent Psychiatry, 32,* 483–493.

American Psychiatric Association. (1994). *Diagnostic and statistical manual of mental disorders* (4th ed.). Washington, DC: Author.

Anderson, J. C., Williams, S., McGee, R., & Silva, P. A. (1987). DSM-III disorders in preadolescent children: Prevalence in a large sample from the general population. *Archives of General Psychiatry, 44*, 69–76.

Barcai, A., & Rosenthal, M. K. (1974). Fears and tyranny: Observations on the tyrannical child. *Archives of General Psychiatry, 30*, 392–395.

Bernstein, G. A. (1991). Comorbidity and severity of anxiety and depressive disorders in a clinic sample. *Journal of the American Academy of Child and Adolescent Psychiatry, 30*, 43–50.

Bernstein, G. A., & Borchardt, C. M. (1991). Anxiety disorders of childhood and adolescence: A critical review. *Journal of the American Academy of Child and Adolescent Psychiatry, 30*, 519–532.

Bernstein, G. A., & Garfinkel, B. D. (1988). Pedigrees, functioning, and psychopathology in families of school phobic children. *American Journal of Psychiatry, 145*, 70–74.

Bernstein, G., & Shaw, K. (1993). AACAP practice parameters for the assessment and treatment of the anxiety disorders. *Journal of the American Academy of Child and Adolescent Psychiatry, 32*, 1089–1098.

Biederman, J., Rosenbaum, J. F., Bolduc-Murphy, E. A., Farone, S. V., Chaloff, J., Hirshfeld, D. R., & Kagan, J. (1993). A 3-year follow-up of children with and without behavioral inhibition. *Journal of the American Academy of Child and Adolescent Psychiatry, 32*, 814–821.

Bowen, R. C., Offord, D. R., & Boyle, M. H. (1990). The prevalence of overanxious disorder and separation anxiety disorder: Results from the Ontario child health study. *Journal of the American Academy of Child and Adolescent Psychiatry, 29*, 753–758.

Bradley, S. J., & Hood, J. (1993). Psychiatrically referred adolescents with panic attacks: Presenting symptoms, stressors, and comorbidity. *Journal of the American Academy of Child and Adolescent Psychiatry, 32*, 826–829.

Costello, E. J. (1989). Developments in child psychiatric epidemiology. *Journal of the American Academy of Child and Adolescent Psychiatry, 28*, 836–841.

de Misquita, P. B., & Gillian, W. S. (1994). Differential diagnosis of childhood depression: Using comorbidity and symptom overlap to generate multiple hypotheses. *Child Psychiatry and Human Development, 24*, 157-172.

Fishbein, M., Middlestadt, S. E., & Ottati, V. (1988). Medical problems among ICSOM musicians: An overview of a national survey. *Medical Problems of Performing Artists, 3*, 1-8.

Gelernter, C. S., Uhde, T. W., & Cimbolic, P. (1991). Cognitive-behavioral and pharmacologic treatment of social phobia: A controlled study. *Archives of General Psychiatry, 48*, 938-945.

Gittleman, R. (1986). *Anxiety disorders of childhood.* New York: Guilford Press.

Gorman, J. M., Liebowitz, M. R., & Fyer, A. J. (1989). A neuroanatomical hypothesis for panic disorder. *American Journal of Psychiatry, 146*, 148-161.

Herzov, L. (1985). School refusal. In M. Rutter & L. Herzov (Eds.), *Child and adolescent psychiatry* (2nd ed.). Oxford, UK: Blackwell.

Judd, L. L. (1994). Social phobia: A clinical overview. 5-9. *Journal of Clinical Psychiatry, 55*(6, Suppl.).

Kagan, J., Reznick, J. S., Clarke, C., Snidman, N., & Garcia-Coll, C. (1984). Behavioral inhibition to the unfamiliar. *Child Development, 55*, 2212-2225.

Kashani, J. H., & Orvaschel, H. (1990). A community study of anxiety in children and adolescents. *American Journal of Psychiatry, 147*, 313-318.

Keller, M. V., Lavori, P., Wunder, J., Beardslee, W. R., Schwarts, C. E., & Roth, J. (1992). Chronic course of anxiety disorders in children and adolescents. *Journal of the American Academy of Child and Adolescent Psychiatry, 31*, 595-599.

Kessler, R. C., McGonagle, K. A., Zhao, S., Nelson, C. B., Hughes, M., Eshleman, S., Wittchen, H. U., & Kendler, K. S. (1994). Lifetime and 12-month prevalence of DSM-III-R psychiatric disorders in the United States: Results from the National Comorbidity Survey. *Archives of General Psychiatry, 61*, 8-19.

Klein, R. G., Koplewicz, H. S., & Kanner, A. (1992). Imipramine treatment of children with separation anxiety disorder. *Journal of the American Academy of Child and Adolescent Psychiatry, 31,* 21–28.

Klein, R. G., & Last, C. G. (1989). *Anxiety disorders in children.* Newbury Park, CA: Sage.

Kovacs, M., Gatsonis, C., Paulauskas, S. L., & Richards, C. (1989). Depressive disorders in childhood, IV: A longitudinal study of comorbidity with and risk for anxiety disorders. *Archives of General Psychiatry, 46,* 776–782.

Last, C. G., Francis, G., Hersen, M., Kazdin, A. E., & Strauss, C. C. (1987). Separation anxiety and school phobia: A comparison using DSM-III criteria. *American Journal of Psychiatry, 144,* 635–657.

Last, C. G., Hersen, M., Kazdin, A. E., Finkelstein, R., & Strauss, C. C. (1987). Comparison of DSM-III separation anxiety and overanxious disorders: Demographic characteristics and patterns of comorbidity. *Journal of the American Academy of Child and Adolescent Psychiatry, 26,* 527–531.

Last, C. G., Perrin, S., Hersen, M., & Kazdin, A. E. (1992). DSM-III-R anxiety disorders in children: Sociodemographic and clinical characteristics. *Journal of the American Academy of Child and Adolescent Psychiatry, 31,* 1070–1076.

Leckman, J. F., Weissman, M. M., Merikangas, K. R., Pauls, D. L., & Prusoff, B. A. (1983). Panic disorder and major depression: Increased risk of depression, alcoholism, panic, and phobic disorders in families of depressed probands with panic disorder. *Archives of General Psychiatry, 40,* 1055–1060.

Links, P. S., Boyer, M. H., & Offord, D. B. (1989). The prevalence of emotional disorders in children. *Journal of Nervous and Mental Disease, 177,* 85–91.

Lipsitz, J. O., Martin, L. Y., Mannuzza, S., Chapman, T. F., Liebowitz, M. R., Klein, D. F., & Fyer, A. J. (1994). Childhood separation anxiety disorder in patients with adult anxiety disorders. *American Journal of Psychiatry, 151,* 927-929.

Livingston, R. (1991). Anxiety disorders. In M. Lewis (Ed.), *Child and adolescent psychiatry: A comprehensive textbook* (pp. 673-684). Baltimore: Williams & Wilkins.

Marks, I. M., & Gelder, M. G. (1966). Different ages of onset in varieties of phobia. *American Journal of Psychiatry, 123,* 218-221.

Marshall, J. R. (1993). Social phobia: An overview of treatment strategies. *Journal of Clinical Psychiatry, 54,* 165-171.

Mattison, R. E., & Bagnato, S. J. (1987). Empirical measurement of overanxious disorder in boys 8-12 years old. *Journal of the American Academy of Child and Adolescent Psychiatry, 26,* 536-540.

McGee, R., Feehan, M., Williams, S., Partridge, F., Silva, P. A., & Kelly, J. (1990). DSM-III disorders in a large sample of adolescents. *Journal of the American Academy of Child and Adolescent Psychiatry, 29,* 611-619.

McClellan, J. M., Rubert, M. P., Riechler, R. J., & Sylvester, C. E. (1990). Attention deficit disorder in children at risk for anxiety and depression. *Journal of the American Academy of Child and Adolescent Psychiatry, 29,* 534-539.

Mitchell, J., McCauley, E., Burke, P. M., & Moss, S. J. (1988). Phenomenology of depression in children and adolescents. *Journal of the American Academy of Child and Adolescent Psychiatry, 27,* 12-20.

Ollendick, T. H., Matson, J. L., & Helsel, W. J. (1985). Fears in children and adolescents: Normative data. *Behaviour Research and Therapy, 23,* 465-467.

Pollack, M. H., Otto, M. W., Rosenbaum, J. F., & Sachs, G. S. (1992). Personality disorders in patients with panic disorder: Association with childhood anxiety disorders, early trauma, comorbidity, and chronicity. *Comprehensive Psychiatry, 33,* 78-83.

Reichler, R. J., Sylvester, C. E., & Hyde, T. S. (1988). Biological studies on offspring of panic disordered probands. In D. J. Dunner, E. S. Gershon, & J. E. Barrett (Eds.), *Relatives at risk for mental disorder* (pp. 131-154). New York: Raven Press.

Robins, L. N. (1971). Follow-up studies investigating childhood disorders. In A. Hareeh & J. K. Wing (Eds.), *Psychiatric epidemiology* (pp. 285-304). London: Oxford Press.

Rosenbaum, J. F., Biedermen, J., Hirshfeld, D. R., Bolduc, E. A., & Chaloff, J. (1991). Behavioral inhibition in children: A possible precursor to panic disorder or social phobia. *Journal of Clinical Psychiatry, 52,* 5–9.

Rutter, M., Tizard, J., & Whitmore, K. (1970). *Education, health, and behavior.* London: Longman.

Schneier, F. R. (1994, Spring). Diagnosis, etiology, and management of social phobias. *Directions in Clinical Psychology, 4*(7), 7-8.

Silver, L. B. (1979). Recognition and treatment of anxiety in children and adolescents. In W. E. Fann, I. Karacan, & A. D. Porkory (Eds.), *Phenomenology and treatment of anxiety* (pp. 65-92). New York: Spectrum.

Spielberger, S. (1973). *Manual for the State-Trait Anxiety Inventory for Children.* Palo Alto, CA: Consulting Psychologists Press.

Strauss, C. C., Last, C. G., Hersen, M., & Kazdin, A. E. (1988). Association between anxiety and depression in children and adolescents with anxiety disorders. *Journal of Abnormal Child Psychology, 16,* 57–68.

Trower, P., & Gilbert, P. (1989). New theoretical conceptions of social anxiety and social phobia. *Clinical Psychology Review, 9,* 19–35.

Turner, S. M., Beidel, D. C., & Costello, A. (1987). Psychopathology in the offspring of anxiety disordered patients. *Journal of Consulting and Clinical Psychology, 55,* 229–235.

Werry, J. S. (1991). Overanxious disorder: A review of its taxonomic properties. *Journal of the American Academy of Child and Adolescent Psychiatry, 30,* 533–544.

Zeitlin, H. (1986). *The natural history of psychiatric disorders in children.* Oxford, UK: Oxford University Press.

Zitrin, C. M., & Ross, D. C. (1988). Early separation anxiety and adult agoraphobia. *Journal of Nervous and Mental Disease, 176,* 621–625.

2

Structured Treatment and Prevention Activities for Sexually Abused Children

Ann Hazzard, PhD

Dr. Hazzard is Associate Professor of Pediatrics and Assistant Professor of Psychiatry at Emory University School of Medicine, Atlanta, GA.

KEY POINTS

- The author discusses two theoretical models that are widely used to conceptualize the emotional and behavioral consequences of childhood sexual abuse — the posttraumatic stress disorder (PTSD) model and Finkelhor's model.

- According to the PTSD model, sexual abuse is an anxiety-producing event (or series of events), after which heightened physiologic reactions, anxious feelings, and distorted cognitions become conditioned to sexual activities.

- Finkelhor's model is based on the premise that four traumagenic dynamics are intrinsic to sexual abuse: self-blame, betrayal, traumatic sexualization, and powerlessness.

- Prevention activities from the Recovery from Abuse Project (RAP) are offered as guidelines for clinicians. RAP is a clinical research project in which a structured treatment for sexually abused girls and their caretakers (who were not the sexually abusers) was developed and evaluated. These activities should prove useful in helping children make sense of the terrifying experiences that have introduced them to sexuality in a developmentally and emotionally damaging manner.

INTRODUCTION

During the past two decades, researchers have documented the negative effects of childhood sexual abuse on the functioning of victimized children. Compared with presumably nonabused children, sexually abused children exhibit significant problems in affective, behavioral, cognitive, and interpersonal functioning (Finkelhor, 1986; Gomez-Schwartz, Horowitz, & Candarelli, 1990). Retrospective studies of adults victimized as children have found documented adverse sequelae of sexual abuse, including low self-esteem and depression (Gold, 1986), posttraumatic stress symptoms (Briere & Runtz, 1988), and difficulty in interpersonal and sexual relationships (Beitchman et al., 1992).

Many articles and books about therapy for sexually abused children and their families are available, including an excellent text by Friedrich (1990). Many authors do not tie therapeutic approaches to theoretical models of the psychological trauma associated with sexual abuse. Atheoretical, nondirective approaches may not be optimally effective because many traumatized children resist discussing their abuse openly or verbally. An additional problem stems from the paucity of outcome studies conducted to inform clinicians about the efficacy of various therapeutic interventions used with sexually abused children. A notable exception is the study by Deblinger, McLeer, and Henry (1990), who documented pre–post improvement following short-term cognitive-behavioral treatment; however, they did not use a control group.

Two theoretical models widely used to conceptualize the emotional and behavioral consequences of childhood sexual abuse are the posttraumatic stress disorder (PTSD) model (McLeer, Deblinger, Atkins, Foa, & Ralphe, 1988) and Finkelhor's model (1986). This chapter discusses the underpinnings of both models and explores their nuances by using a case-study approach. Implications for treatment are highlighted.

THE CASE OF TINA

Tina, a 10-year-old African-American girl, lives with her mother and 4-year-old brother, who has sickle cell anemia. Her mother has a boyfriend who often spends the night. Tina's mother acknowledges a history of past drug abuse but reports only moderate current use of alcohol and marijuana. Tina's mother also has significant difficulty with reading and has received welfare payments since the children were born.

Tina's mother brought her to a pediatric walk-in clinic because, during the past month, Tina began having problems with sleeping and eating, enuresis, occasional vomiting, and poor grooming. On the way to the clinic, Tina told her mother that she had been raped approximately 1 month before by a neighborhood boy named Charles. Her mother had left Tina and her brother alone while she went to the grocery store. Charles came to the door while her mother was gone. Tina reportedly asked who it was and Charles responded, "Me." Thinking it was her mother, Tina opened the door, and Charles raped her. Although Tina clearly was prepubescent (both physically and socially), her mother was distraught and accused Tina of consensual sexual activity. Protective Services was contacted, and Tina was placed in a children's shelter for several days. Her mother calmed down, accepted that Tina had been raped, and assumed a protective stance. Tina was returned home. Criminal charges were filed and pending in juvenile court throughout treatment; Charles remained in the neighborhood. After Tina returned home, enuresis and vomiting stopped; however, she did not want her mother's boyfriend (who was Charles' uncle) to spend the night. She wanted to sleep with her mother and began showering several times a day.

THE PTSD MODEL

According to the PTSD model, sexual abuse is an anxiety-producing, traumatic event or series of events for most children. Heightened physiologic reactions, anxious feelings, and distorted cognitions become conditioned to sexual, abusive activities. Later, children may continue to experience increased automatic arousal and both reexperiencing and avoidance symptomatology. Reexperiencing symptomatology includes intrusive recollections of the abuse, play representations of the abuse, abuse-related dreams, and distress at cues or symbols of the abuse. The child defends against the anxiety-provoking reexperiencing phenomena by avoidance, withdrawal, or emotional numbing. One limitation of the PTSD model is that, except for anxiety, it does not include other affective reactions that a child may have in response to sexual abuse.

Posttraumatic Stress Symptoms:

Anxiety and PTSD symptomatology often must be addressed first to help abused children resume a normal daily routine. Mastering abuse-related anxiety, rather than repressing or dissociating anxiety or abuse memories, is critical to a child's long-term recovery. Many abused children become overwhelmed with negative affect when abuse issues are brought up and typically avoid discussing these events or feelings. The therapist's task is to help the child confront the memories and feelings, cope with and integrate these feelings and memories, and, over time, experience diminished anxiety in response to cues of the abuse. Some lessening and mastery of anxiety can be achieved via gradual and repeated discussion as abuse memories are "reconditioned" to the safety of the therapy setting. Providing children with a rationale for discussion of the abuse is helpful; for example, "Talking about the abuse *here*, where you are safe, can help you get over the scared feelings you have right now whenever you think about what happened." Titrating the child's exposure to anxiety-provoking memories is also important. The therapist might say, "We will only talk about it for 5 minutes" or, "I will only ask you five questions." The therapist may also allow the child to move back and forth between abuse-related and nonthreatening activities.

Asking the child to "draw the abuse" provides an avenue for discussion of the event and may provide important information about what aspects of the experience were particularly salient to the child. An "abuse reminder list" and a "ways to cope" worksheet are useful in identifying cues for anxiety and in developing coping strategies. For the abuse reminder list, the child is asked to list anxiety triggers in any of the following categories: people, places, things, sounds, smells, activities, times of day, or television and books. For the ways to cope worksheet, the therapist, child, and parent(s) develop cognitive or behavioral plans for coping with each anxiety trigger. The goal is to help the child manage the anxiety so that he or she can return to age-appropriate functioning. Tina's triggers on the abuse reminder list were Charles, his sister, his uncle (who was her mother's boyfriend), beds (she was raped on her mother's bed), and genital smells. Tina had been dealing with her anxiety triggers with a mixture of avoidant, regressive, and compulsive behaviors (rarely going outside to play, sleeping with her mother, and showering excessively).

The therapist's goal is to decrease unrealistic or overgeneralized anxiety and to substitute adaptive coping for maladaptive strategies. Presumably, social workers for Protective Services and the therapist have ensured that the child is currently in a situation where he or she is not endangered by unsupervised contact with the perpetrator. However, in some situations, such as Tina's, the child may have some contact with the perpetrator and may feel anxious; this is realistic. In Tina's case, the therapist normalized her anxiety by telling her, "It's normal for you to feel worried when you see him in the neighborhood because seeing him reminds you of how scary it was when he abused you." The therapist also provided behavioral strategies by advising Tina to always be outside with a friend or her mother and cognitive coping thoughts to help Tina recognize that she was safer than before ("You can tell yourself: I don't have to be super scared because he can't hurt me with all these people around. I told what he did so that he knows he'll get in trouble if he tries to bother me again").

Tina's fear of Charles's uncle was further explored to determine if he had been abusive; there was no indication that he had abused Tina. However, his relationship to the offender caused problems in his relationship with Tina's mother, who felt anxious about where his ultimate loyalties lay. She eventually ended the relationship. The therapist attempted to discourage inappropriate generalization of anxiety to all men with the coping thought, "Most men don't abuse children." To deal with Tina's anxiety about beds and sleeping alone, a behavioral program was implemented to encourage her to sleep independently again. Her frequent showering appeared to relate both to the anxiety trigger of genital smells as well as possible feelings of shame and "dirtiness." "I'm clean; he's dirty" was used as a coping thought; with younger children, a "magical" cleansing ritual might help. A behavioral plan was used to gradually decrease her frequency of showers. Consistent praise and support from the parent and the therapist are important in reinforcing the child's mastery of anxiety-provoking situations.

FINKELHOR'S MODEL

Although an alternative to the PTSD model, Finkelhor's model is based on a complementary theory of four traumagenic dynamics intrinsic to sexual abuse (Finkelhor, 1986). According to this model, most sexually abused children must cope with four major issues to varying degrees: self-blame and stigmatization, betrayal, traumatic sexualization, and powerlessness. Many abused children blame themselves for the abuse and feel isolated and different from others. They generally feel betrayed, certainly by the offender and perhaps by other adults who were unable to protect them. As a result, they may develop generalized difficulties with interpersonal trust. Sexually abused children have been introduced to sexuality at a developmentally inappropriate time and in a confusing or anxiety-provoking manner. Therefore, they may react by anxiously avoiding sexuality or, conversely, by sexually acting out. Sexually abused children often feel helpless. Because they were unable to control access to their bodies, they may believe they are unable to control other aspects of their lives.

Self-Blame:

Many sexually abused children feel some degree of guilt about the abuse because of a variety of developmental (e.g., childhood egocentrism) or situational reasons. Elicit the child's attributions of blame for the abuse and offer alternatives to specific self-blaming attributions, rather than initially making a global statement that the abuse is "not your fault," which may inhibit further exploration of the issue.

The "Why Me?" story (Celano, Hazzard, Simmons, & Webb, 1991) is a fill-in-the-blank story in which a girl is abused and wonders why this happened to her. In the course of reading the story with the therapist, the child's attributions about her own abuse generally are reflected in her responses to the story "blanks." Tina's responses suggested that she primarily blamed Charles for the abuse but blamed herself for not telling her mother immediately. Her therapist elicited her fears about telling ("my mother would think I'm fast like the pregnant teens in the neighborhood and kick me out of the house.") The therapist empathized with her concerns, reinforced the importance of telling someone in future problematic situations, and reviewed the difference between consensual sex and rape.

The "Why Pie" is a drawing of a pie that the child is instructed to divide into various-sized pieces, with each piece representing how much he or she blames a given person. Tina's division of the pie revealed that she blamed Charles most, then his mother (for letting him come around), then her mother (for going to the store), and then herself (for asking her mother to go to the store). During this exercise, Tina spontaneously asked why she had to go to the children's shelter. It appeared that her temporary removal from her home had contributed to a sense that she had done something wrong and was partially to blame. The therapist told her that the Protective Services worker felt that her mother was too upset and needed to calm down but empathized with Tina's feelings that she was unfairly "punished" when she had not done anything wrong!

A "Why List" can be used as a supplement to the "Why Pie." Various possible self-blaming attributions are listed and the child is asked to choose any thoughts he or she may have. Among 17 possible self-blaming attributions are:

- Because the person picked me to abuse

- Because I didn't fight back enough

- Because I liked getting affection

- Because I accepted gifts

- Because I didn't obey a parental rule

Therapists are encouraged to empathize with the child's feelings; however, it is important to offer alternatives to the child as well. The therapist might encourage a child to question whether the offender really picked the child because of personal characteristics or because of convenience. The therapist also might point out that all children want affection, but the offender tricked the child by not letting him or her know that sex was part of an unfair deal.

The parents' attributions of blame for the abuse should be assessed. Although most parents (generally mothers) who seek treatment for their abused children blame the perpetrator, there may be subtle elements of child blame or parental self-blame. The therapist's goal is to decrease parents' blame of the child by increasing their empathy for the difficult psychological position faced by an abused child. Parental self-blame may be more or less appropriate depending on the situation. For example, some parents may not have provided appropriate supervision for their children or parent-child communication may have been poor and delayed the child's disclosure. The therapist's goal is to help parents take appropriate responsibility for any contributions they may have made to the abuse situation while discouraging global self-blame or undue guilt.

Betrayal:

Abused children typically feel betrayed by a known offender. An activity that can facilitate the child's expression of affect toward the offender is to write a dictated "Letter to the Offender" (not to be mailed). Tina's letter expressed intense anger toward Charles. Asking what the child wishes would happen to the offender is often informative.

Children also may feel betrayed by their parents, whom they may see as having been unable to protect them or unavailable to talk to them. The "Who I Told" worksheet is helpful in exploring perceived barriers to disclosure as well as the child's perceptions of others' reactions and supportiveness after disclosure. The child is asked to list whom he or she told about the abuse and to paste sticker faces to indicate how each person reacted. In a second column, the child lists whom he or she did not tell and pastes stickers to indicate each person's anticipated reaction. This exercise revealed Tina's reluctance to disclose the abuse to any peers because of concerns about peer rejection; she had also behaviorally withdrawn from peers. The therapist encouraged and supported her through a disclosure to a best friend, who responded appropriately.

In some cases, this exercise may reveal reasons for delayed disclosure to a caregiver. In many families, the therapist may need to identify and remediate parent-child communication problems.

Unresolved feelings of betrayal can lead to later difficulties with interpersonal trust. Some sexually abused children may overgeneralize their fear of exploitation and withdraw from relationships. Others may be overly dependent and seek a great deal of attention because of their frustration of the dependency needs arising from unavailability or betrayal by important others. The overall goal of the therapist is to help the child develop positive, yet realistic and differentiated, expectations about trusting others.

Traumatic Sexualization:

By definition, sexually abused children have been introduced to sexuality in a developmentally and emotionally inappropriate manner. Sex education is important to provide accurate and emotionally corrective information about healthy sexuality. We use an illustrated sex education booklet (Celano et al., 1991) that the therapist reads together with the mother and her child. The booklet addresses body parts, menstruation, intercourse and other sexual activities (including masturbation), and differences between healthy sexuality and sexual abuse. Like most parents, Tina's mother reacted with relief and gratitude to the provision of a structured format for discussing these issues with her child. The activity enhanced mother-daughter closeness and communication as well.

Children receive further practice in differentiating healthy sexuality from sexual abuse in the "Name That Touch Game." Brief situations are read from cards, and children classify each situation as "OK touching" or "not OK touching."

Asking the child to draw a self-portrait of the age he or she would like to be also is informative. Children who have regressed may draw themselves as younger, whereas children who have become pseudomature or prematurely sexualized may draw themselves as older. Interestingly enough, although Tina's behavior was primarily regressive and avoidant, she drew herself at age 21 because she claimed that she could protect herself then. Discussion focused on the ways she can protect herself at her current age and other positive aspects of being 10 years old. This activity provided a springboard for a discussion of expectations and anxieties about future issues, such as dating, having sex, and having children.

Some children may react to their abuse by developing sexual behavior problems, such as sexual acting out with other children, inappropriate seductive behavior, or excessive masturbation. Parents often need help in setting limits on these behaviors in a matter-of-fact manner.

Powerlessness:

To counter the feelings of powerlessness that a sexually abused child may be experiencing, prevention activities may be helpful. Prevention education aims to decrease the risk of future victimization, and prevention activities offer an opportunity to reframe the abuse as having produced positive personal growth. Children can be told, "Let's figure out what you learned from having been abused that can help protect you in the future."

Various sexual abuse prevention materials have been developed and are commercially available; for instance, written materials, such as comic books (Marvel Comics, 1984) and books (Committee for Children, 1986a; Hindman, 1983; Wachter, 1982). We use the second edition of the *Better Safe Than Sorry* videotape (Filmfair Communications, 1986), which includes vignettes such as an acquaintance offering a child a ride and a neighbor asking a girl to try on a negligee that he has bought his wife. Tina was able to recognize the danger in these situations and learn the prevention safety rules of saying no, leaving, and telling someone. Other excellent prevention videos include *Yes, You Can Say No* (Committee for Children, 1986b) and *Child Sexual Abuse: A Solution* (James Stanfield & Company, 1985).

Asking "what if" questions and role playing are also helpful mechanisms to enhance a victim's assertiveness and feelings of personal empowerment. Because date rape is a frequent form of sexual abuse encountered by adolescents, therapists may include a role play of a boy pressuring a girl for sexual activity. The therapist can also help girls clarify their values about choosing to engage in sexual activities, review "pick-up lines" that boys may use, and discuss what makes it hard for girls to say no to boys they like.

THE RECOVERING FROM ABUSE PROJECT

Most of the therapeutic activities described above were developed as part of the Recovering from Abuse Project (RAP), a clinical research project in which a structured treatment for sexually abused girls and nonoffending caretakers (generally mothers) was developed and evaluated (Celano, Hazzard, Webb, & McCall, 1996). A treatment manual describing the activities in more detail is available (Celano et al., 1991). The activities were used with a low-income, primarily African-American population, for which single-mother families were the norm. However, most activities can be adapted for use with other populations.

The RAP program consists of 8-hour individual sessions, with half of each session spent with the child and half spent with the mother — with occasional conjoint activities. Involvement of nonoffending mothers is a critical component of treatment because maternal support is a mediator of outcome for sexually abused children (Conte & Schuerman, 1987; Everson, Hunter, Runyon, Edelsohn, & Coulter, 1989; Gomez-Schwartz et al., 1990). Research is needed to explore the impact of parental support on child outcome in cases where the father was not the perpetrator.

Evaluation:

An evaluation of RAP was conducted by comparing pre- and postassessments of 15 girls and their mothers who participated in RAP with assessments of 17 control families who participated in unstructured "treatment as usual" (Celano et al., 1994). Pre/post measures included the Child Behavior

Checklist (Achenbach & Edelbrock, 1979), the Children's Global Assessment Scale (Shaffer et al., 1983), the Parental Reaction to Incest Disclosure Scale (Everson et al., 1989), the Parental Attribution Scale (Webb, Celano, & Hazzard, submitted), and the Children's Impact of Traumatic Events Scale–Revised (Wolfe, Gentile, Michienzi, Sas, & Wolfe, 1991).

Results of repeated measures (ANOVAs) revealed that both treatment programs yielded decreases in the children's PTSD symptoms and traumagenic beliefs reflecting self-blame and powerlessness and improvement in the children's overall psychosocial functioning. RAP was more effective than the control treatment in increasing abuse-related caretaker support of the child and in decreasing caretaker self-blame and expectations of undue negative impact of the abuse on the child. Although these results need replication, particularly with more diverse samples in terms of race, sex, and socioeconomic status, structured, theoretically based therapeutic activities appear to show promise in the treatment of sexually abused children.

CONCLUDING REMARKS

The RAP program is fairly unique in that it uses structured treatment activities for individual therapy. Other activity workbooks designed for individual therapy include *Flip-Flops, Cartwheels, and High-Tops* (Spinal-Robinson & Wickham, 1992) as well as *Steps to Healthy Touching* (MacFarlane & Cunningham, 1988), which is especially appropriate for children with sexual acting-out problems.

A number of group treatment approaches use structured activities, including group activities for young children (Damon & Waterman, 1986), latency-age children (Celano, 1990; Kitchur & Bell, 1989; Mandell & Damon, 1989; Powell & Faherty, 1990), and adolescents (Blick & Porter, 1982; Hazzard, King, & Webb, 1986). Many activities designed for groups also may be adapted for use with individual clients. Moreover, many multisession, multimedia sexual abuse prevention interventions are designed for classroom or group use. Two excellent programs are *Talking About Touching* (Beland, 1986) and *Feeling Yes, Feeling No* (National Film Board of Canada, 1985).

Mental health clinicians are increasingly being asked to treat children with histories of sexual abuse. The PTSD model and the traumagenic dynamic model are two theoretical frameworks often used to conceptualize the impact of sexual abuse on abused children. Structured treatment activities based on these models are potentially useful in engaging children who often resist working through abuse sequelae and in organizing treatment efforts. An evaluation of RAP suggests that it produces broad client gains and, in some areas, may be more effective than unstructured treatment. The optimal treatment may be a combination of structured activities and more nonspecific clinical interventions designed to respond to the unique needs of particular families.

REFERENCES

Achenbach, T., & Edelbrock, C. (1979). The child behavior profile, II: Boys aged 12–16 and girls aged 6–11 and 12–16. *Journal of Consulting and Clinical Psychology, 47,* 223–233.

Beitchman, J., Zucker, K., Hood, J., DaCosta, G., Alman, P., & Cassavia, E. (1992). A review of the long-term effects of sexual abuse. *Child Abuse and Neglect, 16,* 101–118.

Beland, K. (1986). *Talking about touching.* Seattle, WA: Committee for Children.

Blick, L. C., & Porter, F. S. (1982). Group therapy with female adolescent incest victims. In S. M. Sgroi (Ed.), *Handbook of clinical intervention in child sexual abuse* (pp. 147–175). Lexington, MA: Lexington Books.

Briere, J., & Runtz, M. (1988). Post-sexual abuse trauma. *Journal of Interpersonal Violence, 2*(4), 367–379.

Celano, M. (1990). Activities and games for group psychotherapy with sexually abused children. *International Journal of Group Psychotherapy, 40*(14), 419–429.

Celano, M., Hazzard, A., Simmons, M., & Webb, C. (1991). *Recovering from abuse project.* Unpublished treatment manual (available from Ann Hazzard, Box 26065, Grady Hospital, 80 Butler Street, Atlanta, GA 30335).

Celano, M., Hazzard, A., Webb, C., & McCall, C. (1996). Treatment of traumatogenic beliefs among sexually abused girls and their mothers: An evaluation study. *Journal of Abnormal Child Psychology, 24*(1), 1-17.

Committee for Children (1986a). *Sam's story.* Seattle, WA: Author. (Available from Committee for Children, 2203 Airport Way South, Suite 500, Seattle, WA 98134, 1-800-634-4449.)

Committee for Children (1986b). *Yes, you can say no.* Seattle, WA: Author.

Conte, J. R., & Schuerman, J. R. (1987). Factors associated with an increased impact of child sexual abuse. *Child Abuse and Neglect, 11,* 201–211.

Damon, L., & Waterman, J. (1986). Parallel group treatment of children and their mothers. In K. MacFarlane & J. Waterman (Eds.), *Sexual abuse of young children: Evaluation and treatment.* New York: Guilford.

Deblinger, E., McLeer, S., & Henry, D. (1990). Cognitive-behavioral treatment for sexually abused children suffering posttraumatic stress: Preliminary findings. *Journal of the American Academy of Child and Adolescent Psychiatry, 29,* 747–752.

Everson, M. D., Hunter, W. M., Runyon, D. K., Edelsohn, G. A., & Coulter, M. L. (1989). Maternal support following disclosure of incest. *American Journal of Orthopsychiatry, 59,* 197–207.

Filmfair Communications (1986). *Better safe than sorry* (2nd ed.). Studio City, CA: Author.

Finkelhor, D. (1986). *A sourcebook on child sexual abuse.* Beverly Hills: Sage.

Friedrich, W. N. (1990). *Psychotherapy of sexually abused children and their families*. New York: Norton.

Gold, E. (1986). Long-term effect of sexual victimization in childhood: An attributional approach. *Journal of Consulting and Clinical Psychology, 54*, 471–475.

Gomez-Schwartz, B., Horowitz, J., & Candarelli, A. (1990). *Child sexual abuse: The initial effects*. Newbury Park; CA: Sage.

Hazzard, A., King, H. E., & Webb, C. (1986). Group therapy with sexually abused adolescent girls. *American Journal of Psychotherapy, 40*, 213–223.

Hindman, J. (1983). *A very touching book*. Ontario, OR: Alexandria Associates.

James Stanfield & Company (1985). *Child sexual abuse: A solution*. Santa Monica, CA: Author.

Kitchur, M., & Bell R. (1989). Group psychotherapy with preadolescent sexual abuse victims: Literature review and description of an inner city group. *International Journal of Group Psychotherapy, 39*, 285–310.

MacFarlane, K. & Cunningham, C. (1988). *Steps to healthy touching*. Mt. Dora, FL: Kidsrights.

Mandell, J., & Damon, J. (1989). *Group treatment for sexually abused children*. New York: Guilford.

Marvel Comics (1984). *Spiderman and powerpack*. New York: Author.

McLeer, S. V., Deblinger, E., Atkins, M., Foa, E., & Ralphe, D. (1988). Posttraumatic stress disorder in sexually abused children. *Journal of the American Academy of Child and Adolescent Psychiatry, 27*, 650–654.

National Film Board of Canada (1985). *Feeling yes, feeling no*. Evanston, IL: Perennial Education.

Powell, L., & Faherty, S. (1990). Treating sexually abused latency-age girls. *The Arts in Psychotherapy, 17*, 35–47.

Shaffer, D., Gould, M., Brasie, J., Ambrosini, P., Fisher, P., Bird, H., & Aluwahlia, S. (1983). A Children's Global Assessment Scale (CGAS). *Archives of General Psychiatry, 40,* 1228–1231.

Spinal-Robinson, P., & Wickman, R. E. (1992). *Flip-flops, cartwheels, and high-tops.* Notre Dame, IN: Jalice Publishers.

Wachter, O. (1982). *No more secrets for me.* Boston: Little, Brown.

Webb, C., Celano, M., & Hazzard, A. (submitted). Parental Attribution Scale: Attributions of responsibility for child sexual abuse.

Wolfe, V. V., Gentile, C., Michienzi, T., Sas, L., & Wolfe, D. (1991). The Children's Impact of Traumatic Events Scale: A measure of post-sexual abuse PTSD symptoms. *Behavioral Assessment, 13,* 359–383.

3

Attention-Deficit/ Hyperactivity Disorder

Sam Goldstein, PhD

Dr. Goldstein is Clinical Director of the Neurology Learning and Behavior Center, Salt Lake City, UT. He is also Clinical Instructor, Department of Psychiatry, and Adjunct Professor, Department of Educational Psychology, University of Utah School of Medicine, Salt Lake City, UT.

KEY POINTS

- Attention-deficit/hyperactivity disorder (ADHD) is diagnosed by observing behaviors rather than examining causes. It is confirmed by the intensity, persistence, and clustering of symptoms as opposed to the presence or absence of symptoms.

- Attention deficit, with or without hyperactive-impulsive problems, reflects distinct diagnostic categories. The DSM-IV includes three types of ADHD: inattentive, hyperactive-impulsive, and a combination of the two.

- The cause of ADHD may be biologic or environmental. Possible biologic causes include reactions to medications, a resistance to thyroid hormone, and brain dysfunction.

- The author outlines a multistep process that could be useful in the assessment of ADHD. An in-depth behavioral, emotional, and developmental evaluation and the gathering of extensive data are necessary.

- Treatment must be multidisciplinary, incorporating medical, behavioral, and environmental techniques. A review literature on medications is provided.

- Educational interventions, implementation of a parenting skills training program, development of social skills, and use of cognitive strategies can all be effective treatments for children with ADHD.

INTRODUCTION

Problems characterized as disorders of attention, impulsivity, and hyperactivity in children have long constituted the most chronic of behavior disorders (Wender, 1975) and the largest single source of referrals to child mental health centers (Barkley, 1981). It is not surprising, therefore, that problems related to attention-deficit/hyperactivity disorder (ADHD) result in the most common complaints by parents and teachers. However, behavior characterized by inattentiveness, impulsivity, hyperactivity, and difficulty responding consistently to consequences can be caused by a variety of other childhood disorders.

Symptoms of impulsivity are characteristic of all disruptive disorders in children. Complaints of inattention equally characterize both externalizing and internalizing childhood disorders. Evaluation of these symptomatic problems is complicated because, to date, no "litmus test" for ADHD has been devised. Conners (1975) reported that there are few exclusionary developmental criteria and no unequivocal, positive developmental markers for ADHD, although it is distinct from other childhood disorders. Its diagnosis is confirmed by the intensity, persistence, and clustering of symptoms as opposed to the presence or absence of symptoms (Ross & Ross, 1982).

Although the labels used to describe this cluster of childhood problems have changed many times over the past 100 years, the terms *attention-deficit disorder* and *attention-deficit/ hyperactivity disorder* are most familiar to mental health professionals. Despite the recent publication of the fourth edition of the *Diagnostic and Statistical Manual of Mental Disorders* (DSM-IV) (American Psychiatric Association, 1994), disagreement persists over what causes this set of childhood problems. Researchers have argued that ADHD might best be referred to as a dysfunction of the reward system (Haenlein & Caul, 1987), a learning disability (McGee & Share, 1988), or a self-regulatory disorder (Kirby & Grimley, 1986). Some of the more recent and promising theories propose that ADHD is most accurately described as an impairment of inhibiting behavior and of delaying a response (Barkley, 1994).

DEFINITION

Because of the impact that symptoms of ADHD have on unaffected persons, it has been considered a disruptive behavior disorder. Unlike the other two childhood disruptive disorders (oppositional defiance and conduct disorders), ADHD appears to reflect limited behavior as the result of incompetence and developmental impairment rather than purposeful noncompliance.

ADHD clearly is a behavioral diagnosis (Schaughency & Rothlind, 1991). The DSM-IV includes three types of ADHD: inattentive, hyperactive-impulsive, or a combination of the two (Table 3.1). A fourth diagnosis, referred to as not-otherwise-specified ADHD, can be made when some, but not all, symptoms are present.

Research demonstrates that attention deficit, with or without hyperactive-impulsive problems, reflects different diagnostic categories (Driscoll & Zecker, 1991). The consensus is that children with ADHD associated with a *hyperactive-impulsive* component are impulsive, easily distracted, overactive, and aggressive and experience more conduct problems. Children in the primarily *inattentive* ADHD group are described more often as shy, withdrawn, and sluggish. These children, who manifest more severely depressive symptoms, as well as more motor and learning problems, are more likely to repeat a grade. Both groups are consistently described by teachers and caretakers as inattentive, poor school performers, academically unmotivated, socially unpopular, and possessing low self-esteem (Barkley, 1990; Goldstein & Goldstein, 1990).

Goldstein and Goldstein (1990) posit a definition of ADHD based on the hypotheses of Douglas (1985) and Douglas and Peters (1979). From a common sense perspective, children with ADHD do not pay good attention to activities that are

Table 3.1
DSM-IV Criteria For Attention-Deficit/
Hyperactivity Disorder

A.   Either 1 or 2:

1. **Inattention**: At least six of the following symptoms of inattention have persisted for at least 6 months to a degree that is maladaptive and inconsistent with development level:

    (a)   Often fails to pay close attention to details or makes careless mistakes in schoolwork or other work, and activities
    (b)   Often has difficulty sustaining attention in tasks or play activities
    (c)   Often does not seem to listen to what is being said to him or her
    (d)   Often does not follow through on instructions and fails to finish schoolwork, chores, or duties in the workplace (not due to oppositional behavior or failure to understand instructions)
    (e)   Often has difficulty organizing tasks and activities
    (f)   Often avoids or strongly dislikes tasks (such as schoolwork or homework) that require sustained mental effort
    (g)   Often loses things necessary for tasks or activities
    (h)   Often is easily distracted by extraneous stimuli
    (i)   Often is forgetful in daily activities

2. **Hyperactivity-impulsivity**: At least four of the following symptoms of hyperactivity-impulsivity have persisted for at least 6 months to a degree that is maladaptive and inconsistent with developmental level:

    Hyperactivity

    (a)   Often fidgets with hands or feet or squirms in seat
    (b)   Leaves seat in classroom or in other situations in which remaining seated is expected
    (c)   Often runs about or climbs excessively in situations where it is inappropriate (in adolescents or adults, may be limited to subjective feelings of restlessness)

(d) Often has difficulty playing or engaging in leisure activities quietly
(e) Often is "on the go" or acts as if "driven by a motor"
(f) Often talks excessively

Impulsivity

(g) Often blurts out answers before questions have been completed
(h) Often has difficulty awaiting his or her turn
(i) Often interrupts and intrudes on others

B. Onset no later than 7 years of age

C. Symptoms must be present in two or more situations (e.g., at schoolwork and at home).

D. The disturbance causes clinically significant distress or impairment in social, academic, or occupational functioning.

E. Does not occur exclusively during the course of a pervasive developmental disorder, schizophrenia or other psychotic disorder, and is not better accounted for by a mood disorder, anxiety disorder, dissociative disorder, or a personality disorder

Source: American Psychiatric Association. (1994). *Diagnostic and statistical manual of mental disorders* (4th ed.). Washington, DC: Author. Copyright 1994 American Psychiatric Association. Reprinted with permission.

boring or repetitive, that require effort, or are not of their choosing. Moreover, they become more easily aroused emotionally and physically. As a consequence, they do not permit sufficient time to think before acting and tend to require more frequent, predictable, and salient reinforcers than do their peers. In addition, children with ADHD often precipitate a negative, reinforcing paradigm with the adults in their lives. Thus, unfortunately, they learn to work to avoid bad consequences rather than to earn good ones.

DEVELOPMENTAL COURSE AND COMORBIDITY

Although the basic core problems of children with ADHD are homogeneous, each child's presentation is unique in terms of the manifestation of these problems and associated comorbid factors (Goldstein & Goldstein, 1990). As more scientific data are generated concerning the developmental course and adult outcome of children with ADHD, it appears that the comorbid problems they develop — rather than the ADHD — predict their life outcome. ADHD in isolation best predicts school struggles and difficulty meeting expectations within the home setting; however, it does not predict the significant negative emotional, behavioral, and personality outcomes that have been reported.

Infants with difficult temperaments do not handle changes in routines well. They exhibit a low frustration threshold and a high intensity of response (Carey, 1970; Chess & Thomas, 1986; Thomas & Chess, 1977). In follow-up studies of such infants, as many as 70% developed school problems (Terestman, 1980). These infants appear at greater risk of developing ADHD than do other infants. Further, "difficult" infants exert a significant negative impact on the developing relationship with caregivers — a relationship that is critical in predicting the child's resilience.

Although early symptoms of ADHD may be viewed as transient problems of young children, research data suggest that ignoring these signs results in the loss of valuable treatment time. At least 60%–70% of children later diagnosed with ADHD could have been identified by their symptoms during the preschool years (Cohen, Sullivan, Minde, Novak, and Helwig, 1981). Young children manifesting symptoms of ADHD are more likely to present with speech and language problems than are children not suffering from those symptoms (Baker & Cantwell, 1987) and to develop a wide range of behavioral problems (Cantwell, Baker & Mattison, 1981; Cohen, Davine, & Meloche-Kelly, 1989). Current research cogently suggests that the comorbidity of speech and language disorders with ADHD merits routine screening of children suspect-ed of having ADHD and language disorders, especially dur-ing their younger years. Children with concurrent ADHD and language disorders appear to have a poorer prognosis than those with ADHD alone (Baker & Cantwell, 1992).

Within school settings, children with ADHD appear to be victims of their temperament and of their learning history, which often involves beginning, but not completing, tasks. The teacher's negative reinforcement model tends to focus on misbehavior rather than on termination of the behavior, which may further disrupt the classroom by having a disinhibitory effect on other students. Although some researchers have suggested that children with ADHD are intellectually less competent than their peers (Palkes & Stewart, 1972), it is more likely that weak performance of intellectual tasks results from the impact of impulsivity and inattention on test-taking be-havior rather than an innate lack of intellect. Children with ADHD often underperform, but may not underachieve, dur-ing the elementary years. However, by high school, at least 80% of these children fall behind in a basic academic subject that requires repetition and attention, such as basic math knowledge, spelling, or written language (Barkley, 1990; Goldstein & Goldstein, 1990). A recent series of studies has concluded that approximately 20%–30% of children with ADHD also suffer from a concomitant learning disability (Barkley, 1990). Although it has been hypothesized that ADHD may prevent children from achieving their academic potential (Stott, 1981), the presence of a learning disability may make them look more inattentive than others (McGee & Share, 1988).

In classroom settings, children with ADHD often may be more interested in tasks other than those on which the teacher may be focusing (Douglas, 1972); this leads to significantly more nonproductive activity. In the classroom, children with ADHD also demonstrate an uneven and unpredictable pat-tern of behavior that frequently leads teachers to conclude that these children are noncompliant rather than incompetent.

Further, the overall rates of negative teacher-child interactions involving normal students are higher in classrooms containing children with ADHD (Campbell, Endman, & Bernfeld, 1977). Teachers are more intense and controlling when interacting with children with ADHD (Whalen, Henker, & Dotemoto, 1981). Children with ADHD also have greater difficulty with transition, an important school activity (Zentall, 1988).

Sociometric and play studies suggest that children with ADHD are not chosen as often by their peers to be best friends or partners in activities (Pelham & Milich, 1984). Children with ADHD also seem to be cognizant of their difficulties, an awareness that most likely precipitates lower self-esteem (Glow & Glow, 1980). Moreover, they appear to experience either high-incidence, low-impact problems, which result in poor social acceptance, or low-incidence, high-impact problems, which result in social rejection (Pelham & Milich, 1984). These children have difficulty adapting their behavior to different situational demands (Whalen, Henker, Collins, McAuliffe, & Vaux, 1979). Some researchers suggest that the impulsive behavior pattern of children with ADHD is most responsible for their social difficulty, making those with comorbid hyperactive-impulsive problems at greater risk of developing social difficulty (Pelham & Bender, 1982).

Some primary symptoms of ADHD may diminish in intensity by adolescence (Weiss & Hechtman, 1979). However, many adolescents with ADHD continue to experience significant problems (Goldstein & Goldstein, 1990; Milich & Loney, 1979). At least 80% of adolescents with ADHD continue to manifest symptoms consistent with ADHD, and 60% develop at least one additional disruptive disorder (Barkley, Fischer, Edelbrock, & Smallish, 1989). Between 20% and 60% of adolescents with ADHD are involved in antisocial behavior, with a normal occurrence of 3%–4% (Satterfield, Hoppe, & Schell, 1982). At least 50%–70% of these adolescents develop oppositional defiant disorders, with a significant number progressing to conduct disorders (Barkley et al., 1989). However, the high prevalence of antisocial problems in adolescents with ADHD likely reflects the comorbidity of ADHD with other disruptive disorders, principally conduct disorders (Barkley et al., 1989).

Other studies report that as many as one third of adolescents with ADHD are suspended from school at least once (Ackerman, Dykman, & Peters, 1977), and at least 80% fall behind one or more years in one or more basic academic subjects (Loney, Kramer, & Milich, 1981). Adolescents with a history of ADHD appear at greater risk of developing internalizing problems, including anxiety or depression.

Mannuzza and colleagues (1991) suggested that adults who were diagnosed with ADHD as children do not appear to be at significantly greater risk of developing any disorders other than antisocial problems and substance abuse. These authors found that in a young adult population with a history of ADHD, 43% still manifested full-blown ADHD, 32% met the diagnostic criteria for antisocial personality disorder, and 10% were drug abusers. This finding contrasts with other results that indicate a greater risk of internalizing marital and vocational problems in adults who were diagnosed with ADHD as children (Biederman, Munir, & Knee, 1987; Weiss & Hechtman 1993).

EPIDEMIOLOGY

Initial efforts at identifying hyperactive and inattentive children showed that half the boys and almost half the girls in elementary school presented with symptoms of ADHD (Lapouse & Monk, 1958). Later studies cited incidence rates as high as 20% (Yanow, 1973). However, it is important to consider that incidence is based on a number of issues, including diagnostic criteria, the manner in which data are collected (observation, direct assessment, questionnaires, etc.), the cut-off score used to differentiate the affected from the unaffected group, and the location in which data are collected (clinic versus community). With regard to the location, the occurrence of comorbid problems appears to almost double in clinic-based samples as compared with community-based ones.

When consistent diagnostic criteria are applied across situations using valid means of assessment, the incidence rate of attention deficit drops between 1% and 6% (Goldstein, 1995). Some authors have estimated the incidence of ADHD among children and adolescents to be between 3% and 5% (Barkley, 1990; Goldstein & Goldstein, 1990). Again, these estimates vary for a number of reasons. However, the argument as to the specific number of children with ADHD is a moot point. ADHD is a behavioral diagnosis; it is not a diagnosis based on cause. Therefore, a wide range of factors may influence the exact number of children within a population meeting the diagnostic criteria of ADHD.

Research has indicated that ADHD is approximately five to nine times more prevalent in boys than girls (Ross & Ross, 1982). However, the majority of studies drawing that conclusion were based on clinic-referred samples. The ratio of boys to girls in epidemiologic studies appears to be closer to 3:1 (Goldstein & Goldstein, 1990). When boys and girls were compared with same-sex normative groups and when controls were present for symptoms of hyperactivity and antisocial behavior, the occurrence of attention problems was equal in boys and girls (McGee, Williams, & Silva, 1987). Although it has been suggested that girls with ADHD may experience more mood, affect, and emotional problems (Kashani, Chapel, & Ellis, 1979) or greater cognitive and language impairments (Berry, Shaywitz, & Shaywitz, 1985), it appears that boys and girls with ADHD generally experience similar problems. Differences observed between boys and girls with ADHD are more attributable to societal beliefs, attributions, and treatment of boys versus girls than to different behaviors caused by ADHD.

Current research suggests that less than 15% of clinic-referred children and adolescents diagnosed with ADHD suffer solely from this disorder (Goldstein, 1995). Of the remaining 85% of these children and adolescents, approximately 40% have one other disorder, 30% have two other disorders, and 15% have at least three other disorders (Goldstein & Goldstein, 1992). Therefore, it is not surprising that therapists encounter the highest rates of diagnostic comorbidity when working with this client population.

CAUSE

The cause of ADHD can be viewed as environmental or biologic. However, the diagnosis is based on observed behavior rather than on cause. Accumulating evidence from genetic, biochemical, neurobehavioral, and neuroimaging studies strongly suggests a neurologic etiology for ADHD in most children (Hynd, Hern, Voeller, & Marshall, 1991). However, it cannot as yet be concluded that all children with ADHD demonstrate symptoms reflecting a neurologic dysfunction. Causes of ADHD may result from environmental factors, including heredity (Morrison & Stewart, 1973). Nonetheless, a number of commonly suspected environmental causes (e.g., diet, candidal yeast, and vestibular dysfunction) have not been linked scientifically to ADHD (Ingersoll & Goldstein, 1993).

Medications (e.g., phenobarbital [Luminal] and phenytoin [Dilantin]) used to treat other medical illnesses may precipitate ADHD symptoms (Goldstein & Goldstein, 1990). Researchers at the National Institutes of Health (Hauser et al., 1993) demonstrated a relationship between generalized resistance to thyroid hormone and ADHD. Thyroid hormone regulates a number of functions in the body. Too little thyroid hormone can retard growth in children and lead to feelings of fatigue and depression. Some persons with a sufficient amount of thyroid hormone have a genetic defect in their thyroid-receptor cells that prevents them from benefiting from thyroid hormone. In such individuals, the hormone is unable to bind with the cells, thereby causing high levels of thyroid hormone in the blood and manifesting in symptoms similar to those seen in persons with insufficient amounts of hormone. This condition is referred to as *generalized resistance to thyroid hormone*.

Hauser and associates (1993) found that persons with generalized resistance to thyroid hormone are much more likely than persons without this condition to demonstrate symptoms of ADHD. If a person has this condition, he or she also may have ADHD; however, the reverse is not necessarily true. This genetic linkage study suggests that the genes responsible for generalized resistance to thyroid hormone may reside close to those responsible for ADHD. Nevertheless, it does not suggest that these genes are directly responsible for ADHD.

From a biologic perspective, ADHD can be viewed as the result of brain dysfunction. Neurotransmitters involving dopamine, serotonin, and norepinephrine have been implicated as essential building blocks for effective attention and impulse control. Research studies have hypothesized that the locations of the biochemical causes of ADHD include the right hemisphere and frontal lobes of the brain (Zametkin & Rapoport, 1987).

ASSESSMENT

Because of the pervasive, multisetting nature of problems related to ADHD and the high comorbidity with other childhood disorders, an assessment for ADHD involves a thorough emotional, developmental, and behavioral evaluation. The comprehensive evaluation should collect data concerning the child's behavior at home, with friends, and at school; academic and intellectual achievement; medical status; and emotional development. Barkley (1991) recommended that assessment for ADHD include the use of standardized behavior-rating scales, a review of laboratory measures when available, and observations in both the classroom and the clinic. Direct interviews with teachers and adults, as well as other forms of face-to-face assessment with the child, are necessary depending on specific, identified problems (Goldstein & Goldstein, 1990). Within the classroom setting, off-task behavior, excessive motor activity, and negative vocalization appear to be the most visible manifestations of ADHD (DuPaul, Guevremont, & Barkley, 1992).

A Multistep Process for Assessment:

When ADHD is suspected, assessment involves a multistep process.

- A complete history must be obtained. This is not a cursory process. Sufficient time (1–1½ hours) should be set aside to obtain a narrative of the child's development, behavior, extended family history, family relations, and current functioning. Within the context of the interview, efforts should be made to trace a developmental course that appears to fit ADHD as well as to identify core symptoms and those related to other childhood disorders. Obtaining thorough knowledge of the diagnostic criteria for common and uncommon (e.g., high-functioning autism) childhood internalizing and externalizing disorders should be of paramount concern.

- Data obtained from the history should be supplemented by the completion of a number of standardized, factor-analyzed questionnaires concerning children's problems. At least two adults who interact with the child on a regular basis—ideally a parent and a teacher—should be requested to complete questionnaires. For general child assessment, the most valuable questionnaire is the Child Behavior Checklist (Achenbach & Edelbrock, 1991). This questionnaire organizes childhood behavior on the disruptive–nondisruptive continuum. The Conners

Teacher Rating Scales (Conners, 1989), Comprehensive Teacher's Rating Scale (Ullmann, Sleator, & Sprague, 1988), Childhood Attention Problems (CAP) Scale (Edelbrock, 1990), and Academic Performance and ADHD Rating Scales (DuPaul, 1990) also are helpful. However, these questionnaires alone do not provide sufficient information for diagnosis; they simply provide an organized report of behavior. They describe what the observer sees, but not why it is being seen.

- Based on the history and questionnaires, the clinician should be able to generate a consistent set of data and a series of hypotheses for the child's behavior across a variety of settings.

- Requests should be made to review school records, including report cards and the results of any group achievement testing. If weak performance or learning disabilities are suspected, or if the child is already receiving special education services, the therapist should review all assessment data as well as the child's individualized education plan. It is then proper to decide which tests and what amount of time should be used to arrive at the most accurate evaluation of the child. Clinicians should be cautioned that *no specific tests to evaluate ADHD are available*. The primary purpose of vis-à-vis assessment with the child should involve addressing issues related to the child's emotional status, self-esteem, cognitive development, and any specific learning disabilities. Observation of the child's behavior during assessment also may yield clues regarding his or her interpersonal style and temperament.

- Although a number of paper-and-pencil tasks have

been used over the years in research settings to identify symptoms of ADHD, most do not lend themselves easily to clinical use. In research studies, some of these tests, such as the Matching Familiar Figures Test (Kagan, 1964), appear to have high positive and negative predictive power for identifying impulsive children. However, in clinical practice, such instruments have not been reliable for confirming the diagnosis of ADHD. Computerized instruments designed to measure sustained attention and the ability to inhibit impulsive responses (Gordon, 1983; Greenberg, 1991) have become increasingly popular among mental health professionals. Although these instruments may have a high positive predictive power (i.e., if the child fails the task, it strongly confirms the presence of symptoms related to ADHD), they possess poor negative predictive power (if the child passes the task, conclusions cannot be drawn one way or the other concerning the diagnosis). Nonetheless, many therapists rely on such instruments to provide additional data for the diagnostic process rather than a specific data point to confirm or disconfirm the diagnosis of ADHD.

TREATMENT

Treatment of ADHD should be multidisciplinary, multimodal, and maintained over a long period (Barkley, 1991; Goldstein & Goldstein, 1990, 1992). By far, the most effective short-term interventions for children and adolescents with ADHD reflect the combined use of medical, behavioral, and environmental techniques. Medication reduces the manipulative power of the child's behavior in eliciting certain responses from teachers, peers, and family members; behavior management increases the salience of behaving in a way more consistent with the environment's expectations; and environmental manipulation (e.g., locking the cabinets) reduces the risk of problems within the natural setting.

If the core problems of children with ADHD reflect an inability to permit sufficient time to think or respond consistently to consequences, the underlying theoretical basis for managing ADHD problems must evolve from these deficits and the subsequent difficulties that these children experience. Regardless of the treatment modality used, the basic underlying premise in managing ADHD in children must involve increasing their capacity for thoughtful patience and consideration. Medical, behavioral, environmental, and even adjunctive interventions (such as cognitive training) must flow logically from this theorem. Children with ADHD must be helped to think logically and concentrate longer.

MEDICATION

The literature attests to the benefits of methylphenidate (Ritalin) in reducing key symptoms of ADHD, including inattentiveness, motor overactivity, and impulsiveness (Klein, 1987). Stimulants have consistently been reported to improve academic attainment and productivity; accuracy of classwork (Douglas, Barr, O'Neil, & Britton, 1986); attention span; reading comprehension; and even complex problem solving (Balthazor, Wagner, & Pelham, 1991; Pelham, 1986). Related problems also improve, including peer interactions and peer status (Whalen & Henker, 1991).

Approximately 90% of children in the United States who take medication for ADHD receive the stimulant methylphenidate. An additional 8%–9% of children with ADHD take other stimulants (i.e., dextroamphetamine [Dexedrine], pemoline [Cylert], and methamphetamine [Desoxyn]). Less than 1% of treated children presently are given a nonstimulant for ADHD; the majority of this small group receives one of the tricyclic antidepressants (e.g., imipramine [Tofranil], desipramine [Norpramin, Pertofrane], or nortriptyline [Aventyl, Pamelor]. Although other drugs, including the antihypertensive clonidine (Catapres) and the selective serotonin reuptake inhibitors (e.g., fluoxetine [Prozac], paroxetine [Paxil], and sertraline [Zoloft]), are being used on a limited clinical basis in children with ADHD, research has not consistently demonstrated that they are as effective as stimulant medications. Nonetheless, for children for whom stimulants are contraindicated (e.g., those with Tourette's syndrome, severe depression, or anxiety), these medications may serve as reasonable alternatives.

The response of children with ADHD to the administration of methylphenidate often is remarkably positive. Placebo-controlled, double-blind trials demonstrated that 75%–80% of children with ADHD responded to methylphenidate, whereas only 30%–40% responded to placebo (Barkley, 1990; Goldstein & Goldstein, 1990; Greenhill & Osman, 1991). Conducted in classroom settings, these trials found that time spent on a task, work completion, accuracy of work, and general conduct improved dramatically; conflicts with peers and siblings declined; and negative interactions between parents and the child with ADHD also declined.

The effect of methylphenidate on academic performance has been controversial. It was initially suggested that there was little improvement in academic performance with the use of methylphenidate despite the dramatic improvement in behavior. It was also suggested that dosages of methylphenidate that optimized behavior did not improve learning, and dosages that improved learning did not optimize behavior.

DuPaul and Rapport (1993) examined 31 children with attention-deficit disorder in a double-blind, placebo-controlled trial of four doses of stimulant medication. Methylphenidate exerted a significant positive effect on classroom measures of attention and academic efficiency to the point that these problems were no longer statistically deviant in the ADHD population. However, on individual examination, 25% of the children with ADHD failed to demonstrate normalized levels of classroom performance, suggesting that although stimulant medications are beneficial, a need for ancillary interventions for the ADHD population remains.

Almost all children with ADHD who do not respond to one stimulant may derive clinical benefit in the classroom from another (Elia, Borcherding, Rapoport, & Keysor, 1991). However, what defines a good response is debatable. When a good response is defined as a reduction in cardinal symptoms of ADHD and improvement in behavior and compliance at school, at least 80% of children appropriately diagnosed with ADHD respond to medication (Barkley, 1990; Goldstein & Goldstein 1990). However, when a good response is defined by performance on a cognitive task, such as *paired associate learning*, a greater number of children with ADHD are unresponsive to stimulants (Swanson, Cantwell, Lerner, McBurnett, & Hanna, 1991).

Improvement appears to be related directly to the amount of methylphenidate prescribed. Although these improvements may be significant statistically, they are not as dramatic as the effects on behavior. Increasing single doses of methylphenidate beyond 15–20 mg may cause deterioration of behavior that follows a time course similar to that of the improvement seen at lower dosages.

Long-term effects of methylphenidate have been debated. Studies using stimulant medication in children have demonstrated consistent short-term benefits but have not demonstrated significant long-term benefits into adulthood. When outlook was measured in terms of socioeconomic status, vocation, marriage, drug addiction, or criminal behavior, minimal long-term positive effects of stimulants were demonstrated. Some studies suggested that multidisciplinary treatment, including medication, may have a positive impact on long-term outlook. However, the immediate short-term benefits of stimulant medication far outweigh the liabilities and, thus, appear to justify the continued use of these medications in the treatment of ADHD.

Table 3.2 contains an overview of common medications and

respective dosages used in the treatment of ADHD. Sustained-release methylphenidate was developed to allow a longer-acting preparation. Initial tests suggested it had an 8-hour half-life and was effective in the treatment of ADHD symptoms in a once-a-day dosage. However, subsequent studies and clinical experience have indicated that sustained-release methylphenidate has a variable onset and duration of action and usually is not as useful as the regular formula. Because methylphenidate is effective for approximately 4 hours, it often is used in multiple dosages. Many physicians start with a single daily dose and then evaluate onset and withdrawal; second and third doses are provided as needed.

EDUCATIONAL INTERVENTIONS

Abramowitz and O'Leary (1991) reported on the various effective educational interventions for ADHD-related problems in the classroom, including positive- and negative-contingent teacher attention, token economies, peer-mediated and group contingencies, time-out, home-school contingencies, reductive techniques based on reinforcement, and cognitive-behavioral strategies. Environmental and task modifications are also critical for classroom success for the child suffering from ADHD. However, additional research is clearly needed, especially in the area of school-based intervention for adolescents with ADHD.

A summary of the classroom research data dealing with ADHD in children has led to a number of general conclusions (Barkley, 1990; Goldstein & Goldstein, 1990; Parker, 1992):

- Classrooms should be organized and structured with clear rules, a predictable schedule, and separate desks.

- Rewards should be consistent, immediate, salient, and frequent.

Table 3.2
MEDICATION CHART FOR TREATING ATTENTION-DEFICIT DISORDERS

Drug	RITALIN Methylphenidate	RITALIN–SR Methylphenidate *Sustained-release formula*	DEXEDRINE Dextroamphet- amine
Dosing	Start with a morning dose of 5 mg/d and increase up to 0.3–0.7 mg/kg body weight 2.5–60 mg/d*	Start with a morning dose of 20 mg and increase up to 0.3–0.7 mg/kg body weight. Sometimes 5 or 10 mg standard tablet in morning for quick start, up to 60 mg/d*	Start with a morning dose of 5 mg 0.3–0.7 mg/kg body weight. Give in divided doses 2–3 times per day 2.5–40 mg/d*
Common Side Effects	Insomnia, decreased appetite, weight loss, headache, irritability, stomach-ache	Insomnia, decreased appetite, weight loss, headache, irritability, stomach ache	Insomnia, decreased appetite, weight loss, headache, irritability, stomach ache
DBH† (hr)	3–4	7	3–4 (tablets) 8–10 (spansule)
Pros	Works quickly (within 30–60 min); effective in 70% of patients; good safety record	Particularly useful for adolescents with ADHD to avoid noontime dose; good safety record	Works quickly (within 30–60 min); may avoid noontime doses in spansule form; good safety record
Precautions	Not recommended in patients with marked anxiety, motor tics, or family history of Tourette's syndrome	Not recommended in patients with marked anxiety, motor tics, or family history of Tourette's syndrome	Not recommended in patients with marked anxiety, motor tics, or family history of Tourette's syndrome

* *Daily dosage*
†*Duration of behavioral effects*

CYLERT Pemoline	TOFRANIL Imipramine	NORPRAMIN Desipramine	CATAPRES Clonidine
Start with a dose of 18.75–37.5 mg and increase up to 112.5 mg as needed in single morning dose 18.75–112.5 mg/d*	Start with a dose of 10 mg in evening if weight <50 lb and increase 10 mg every 3–5 days as needed; start with a dose of 25 mg in evening if weight is >50 lb and increase 25 mg every 3–5 days as needed. Given in single or divided doses morning and evening 25–110 mg/d*	Start with a dose of 10 mg in evening if weight <50 lb and increase 10 mg every 3–5 days as needed; start with a dose of 25 mg in evening if weight is >50 lb and increase 25 mg every 3–5 days as needed. Given in single or divided doses morning and evening 25–110 mg/d*	Start with a dose of 0.025–0.05 mg/d in evening and increase by similar dose every 3–7 days as needed. Given in divided doses 3–4 times per day 0.15–3 mg/d*
Insomnia, agitation, headaches, stomach aches; infrequently, abnormal liver function tests reported	Dry mouth, decreased appetite, headache, stomach ache, dizziness, constipation, mild tachycardia	Dry mouth, decreased appetite, headache, stomach ache, dizziness, constipation, mild tachycardia	Sleepiness, hypotension, headache, dizziness, stomach ache, nausea, dry mouth
12–24	12–24	12–24	3–6 (oral form)
Given only once a day	Helpful for ADHD patients with comorbid depression or anxiety; lasts throughout the day	Helpful for ADHD patients with comorbid depression or anxiety; lasts throughout the day	Helpful for ADHD patients with comorbid tic disorder or severe hyperactivity or aggression
May take 2–4 weeks for a clinical response; regular blood tests needed to check liver function	May take 2–4 weeks for clinical response; to detect preexisting cardiac conduction defect, a baseline ECG†† may be recommended; discontinue gradually	May take 2–4 weeks for clinical response; to detect preexisting cardiac conduction defect, a baseline ECG†† may be recommended; discontinue gradually	Sudden discontinuation could result in rebound hypertension; to avoid daytime tiredness, starting dose should be given at bedtime and increased slowly

†† ECG, electrocardiogram.

- A response-cost reinforcement program is recommended as an integral part of the classroom.

- Feedback from teachers should be constant.

- Minor disruptions that do not bother others should be ignored.

- Academic materials should be matched to the child's ability.

- Tasks in the classroom should vary but should generally be of interest to the child.

- Transition times, as well as recess and assemblies, should be supervised closely.

- Teachers and parents should maintain close communication, especially in the lower grades.

- Teachers' expectations should be adjusted to meet the child's skill level, both behaviorally and academically.

- Teachers should be educated concerning the issues of ADHD in the classroom and develop a repertoire of interventions to effectively manage this pattern of behavior to minimize the negative impact of the child's temperament on the child and on the entire classroom population.

Thus far, school-based interventions for secondary students are less developed and include weekly progress reports, work with an academic coach, study skills, test-taking and organizational training, and mature versions of classroom interventions used with younger students. A specific focus for secondary school students includes academic problems most commonly encountered by students with ADHD, including problems with written language, spelling, and basic mathematics.

Zentall (1994) suggested that students with ADHD possess an active learning style with a demonstrated need to move, talk, respond, question, choose, debate, and even provoke. Suggestions for classroom interventions and Zentall's instructional model flow logically from three guideposts: *move, talk/question, and learn*. Activating these premises would entail a new and challenging classroom paradigm.

PARENTING SKILLS

Parents must be counseled to understand that to manage their child's ADHD at home requires accurate knowledge of the disorder and its complications. They must be consistent, predictable, and supportive of their child in their daily interactions. Significant research on childhood resilience clearly reflects that the best outcomes for children facing adversity are achieved through the habitual relationships they develop with their caregivers (Fonagy, Steele, Steele, Higgitt, & Target, 1994; Werner, 1994).

The following guidelines are recommended when working with parents of children with ADHD. These guidelines can be implemented on an individual basis or incorporated into a comprehensive parent-training program.

- *Education.* Parents must be urged to become educated consumers. They must understand this disorder thoroughly because it will affect their child throughout his or her entire life.

- *Incompetence versus noncompliance.* Parents must develop an understanding and be able to distinguish between problems of incompetence (nonpurposeful problems resulting from the child's inconsistent application of skills leading to performance and behavioral deficits) and problems of noncompliance (purposeful problems that occur when children do not wish to do as they are asked or directed). However, because at least half of children with ADHD also experience other disruptive, noncompliant problems, parents must develop a system to differentiate between these two issues and possess a set of interventions for both.

- *Appropriate commands.* Parents must be taught to tell their child specifically what to do in a clear, operationally defined way. More often than not, parents of children with ADHD, give too many unclear and abrupt commands, such as "stop that" or "pay attention," out of frustration.

- *Rewards.* Children with ADHD require frequent, predictable, and consistent rewards. Both social (praise) and tangible rewards (toys, treats, privileges) must be provided more frequently when a child with ADHD is compliant or succeeds. It is likely that the child with ADHD receives less positive reinforcement than his or her siblings. Parents must work to keep a balance as well as to avoid the issue of negative reinforcement (paying attention to the child when he or she acts inappropriately and removing attention when appropriate behavior is exhibited). Negative reinforcement often leads to immediate compliance; however, in the long term, it reinforces, rather than discourages, inappropriate behavior.

- *Timing.* Parents must recognize that consequences (both rewards and punishments) must be provided quickly and consistently.

- *Response cost.* A modified response-cost program (you can lose what you earn) must be used at home with a child with ADHD. This system can provide the child with all reinforcers the first day. He or she must then work to keep them. Parents have the option of allowing the child to earn at least three to five times the amount of rewards for good behavior versus what is lost for negative behavior (e.g., earn five chips for doing something right, lose one chip for doing something wrong).

- *Planning.* Parents must be helped to understand the forces that affect their child. They must not personalize the child's problems. When the child acts the way his or her parents hope he or she will, it is natural for them to feel that they are being good parents. When the child does not meet expectations, parents tend to judge themselves severely. Parents must learn to respond to their child's limits in a proactive way. They should be guided to avoid placing their child in a situation that exacerbates the ADHD.

- *Take care of yourself.* Families with a child suffering from ADHD experience greater stress, more marital disharmony, potentially more severe emotional problems between the parents, and often succeed or fail based on reactions to the child's behavior. Parents must understand the impact their child with ADHD has on other family members and defuse family tensions in a constructive manner. Parents should do their best to anticipate and forestall potential problems.

- *Take care of your child.* Parents must recognize that the relationship they develop with their child with

ADHD is likely to be strained. They must take extra time to balance the scales and maintain a positive relationship. They should be urged to find enjoyable activities and engage in those activities with their child as often as possible, at least a number of times per week.

Parents of a child with ADHD must recognize that if they approach each day with a sense of hope, encouragement, acceptance, and honesty, they will empower their child. If they approach each day with a sense of despair, discouragement, anger, and blame, they will jeopardize their child's external locus of control and foster a perception on the child's part of his or her own powerlessness and hopelessness.

DEVELOPMENT OF SOCIAL SKILLS

Peer-relation problems occur in approximately half of all children with ADHD (Guevremont, 1993). It has been suggested that social skills problems for children with ADHD result from either low-occurrence, high-impact problems (aggressive behavior), or from high-occurrence, low-impact problems (poor knowledge of basic skills). Alone or in combination, these factors result in peer rejection and neglect. Cognitive training in the form of enhancing social skills has not yielded consistent benefit for children with ADHD. Still, as Guevremont (1993) noted, questions concerning the benefits of social-skills training for children with ADHD must be asked within the context of specific goals.

Appropriate goals for teaching social skills to children with ADHD should include providing successful peer contacts and a positive experience, teaching adaptive social skills when they are lacking, promoting generalization to the natural setting to increase successful peer interactions, and improving the child's popularity.

In some studies, the failure of social skills training may

have resulted from a lack of effective generalization and not necessarily from inadequacies in the training (Goldstein & Goldstein, 1990). Most social skills programs for children with ADHD are brief, occur in a clinic with children whom they do not know, and are far removed from their natural setting. When these variables are manipulated positively, social skills training appears to hold greater benefit for children with ADHD.

A sample program called *Making and Keeping Friends* (Sheridan, 1993) offers a glimpse into the future of social skills training for ADHD children. This social skills intervention package was developed to teach or strengthen social skills in children with ADHD, introduce parents to methods of helping their children in social situations, and engage teachers in social skills intervention via a consultation model. The latter two factors enhance and increase generalization, thereby improving opportunities to achieve healthy socialization for children with ADHD.

The *Making and Keeping Friends* program begins with screening for appropriate group members. This particular 16-week program, developed for children ages 9–12, teaches three general areas of social skills: social entry, maintaining interactions, and problem solving. Specific social skills taught include learning how to start a conversation, joining an ongoing activity, recognizing and expressing feelings, having a conversation with others, playing cooperatively, solving problems, dealing with arguments or conflict, teasing, being left out, using self-control, and accepting "no" for an answer. This program also includes an extensive manual for parents, and skills are taught to parents in weekly meetings. In addition to acquainting parents with what their children are being taught, the program focuses on promoting use of these skills in daily life.

Similar programs have been developed and are being researched with children of all ages. The work of Goldstein and colleagues (Goldstein, Sprafkin, Gershaw, & Klein, 1980; McGinnis, Goldstein, Sprafkin, & Gershaw, 1984) exemplifies research with these other populations. Rating scales and check-lists are completed to obtain a thorough overview of specific appropriate and inappropriate behaviors observed by adults in the target child as well as situations in which those problems occur.

COGNITIVE STRATEGIES

During the past decade, there has been a tremendous upsurge of scientific and public interest in ADHD. Great strides have been made in understanding and managing this disorder. However, many questions have yet to be answered concerning effective treatments.

The repeatedly and scientifically proven treatments reviewed in this chapter ostensibly have benefited children with ADHD beyond a level of chance. However, certain treatments have been advocated as proven and beneficial for children with ADHD. Such interventions are controversial because they have been instituted without consistent research supporting their effectiveness. Many are supported through testimonials, single case studies, and marketing ploys offering "proof" of the effectiveness of the treatment. Examples include the suggested use of megavitamins, oil of evening primrose, dietary manipulation, and antimotion sickness medications (e.g., dimenhydrinate [Dramamine]) to abate ADHD symptoms.

The use of cognitive strategies also has been heralded as a beneficial treatment for ADHD with limited scientific support. Beginning in the early 1970s, these strategies (learning to think differently and thereby act differently) were repeatedly tested and suggested as effective for children with ADHD. These strategies emphasized teaching a child with ADHD to approach a task or problem analytically by asking himself or herself questions such as: *What is my problem? What alternatives do I have? How can I implement an alternative? How am I doing?* After initial training on tasks such as puzzles and mazes, children are taught to apply their new skills to schoolwork and social situations. For example, to help children learn to cope with difficult social situations in a less impulsive manner, training programs include role playing and problem solving. In the home setting, cognitive and self-control training has been used to teach children with ADHD to think through and resolve problems more efficiently. In the classroom, cognitive training has been used to help children control their behavior, follow rules, and remain on task (Braswell & Bloomquist, 1991).

Unlike other controversial treatments for children with ADHD, cognitive training approaches have been studied in controlled experiments using sophisticated measurement techniques and statistical procedures. However, the emerging scientific literature suggests that these approaches have not met the treatment potential attributed to them 20 years ago. Although these strategies may be helpful for children with other disorders, such as learning disabilities or problems controlling anger, they have not been as effective in the management of ADHD. In combination with medication, behavior management, or environmental manipulation, cognitive training may yield some additional benefits. However, the amount of benefit obtained must be weighed against the cost and significant amount of time required to implement this form of treatment. Cognitive interventions that have proved beneficial for children with ADHD take place over many sessions and must incorporate strong generalized components.

CONCLUSION

Because ADHD is a biopsychosocial disorder, clinicians must possess a thorough knowledge of the developmental course, definition, evaluation procedures, and proven treatments for the disorder. Although nonprescribing clinicians often are well aware of cognitive and behavioral treatment strategies for children's disorders, their knowledge of medications used to treat emotional and behavioral problems, as well as their ability to communicate with treating physicians, may be lacking.

Furthermore, therapists must understand the educational system and available special services. The majority of children with ADHD require some type of assisted intervention at school, either through special education via the Individuals with Disabilities Education Act (IDEA) or through accommodations through Section 504 of the Americans with Disabilities Act (ADA).

The evaluative process does not end with making the diagnosis. Even the best diagnosis may not yield compliance with recommendations for treatment if parents do not understand the diagnostic process, the means by which the diagnosis was determined, and the reasons that certain treatment recommendations should be followed.

Clinicians also must recognize that the best predictors of outcome for a child with ADHD appear to lie within the child's social frame of reference, rather than within the child himself or herself. Parents must be helped to recognize that the most powerful predictors of positive adult outcome for children with ADHD include parents who are competent, develop a warm relationship with their child, are available, take an interest in the child's education, foster the child's self-worth, and meet the child's physical needs (Fonagy et al., 1994). Clinicians should help parents understand that as long as the balance between stressful life events and surrounding protective factors is favorable, children with ADHD stand a significantly better chance of entering adulthood successfully.

The topic of ADHD continues to be the most widely researched area in childhood development. Although new information is made available virtually on a daily basis, it is not likely that more effective medications or other treatments will be discovered in the foreseeable future. In the immediate future, factors relating to issues of resilience (i.e., those factors that help all affected children survive the disorder) will be emphasized because current research suggests that these factors — especially those related to family relations, school, and social success — play a larger role than once thought in determining the success or failure of adults who endured ADHD as children.

REFERENCES

Abramowitz, A. J., & O'Leary, S. G. (1991). Behavioral interventions for the classroom: Implications for students with ADHD. *School Psychology Review, 20,* 220–234.

Achenbach, T. M., & Edelbrock, C. S. (1991). *Normative data for the child behavior checklist — revised.* Burlington, VT: University of Vermont, Department of Psychiatry.

Ackerman, P. T., Dykman, R. A., & Peters, J. E. (1977). Teenage status of hyperactive and nonhyperactive learning-disabled boys. *American Journal of Orthopsychiatry, 47,* 577–596.

American Psychiatric Association (1994). *Diagnostic and statistical manual of mental disorders* (4th ed.). Washington, DC: Author.

Baker, L., & Cantwell, D. P. (1987). A prospective psychiatric follow-up of children with speech/language disorders. *Journal of the American Academy of Child and Adolescent Psychiatry, 26,* 546–553.

Baker, L., & Cantwell, D. P. (1992). Attention deficit disorder and speech/language disorders. *Comprehensive Mental Health Care, 2,* 3–16.

Balthazor, M. J., Wagner, R. K., & Pelham, W. E. (1991). The specificity of the effects of stimulant medication on classroom learning-related measures of cognitive processing for attention deficit disorder children. *Journal of Abnormal Child Psychology, 19,* 35–52.

Barkley, R. A. (1981). *Hyperactive children: A handbook for diagnosis and treatment.* New York: Guilford Press.

Barkley, R. A. (Ed.). (1990). *Attention-deficit/hyperactivity disorder: A handbook for diagnosis and treatment.* New York: Guilford Press.

Barkley, R. A. (1991). Diagnosis and assessment of attention-deficit hyperactivity disorder. *Comprehensive Mental Health Care, 1,* 27–43.

Barkley, R. A. (1994). More on the new theory of ADHD. *The ADHD Report, 2,* 1–4.

Barkley, R. A., Fischer, M., Edelbrock, C. S., & Smallish, L. (1989). The adolescent outcome of hyperactive children diagnosed by research criteria, I: An 8-year, prospective follow-up study. *Journal of the American Academy of Child and Adolescent Psychiatry, 29,* 546–557.

Berry, C. A., Shaywitz, S. E., & Shaywitz, B. A. (1985). Girls with attention deficit disorder: A silent minority? A report on behavioral and cognitive characteristics. *Pediatrics, 76,* 801–809.

Biederman, J., Munir, K., & Knee, D. (1987). Conduct and oppositional disorder in clinically referred children with attention deficit disorder: A controlled family study. *Journal of the American Academy of Child and Adolescent Psychiatry, 26,* 724–727.

Braswell, L., & Bloomquist, M. L. (1991). *Cognitive-behavioral therapy with ADHD children: Child, family, and school interventions.* New York: Guilford Press.

Campbell, S. B., Endman, M. W. & Bernfeld, G. (1977). A 3-year follow-up of hyperactive preschoolers into elementary school. *Journal of Child Psychology and Psychiatry, 18,* 239-249.

Cantwell, D. P., Baker, L. & Mattison, R. (1981). Prevalence, type, and correlates of psychiatric disorder in 200 children with communication disorder. *Journal of Developmental and Behavioral Pediatrics, 2,* 131–136.

Carey, W. B. (1970). A simplified method for measuring infant temperament. *Journal of Pediatrics, 77,* 188–194.

Chess, S., & Thomas, A. (1986). *Temperament in clinical practice.* New York: Guilford Press.

Cohen, N. J., Davine, M., & Meloche-Kelly, M. (1989). Prevalence of unsuspected language disorders in a child psychiatric population. *Journal of the American Academy of Child and Adolescent Psychiatry, 28,* 107–111.

Cohen, N. J., Sullivan, S., Minde, K. K., Novak, C., & Helwig, C. (1981). Evaluation of the relative effectiveness of methylphenidate and cognitive behavior modification in the treatment of kindergarten-aged hyperactive children. *Journal of Abnormal Child Psychology, 9,* 43–54.

Conners, C. K. (1975). Minimal brain dysfunction and psychopathology in children. In A. Davids (Ed.), *Child personality and psychopathology: Volume 2: Current topics* (pp. 87–133). New York: Wiley Interscience Press.

Conners, C. K. (1989). *Conners teacher rating scales.* Toronto: Multi-Health Systems.

Douglas, V. I. (1972). Stop, look, and listen: The problem of sustained attention and impulse control in hyperactive and normal children. *Canadian Journal of Behavioral Science, 4,* 259–282.

Douglas, V. I. (1985). The response of ADD children to reinforcement: Theoretical and clinical implications. In L. N. Bloomingdale (Ed.), *Attention deficit disorder: Identification, course, and rationale* (pp 110–135). Jamaica, NY: Spectrum.

Douglas, V. I., Barr, R. G., O'Neil, M. E., & Britton, B. G. (1986). Short-term effects of methylphenidate on the cognitive, learning, and academic performance of children with attention deficit disorder in the laboratory and classroom. *Journal of Child Psychology and Psychiatry, 27,* 191–211.

Douglas, V. I., & Peters, K. G. (1979). Toward a clearer definition of the attentional deficit of hyperactive children. In G. A. Hale & M. Lewis (Eds.), *Attention and the development of cognitive skills* (pp. 225–243). New York: Plenum Press.

Driscoll, M. S., & Zecker, S. G. (1991). Attention deficit disorder: Are there subtypes? A review of the literature from 1980 to 1989. *Learning Disabilities, 2,* 55–64.

DuPaul, G. J. (1990). *Academic performance rating scale and ADHD Rating Scale.* Worcester, MA: Department of Psychiatry, University of Massachusetts.

DuPaul, G. J., Guevremont, D. C., & Barkley, R. A. (1992). Behavioral treatment of attention-deficit/hyperactivity disorder in the classroom: The use of the attention training system. *Journal of Behavioral Modification, 16,* 204–225.

DuPaul, G. J., & Rapport, M. D. (1993). Does methylphenidate normalize the classroom performance of children with attention-deficit disorder? *Journal of the American Academy of Child and Adolescent Psychiatry, 32,* 190–198.

Edelbrock, C. S. (1990). Childhood attention problems (CAP) scale. In R. A. Barkley (Ed.), *Attention-deficit/hyperactivity disorder: A handbook for diagnosis and treatment* (p. 211). New York: Guilford Press.

Elia, J., Borcherding, B. G., Rapoport, J. L., & Keysor, C. S. (1991). Methylphenidate and dextroamphetamine treatments of hyperactivity: Are there true nonresponders? *Psychiatry Research, 36,* 141–155.

Fonagy, P., Steele, M., Steele, H., Higgitt, A. & Target, M. (1994). The Emanuel Miller Memorial Lecture, 1992: The theory and practice of resilience. *Journal of Child Psychology and Psychiatry, 35,* 231–257.

Glow, R. S., & Glow, P. H. (1980). Peer- and self-rating: Children's perception of behavior relevant to hyperkinetic impulsive disorder. *Journal of Abnormal Child Psychology, 8,* 471–490.

Goldstein, S. (1995). *Understanding and managing children's classroom behavior.* New York: Wiley Interscience Press.

Goldstein, S., & Goldstein, M. (1990). *Managing attention disorders in children: A guide for practitioners.* New York: Wiley Interscience Press.

Goldstein, S., & Goldstein, M. (1992). *Hyperactivity: Why won't my child pay attention?* New York: Wiley Interscience Press.

Goldstein, A. P., Sprafkin, R. P., Gershaw, N. J., & Klein, P. (1980). *Skillstreaming the adolescent: A structured learning approach to teaching prosocial skills.* Champaign, IL: Research Press.

Gordon, M. (1983). *The Gordon diagnostic system.* Dewitt, NY: Gordon Systems.

Greenberg, L. (1991). *Test of variables of attention (TOVA).* St. Paul, MN: Attention Technology, Inc.

Greenhill, L. L., & Osman, B. B. (1991). *Ritalin: Theory and patient management.* New York: Mary Ann Liebert Publishers.

Guevremont, D.C. (1993). Social skills training: A viable treatment for ADHD? *ADHD Report, 1*(1), 6,7.

Haenlein, M., & Caul, W. F. (1987). Attention deficit disorder with hyperactivity. A specific hypothesis of reward dysfunction. *Journal of the American Academy of Child and Adolescent Psychiatry, 26,* 356-362.

Hauser, P., Zametkin, A. J., Martinez, P., Vitiello, B., Matochik, J. A., Mixson, A. J., & Weintraub, B. D. (1993). Attention-deficit/hyperactivity disorder in people with generalized resistance to thyroid hormone. *New England Journal of Medicine, 328,* 997.

Hynd, G. W., Hern, K. L., Voeller, K. K., & Marshall, R. M. (1991). Neurobiological basis of attention-deficit disorder (ADD). *School Psychology Review, 20,* 174-186.

Ingersoll, B. D., & Goldstein, S. (1993). *Attention deficit disorder and learning disabilities: Realities, myths, and controversial treatments.* New York: Doubleday.

Kagan, J. (1964). *The matching familiar figures test.* Unpublished, Harvard University, Cambridge, MA.

Kashani, J., Chapel, J., & Ellis, J. (1979). Hyperactive girls. *Journal of Operational Psychiatry, 10,* 145-149.

Kirby, E. A., & Grimley, L. K., (1986). *Understanding and treating attention deficit disorder.* New York: Pergamon Press.

Klein, R. G. (1987). Pharmacology of childhood hyperactivity: An update. In H. Y. Meltzer (Ed.), *Psychopharmacology: The third generation of progress* (pp. 158-193). New York: Raven Press.

Lapouse, R., & Monk, M. A. (1958). An epidemiologic study of behavior characteristics in children. *American Journal of Public Health, 48,* 1134–1144.

Loney, J., Kramer, J., & Milich, R. S. (1981). The hyperactive child grown up: Predictors of symptoms, delinquency, and achievement at follow-up. In K. D. Gadow & J. Loney (Eds.), *Psychosocial aspects of drug treatment for hyperactivity* (pp. 310–343). Boulder, CO: Westview Press.

Mannuzza, S., Klein, R. G., Bonagura, N., Malloy, P., Giampino, T. L., & Addalli, K. A. (1991). Hyperactive boys almost grown up. V. Replication of psychiatric status. *Archives of General Psychiatry, 48,* 77–83.

McGee, R., & Share, D. L. (1988). Attention-deficit disorder hyperactivity and academic failure: Which comes first and what should be treated? *Journal of the American Academy of Child and Adolescent Psychiatry, 27,* 318–325.

McGee, R., Williams, S., & Silva, P. A. (1987). A comparison of girls and boys with teacher-identified problems of attention. *Journal of the American Academy of Child and Adolescent Psychiatry, 26,* 711–716.

McGinnis, E., Goldstein, A. P., Sprafkin, R. P., & Gershaw, N. J. (1984). *Skill-streaming the elementary school child: A guide for teaching prosocial skills.* Champaign, IL: Research Press.

Milich, R. S., & Loney, J. (1979). The role of hyperactive and aggressive symptomatology in predicting adolescent outcome among hyperactive children. *Journal of Pediatric Psychology, 4,* 93–112.

Morrison, J., & Stewart, M. A. (1973). The psychiatric status of legal families of adopted hyperactive children. *Archives of General Psychiatry, 28,* 888–891.

Palkes, H. S., & Stewart, M. A. (1972). Intellectual ability and performance of hyperactive children. *American Journal of Orthopsychiatry, 42,* 35–39.

Parker, H. C. (1992). *The ADD hyperactivity workbook for schools.* Plantation, FL: ADD Warehouse.

Pelham, W. E. (1986). The effects of psychostimulant drugs on learning and academic achievement in children with attention-deficit disorders and learning disabilities. In J. K. Torgeson & B.Y.L. Wong (Eds.), *Psychological and educational perspectives on learning disabilities* (pp. 48–67). San Diego: Academic Press.

Pelham, W. E., & Bender, M. E. S. (1982). Peer relationships and hyperactive children: Description and treatment. In K. Gadow & I. Bailer (Eds.), *Advances in learning and behavioral disabilities* (Vol. 1, pp. 111-148). Greenwich, CT: JAI Press.

Pelham, W. E., & Milich, R. (1984). Peer relations of children with hyperactivity/attention-deficit disorder. *Journal of Learning Disabilities, 17,* 560-568.

Ross, D. M., & Ross, S. A. (1982). *Hyperactivity: Current issues, research, and theory* (2nd ed.). New York: Wiley.

Satterfield, J. H., Hoppe, C. M., & Schell, A. M. (1982). A perspective study of delinquency in 110 adolescent boys with attention deficit disorder and 88 normal adolescent boys. *American Journal of Psychiatry, 139,* 795-798.

Schaughency, E. A., & Rothlind, J. (1991). Assessment and classification of attention-deficit/hyperactivity disorders. *School of Psychology Review, 20,* 187-202.

Sheridan, S. (1993). *Making and keeping friends.* Unpublished Manuscript, University of Utah, Salt Lake City, UT.

Stott, D. H. (1981). Behavior disturbance and failure to learn: A study of cause and effect. *Educational Research, 23,* 163-172.

Swanson, J. M., Cantwell, D., Lerner, M., McBurnett, K., & Hanna, G. (1991). Effects of stimulant medication on learning in children with ADHD. *Journal of Learning Disabilities, 24,* 219-230.

Terestman, N. (1980). Mood quality and intensity in nursery school children as predictors of behavior disorder. *American Journal of Orthopsychiatry, 50,* 125-138.

Thomas, A., & Chess, S. (1977). *Temperament and development.* New York: Brunner/Mazel.

Ullmann, R. K., Sleator, E. K., & Sprague, R. L. (1988). *ADD-H: Comprehensive teacher's rating scale.* Champaign, IL: Metri-Tech.

Weiss, G., & Hechtman, L. (1979). The hyperactive child syndrome. *Science, 205,* 1348-1354.

Weiss, G., & Hechtman, L. (1993). *The hyperactive child grown up* (2nd ed.). New York: Guilford Press.

Wender, P. H. (1975). The minimal brain dysfunction syndrome. *Annual Review of Medicine, 26,* 45–62.

Werner, E. E. (1994). Overcoming the odds. *Developmental and Behavioral Pediatrics, 15,* 131–136.

Whalen, C. K., & Henker, B. (1991). Social impact of stimulant treatment for hyperactive children. *Journal of Learning Disabilities, 24,* 231–241.

Whalen, C. K., Henker, B., Collins, B., McAuliffe, S., & Vaux, A. (1979). Peer interaction in a structured communication task: Comparisons of normal and hyperactive boys and of methylphenidate (Ritalin) and placebo effects. *Child Development, 50,* 388-401.

Whalen, C. K., Henker, B., & Dotemoto, S. (1981). Teacher response to methylphenidate (Ritalin) versus placebo status of hyperactive boys in the classroom. *Child Development, 52,* 1005–1014.

Yanow, M. (1973). Report on the use of behavior modification drugs on elementary school children. In M. Yanow (Ed.), *Observations from the treadmill* (pp. 27-46). New York: Viking Press.

Zametkin, A. J., & Rapoport, J. L. (1987). Neurobiology of attention deficit disorder with hyperactivity: Where have we come in 50 years? *Journal of the American Academy of Child and Adolescent Psychiatry, 26,* 676–686.

Zentall, S. S. (1988). Production deficiencies in elicited language but not in the spontaneous verbalizations of hyperactive children. *Journal of Abnormal Child Psychology, 16,* 657–673.

Zentall, S. (1994). Modifying classroom tasks and environments. In S. Goldstein (Ed.), *Understanding and managing classroom behavior.* New York: Wiley Interscience Press.

4

Homelessness and Depression in Children: Implications for Intervention

Janet Wagner, PhD, RN, Cathryne L. Schmitz, PhD, ACSW, and Edna Menke, PhD, RN

Dr. Wagner is Dean, Health and Human Services Division, Columbus State Community College, Columbus, OH. Dr. Schmitz is Assistant Professor, Saint Louis University School of Social Service, St. Louis, MO. Dr. Menke is Associate Professor, The Ohio State University College of Nursing, Department of Family and Community Medicine, Columbus, OH.

KEY POINTS

- Homelessness imposes severe mental, physical, and social deprivation on a significant number of children in the United States. The extreme poverty of homeless families puts them at high risk for negative consequences effecting the physical and mental health of the children.

- The results of two studies discussed in this chapter indicate a high incidence of depression in homeless school-age children. One study also suggests a posi- tive correlation between high levels of depression and anxiety.

- The needs of depressed homeless children can be met most effectively through the services of an interdisciplinary service team, coordinated by a case manager. Such a team consists of professionals with multiple skills and tools; together, they can provide interventions in nursing, social work, counseling, and child psychiatry.

Supported by the Ohio Department of Mental Health (grants no. 89.1019 and 92.1051) and the National Center for Nursing Research at the National Institutes of Health (grant no. 1R15NR02462)

INTRODUCTION

Children are emerging as the most frequent victims of poverty and homelessness as these problems become more severe in the United States. Children comprise the nation's fastest growing group among the homeless (Bassuk & Rubin, 1987; *The Crisis in Homelessness*, 1987). According to the Children's Defense Fund (1995), 22.7% of all U.S. children—including 42% of children in young families—are currently living below the federal poverty level, and children account for one in four homeless individuals, with 100,000 children homeless every night.

Research on the devastating effects of homelessness on families has been limited. The overall response to the needs of homeless families and children has been inadequate, and services remain fragmented and deficient. In addition to posing a physical threat, common sense and available studies suggest that homelessness puts children at risk for developing depression (Bassuk & Rubin, 1987).

This chapter reviews factors that can precipitate depression in homeless children, reports the results of research that indicates the extent of the self-reported depression among homeless school-age children, and discusses the implications for interdisciplinary intervention designed to alleviate stress and mitigate the long-term impact of depression in homeless children. An explanation of case management, with a case example, completes the discussion.

BACKGROUND

Depression probably develops from a combination of physical, psychological, social, and environmental factors (Akiskal, 1979). Two discrete groups of theories have been noted: those that attribute depression to biologic causes and those that attribute depression to psychosocial causes (Kazdin, 1988). Most theories recognize the effect of negative life events; for example, in the *Diagnostic and Statistical Manual of Mental Disorders* (DSM-IV), the American Psychiatric Association (1994) applies a diagnostic label—"adjustment disorder with depressed moods"—to depressive symptoms that develop as a result of psychosocial stressors. Although the etiology of depression is complex, loss exceeding coping ability can be correlated with the development of depressive disorders (Beck & Rosenberg, 1986; Paykel, 1969).

DEPRESSION IN CHILDREN

Several subtypes of depression, with features similar to adult depression, have been identified in children (Puig-Antich & Gittleman, 1982). "Dysphoric mood and loss of interest in usual activities are acknowledged features of most forms of depression, although other signs, such as sleep disruption, may be present" (Wagner & Menke, 1991a, p. 20). Commonly used factors in differential diagnosis include precipitating events along with the severity, duration, and comorbidity with other psychiatric disorders (Kazdin, 1988). The course of childhood depression remains unclear; however, it is believed to have periods of remission and recurrence (Stark, Reynolds, & Kaslow, 1987).

How Depression Affects Children:

The consequences of childhood depression may be long lasting and far reaching. Children can experience deficits in multiple areas of their lives that can severely impair their interpersonal skills during depressive episodes (Puig-Antich et al., 1985). Depression can interfere with social relationships, limiting a child's ability to initiate conversations, make friends, or participate in social activities (Helsel & Matson, 1984). Self-destructive behaviors and significant disruption in normal development are other possible end results (Carlson, 1983; Puig-Antich et al., 1985). Depression may prevent a child from attaining his or her full potential and hinder the development of the skills necessary for effective functioning in future adult roles (Puig-Antich et al., 1985).

Factors That May Precipitate Depression in Homeless Children:

Homelessness is a life event often marked by economic and emotional upheaval involving drastic change, loss, and absence. According to Wagner and Menke (1991c), the typical homeless family has faced potentially negative life events during the 12 months preceding homelessness. Low-income families live precariously, frequently spending up to 70% of their income on rent, with no cushion for changes in income or housing costs (Mihaly, 1989). Bassuk and Rubin (1987) report that the most common events precipitating homelessness are eviction for nonpayment of rent and interpersonal conflict; Mills and Ota (1989) found that eviction, domestic conflict, and unsafe living conditions are common precipitating factors.

Marked by chaos and confusion (Boxill & Beaty, 1990), homelessness can develop into a terrifying crisis in a child's life. Children faced with the loss of their homes also often experience the loss of neighborhood, school, belongings, and friends. Moreover, homeless children are likely to be chastised and ostracized by peers (Gerwirtzman & Fodor, 1987). For children, the state of being homeless is generally also accompanied by a diminution of parental emotional support as adult family members attempt to provide for the family's physical needs. The mother-child relationship may be altered, and the child may lose any sense of permanence (Boxill & Beaty, 1990).

Incidence of Depression in Homeless Children:

Mental health professionals differ in their estimates of the prevalence of depressive disorders in children; however, general community surveys indicate that approximately 10% of children in the general population exhibit feelings of depression, and 60% of the children referred for psychiatric problems experience these feelings (Tongue, 1990). Research on homeless children by Bassuk and Rubin (1987) and Wagner and Menke (1991b) indicates that more than half of these children exhibit at least some depressive symptoms.

Although homelessness may not precipitate a diagnosable depressive reaction in all children, it is difficult to believe it does not have a profound effect in many children. In addition to all of their other problems, homeless children experience higher levels of dysphoria and depression than do other children their age (Bassuk & Rubin, 1987; Wagner & Menke, 1991a). Although many factors, including genetic predisposition, have an impact on the long-term effects of depression related to the experience of homelessness, research suggests that even mild depression may place children at risk for the development of a major depressive disorder (Brantly & Takacs, 1991).

THE COLUMBUS, OHIO STUDIES

Two studies conducted in Columbus, Ohio examine the physical and emotional well-being of children and families living in poverty (Schmitz, 1993; Schmitz, Wagner, & Menke, in press; Wagner & Menke, 1991b, 1993). Children in both studies exhibit depressive symptomatology; children in the second study show a positive correlation between high levels of depression and high levels of anxiety (Wagner, Menke, & Schmitz, 1992) and indicate a relationship between academic performance and both depression and anxiety (Schmitz, 1993). This is consistent with the Institute of Medicine's (1989) review of related research, which also finds a correlation between high levels of depression and high levels of anxiety, as does a study by Marchesano (1993), which adds a finding of a relationship between childhood depression and academic performance. Both Columbus studies provide evidence of depressive symptomatology; the second study provides evidence of a correlation between high levels of depression and high levels of anxiety in homeless children. This comorbidity indicates increased risk. These findings constitute additional evidence of increased short- and long-term risk for homeless children.

Method:

Data from 76 latency-age homeless children and their mothers in the first study (Wagner & Menke, 1991a, 1991b) and 71 in the second study (Schmitz, 1993; Wagner & Menke, 1993) were examined. The 76 latency-age children from the first study were part of a larger study that included 251 homeless families with children birth through 11 years; the 71 children in the second study were part of a study of 133 children living in poverty, 71 of whom were homeless at the time of the interview. The children in the first study were 8–11 years of age; the children in the second study were 8–12 years of age.

Selection Criteria

Children included in the Columbus studies lived with mothers who perceived themselves and their families to be homeless. They were in a living arrangement in which the actual stay or the intent to stay was fewer than 45 days. The studies included children who lived with their mothers in shelters, who were staying with other families or friends, or who lived in cars, vans, or barns. In accordance with criteria set by the study by Roth, Dean, Lust, and Saveanu (1985), families living in shelters for battered women were excluded. The children in the Columbus studies were members of homeless families solicited from shelters, transitional housing facilities, cheap hotels, churches, agencies that work with homeless families, and places where homeless persons frequently congregate (libraries, soup kitchens, and bus depots).

Instrumentation:

Each mother and child participated in a face-to-face interview and completed a number of standardized instruments. The interviews were conducted in the places where the mothers and children were temporarily sleeping. In both studies, each child completed the Children's Depression Inventory (CDI) (Kovacs, 1985). The second study also measured the children's anxiety using the Reynolds Manifest Anxiety Scale (Reynolds & Richmond, 1985). Demographic and background information about the children was collected from the mothers, using the mother version of the Homeless Children Interview Schedule.

The Homeless Children Interview Schedule-Mother Version contained questions regarding demographic information, health history, obstetric history, social history, general well-being, social network, and health care practices. The instrument used in the first study was derived from an interview used in a previous study and from a survey developed by Roth and colleagues (1985). The core of the instrument remained the same for the second study, with minor modifications.

The CDI is a self-rated, symptom-oriented scale for school-age children and adolescents (Kovacs, 1985). The inventory consists of 27 items regarding behavioral, affective, cognitive, somatic, and interpersonal aspects of depression. The total score can range from 0 to 54. A cutoff score of 9 indicates a need for further assessment and a score of 15 or above provides a good indicator of psychopathology (Fristad, Weller, Weller, & Teare, 1988). Test-retest reliability coefficients for the CDI have ranged from 0.50 to 0.84 (Kovacs, 1985).

The Reynolds Manifest Anxiety Scale is a 37-item test designed for children (Reynolds & Richmond, 1979, 1985) that originates from the adult Taylor Manifest Anxiety Scale (Castaneda, McCandless, & Palermo, 1956). It includes 25 items and a 9-item lie scale. All items are answered in a "yes" or "no" fashion and are aimed at those with a third-grade reading level; therefore, this test must be administered orally to children who have not achieved a third-grade reading level. Three subscales are included: (a) physiologic signs of anxiety, (b) indicators of worry and hypersensitivity, and (c) fear/

concentration (Reynolds & Richmond, 1979, 1985). Reynolds (1980) found support for construct validity as a measure of both chronic and situational anxiety. Test-retest reliability ranged from 0.60 to 0.88 for sixth- to eighth-grade boys and girls (Wisniewski, Mulick, Genshaft, & Coury, 1987).

Results:

The results from the Columbus studies provide evidence of the emotional impact of homelessness on children. Wagner and Menke (1991a, 1991b) found that 80% of the children had CDI scores indicating depressive symptoms and 34% had scores high enough to indicate the need for additional clinical evaluation for depression. The second study (Schmitz, 1993) found levels of depression almost as high—67% with symptomatology and 21% needing clinical evaluation. The second study also found 62% of the children exhibited some symptoms of anxiety, with almost a third needing further evaluation. A positive correlation existed in this study between anxiety and depression (r=49, p<.0001). The correlation adds evidence to previous studies showing a relationship between depression and anxiety.

Demographic Information
Table 4.1 summarizes the demographic characteristics of the homeless children 8–12 years of age from both studies gathered from The Homeless Children Interview Schedule—Mother Version.

Scores on Depression
The scores on the CDI for the studies samples ranged from 0 to 31, with a mean of 10.7 (SD=7.6), in the first study, and from 2 to 27, with a mean of 9.3 (SD=6.69), in the second study. Cronback alpha coefficients of 0. 83 for the first study and 0.80 for the second study were computed.

Just over a quarter (26%) of the subjects had scores of 9 or below, with 74% having scores above 9, indicating some depressive symptoms. Furthermore, 28% had scores of 15 or higher, indicating the potential for major difficulty. Seven children (5%) across the two studies had extreme scores that ranged from 27 to 31. A summary of scores on depression is presented in Table 4.2.

Table 4.1
DEMOGRAPHIC INFORMATION ON CHILDREN AND FAMILIES

Variable	Study One n = 76		Study Two n = 71	
	n	%	n	%
Gender				
Female	43	57	36	51
Male	33	43	35	49
Race				
African-American	55	72	47	66
Euro-American	21	28	19	27
Biracial	–	–	5	7
Age				
8 years	23	30	18	25
9 years	16	21	13	18
10 years	22	29	18	25
11 years	15	20	14	20
12 years	–	–	8	11

NB: percentages may add up to only 99% due to rounding.

Table 4.2
SUMMARY OF SCORES ON DEPRESSION

	Study One n = 76		Study Two n = 71	
	n	%	n	%
Scores $\leq$ 9	15	20	23	32
Scores $\geq$ 9	35	46	33	46
Scores $\geq$ 15	21	28	13	18
Scores $\leq$ 27	5	6	2	3

NB: percentages may add up to only 99% due to rounding.

Scores on Anxiety

The Reynold's Manifest Anxiety was used to measure children's anxiety in the second Columbus study. A Cronbach alpha of 0.87 was computed for the study. The scores ranged from 34 to 79 with a mean score of 53.7 (SD=10.7). Almost two thirds (62%) had scores above the standardized mean of 50 and 30% had scores above the clinical cutoff (60), indicating a need for further assessment. Table 4.3 lists a summary of scores on anxiety.

Table 4.3
SUMMARY OF SCORES ON REYNOLD'S MANIFEST ANXIETY

		n = 71	%
Scores ≤	50	27	38
Scores	51–59	23	32
Scores ≥	60	21	30

Discussion:

The results of the Columbus studies support the findings of previous research. Almost three quarters (74%) of the children identified as homeless had scores indicating some depressive symptoms, and more than one quarter (26%) of the children had scores indicating a need for more thorough clinical assessment (Fristad, Weller, Weller, & Teare, 1988). The presence of extreme scores in 5% of the children in these samples should sensitize health care and mental health providers to the intensity of the desperation and despair that children in these circumstances may feel, while alerting them to the potential for self-destructive behavior. The findings support the conclusion that depression is a potential serious mental health problem for homeless children.

The number of other stressors to which the child has been

exposed (Rutter, 1990), the meaning of the stressors to the child, and the child's particular coping style may mediate the stress response (Lazarus & Folkman, 1984) and alter its impact. Depressed homeless children may exhibit crisis reactions or grief behaviors as well as numerous other signs and symptoms. High suicide risk (as determined by high depressive scores and the presence of a suicide plan) may require immediate intervention and added support services to provide safety and structure. Health care professionals must assess the child's potential for self-destructive behaviors and implement a series of targeted interventions involving primary health and mental health professionals and possible referrals to social welfare agencies.

Evidence indicates that some factors may help protect children. Although research is just beginning in this area, a series of studies has been designed to uncover the factors that appear to protect children from the adverse effects of severe stressors. Garmezy (1981) and Rutter (1990) have identified some of these protective factors, including:

- Good physical health

- Easy temperament

- High self-esteem

- Positive social orientation

- Independent nature

- Ability to plan actions

- Ability to process the negative experience cognitively

- Ability to remove or distance oneself from an unalterable situation

- Success in some endeavor

- Strong family cohesion

- External social support systems

- Positive school experiences

These findings, along with more traditional approaches, can serve as preliminary guidelines for developing assessment protocols as well as a framework for designing an intervention plan to help ameliorate the lasting effects of stressors.

Implications for Practice — Crisis Intervention:

After an extensive review of the research on the prevalence and treatment of mental, behavioral, and developmental disorders of children, the Institute of Medicine (1989) finds "a growing body of evidence [that] supports the effectiveness of many treatments used in clinical care" (p. 202). They found evidence that many major childhood disorders, including depression and anxiety, are responsive to treatment. Although research is needed to determine which treatment or combination of treatments may be the most effective, "conventional treatments are demonstrably better than no treatment" (p. 202). Crisis intervention may be the ideal focus for beginning treatment with homeless children and families. In this situation, crisis intervention may become a forum for the safe expression of the emotions generated by homelessness, help promote family cohesion, and provide a mechanism for the generation of alternative solutions to the homeless problem.

Varying schools of thought attribute depression to differing agents, which, in turn, imply alternative treatment models (Kazdin, 1988). Examples include psychosocial interventions, such as individual or group counseling, and family therapy/ support; pharmacologic intervention; and case management. As a part of the process, cognitive therapy, social skills training, behavior therapy, self-control therapy, art and play therapies, increases in pleasant activities, and relaxation training have been used (Bufe, 1991; Kazdin, 1988). Case management as a method of service delivery can ensure the ongoing coordination of these services and therapeutic interventions.

CASE MANAGEMENT: AN INTERDISCIPLINARY APPROACH

The needs of depressed homeless children can be met most thoroughly through the services of an interdisciplinary service team, coordinated by a case manager (Wagner & Menke, 1992). An interdisciplinary team consists of professionals with multiple skills and tools for assessing the many needs of the family, as well as addressing the health, social service, support, and treatment needs of the child and the family simultaneously. As a team, they can provide the variety of interventions depressed homeless children need: nursing (primary and advanced practice), social work, counseling, and child psychiatry.

The clinical case management model developed by Kanter (1989) is appropriate for working with homeless families. The role of the clinical case manager involves an integration of clinical skill and environmental manipulation along with systems coordination, service brokering, and support in advocating for the child and the family. This model involves an integration between therapeutic and case management modalities. The relationship allows for a facilitation of service delivery while enhancing the coping skills and resourcefulness of both the individuals within the family and the family unit.

The case manager should at least work with the child and his or her family until they become emotionally stable and physically secure in a setting such as a shelter. Ideally, the case manager would continue to follow the family until they are settled in permanent housing or, at the very least, long-term transitional housing.

Goals for intervention during the early phase include:

- Helping the family meet the physical needs of the child

- Managing the emotional distress of both child and parent(s) by providing emotional support and assistance with coping strategies

- Nurturing hope and helping the family gain access to a social support system

- Providing crisis intervention and systems advocacy through proactive case management services

System advocacy is necessary to help the family meet their immediate physical needs for food and shelter, work on permanent planning and long-range goals, and develop a consistent system of social support.

In practice, primary health or mental health providers engaged in outreach activities (e.g., staffing emergency rooms, urgent care centers, public health clinics, schools, or soup kitchens) will be the persons who will have initial contact with homeless families. These front-line workers are responsible for the initial assessment. Accurate identification of homeless families, however, is not easy and may require that these staff members take a careful and specific housing history as a routine part of their assessment procedures.

Because some children exhibit the symptoms of adverse effects, whereas others do not, assessment must also involve inquiry into factors that may either protect or place the child at higher risk. Clearly, once a child has been identified as being at risk for depression, the immediate physical safety of the child is the highest priority. Health care professionals must assess the child's potential for self-destructive behaviors and implement a series of targeted interventions involving primary health and mental health professionals and possible referrals to social service agencies.

Care specific to the depressed child involves the initiation of a therapeutic modality specifically designed and individualized for the child and family. In general, school-age homeless children need information concerning their situation, permission to express their feelings, emotional support, and assistance with developing coping strategies. The choice or combination of therapies used to work with these children depends on the treatment goals for the particular child and family. Frequently used therapies can be delivered through individual intervention, group intervention, or family intervention.

Various studies confirm the effectiveness of behavioral, cognitive, and other psychosocial interventions in working with depressed children (Casey & Berman, 1985; Kazdin, 1989; Tuma, 1989). Although it is not clear which approach would be best for any given situation, a combination of modalities and interventions may be more effective in the long run. Treatment of the child suffering from depression may also include pharmacotherapy (Kazdin, 1988). Most researchers agree that drug therapy is more effective in combination with other modalities (Institute of Medicine, 1989; Tuma, 1989).

Obviously, aggressive crisis intervention, system intervention, case management, and ongoing therapeutic intervention(s) must be provided either to prevent or to mitigate the damaging effects of the homeless experience. Intervention should specifically address each child's particular family circumstance and lifestyle (Wagner & Menke, 1991a).

Whatever the treatment or strategies used, parents or guardians need to be aware of the issues and, if possible, involved in all planning, decision making, and intervention. Support services and counseling targeted toward the parents/guardians will also benefit child functioning both directly and indirectly. Level of stress, ability to cope, and depression or anxiety in the parents/guardians affect the child's environment and sense of safety. Adjunctive activities, such as anticipatory guidance and parenting education, may be useful in helping to maintain the advances the child makes in therapy as well as in increasing family cohesion.

Case Example:

Visibly taut, Sandra Williams has just arrived with her two children in the emergency room of the local hospital. She is an articulate, well-groomed, 33-year-old African-American woman. Mihala, her 4-year-old daughter, has a high fever and is grabbing at her ear, screaming. The triage nurse notices that family members look tired and stressed. The mother appears attentive to her children, and the nurse wonders why she waited to seek medical attention.

The nurse discovers Sandra is unemployed and has neither insurance nor money. Because Mihala appears to be in severe distress, the nurse decides to have the physician examine her first, but also notes the need to finish assessing the family after Mihala has been examined.

Because Mihala has a high fever, a severe ear infection, and a history of seizures, the physician decides to keep her for observation. Once the child is resting, the nurse sits down with Sandra and her 8-year-old son, Jeremy. As the nurse talks, Sandra begins to cry. She is tired and hungry. She admits that she and the children have been living out of a car for 2 days. Although they ate in a soup kitchen the last 2 nights, they have not eaten today.

Each community has a collaborative, intersystem team that responds to the needs of families in distress. The members of this team have access to a fund available for use across systems to meet immediate financial needs of a family not covered elsewhere. The nurse uses these funds to arrange for a meal to be brought to the family. As they eat and slowly begin to relax, the mother tells her story.

Although her family did not have much money when she was a child, they were never homeless and never had to resort to government services. She did well in school, but quit high school one semester short of graduation. Her family was furious and told her she had to support herself if she was not enrolled in school. She was able to get by and took evening courses to be a computer operator.

At the age of 24, she married. Although Sandra and her husband had two children, she and her husband gradually drifted apart. Shortly after Mihala's birth, he was laid off and left town. Sandra has not heard from him since. It was difficult to live on one income but she and the children survived. After buying food and paying for rent, child care, and the children's medical insurance, there was little money left for clothes or entertainment. Her parents and grandmother helped when they could.

Then, 6 months ago, Sandra lost her job. With no savings, she could not pay the rent and was evicted after 2 months. She moved in with her parents, but felt pressured by them and left to live with a friend after several months. However, her friend's landlord said there were too many people in the apartment, and she left there 2 days ago. With no money, she did not know where to turn. She was ashamed to go back to her family, especially since she had applied for Aid to Families with Dependent Children (AFDC) and no one else in the family had ever sought state assistance. Although Sandra applied for AFDC a month ago and has gone back several times, the computer indicated she was still employed and, therefore, ineligible for benefits.

At this point, the nurse tells her about a program at the local family center that can provide a social work case manager who can guide her through the assistance process. The nurse initiates the contact after obtaining Sandra's permission. The case manager continues the assessment with Sandra and her children over the next several days while immediately starting the search for housing, food, and follow-up medical care. The case manager also makes sure the family has gas money and works with Sandra to straighten out her eligibility for AFDC.

The members of an interdisciplinary team need easy access to other members for referral and coordination. The system should provide 24-hour access to case management services and flexible funds for assisting families in crisis. The case management function can originate out of one system or be spread across systems, but a structure must be in place; one team member should be recognized as having primary responsibility. The case manager should provide a level of counseling during the time he or she spends with the family and coordinate intervention with other mental health providers.

Although the Williams family does not appear to have substance abuse problems, some families do. The interdisciplinary team should include members from the medical, mental health, substance abuse, and social service systems. The team should connect on a regular basis to coordinate activities, focusing first on safety, emergency, and survival needs such as food, housing, and medical care. A case manager with connections to housing, financial assistance, and education/training resources is vital in coordinating the family's recovery.

Based on the time spent with the Williams family, the case manager determines that Jeremy is a good student who has consistently earned A's and B's. He is especially proficient in math and science and wants to be a biologist or math teacher. However, Sandra has noticed a gradual change since they lost their home. After having moved from his grandparents' house and changing schools twice, Jeremy has grown increasingly distracted, withdrawn, and unable to concentrate. He has been out of school for 2 days and he misses his friends and teachers.

Because Jeremy shows signs of depression, Sandra is feeling hopeless and isolated, and, in turn, Mihala seems scared and anxious. Therefore, the case manager refers Sandra and her children to a family counselor for assessment of depression and anxiety in all three family members. She also knows the worker can provide ongoing support as the family rebuilds its life. The counselor assesses the mental health needs of the family and plans treatment in consultation with Sandra.

The case manager spends several weeks with the Williams family, helping them obtain short- and long-term housing assistance. The case manager also works with the teacher and the class as Jeremy reenrolls in school — to ensure that he is well received and that his home situation is not a source of ridicule. Once the family has stable assistance and is settled in permanent housing, the case manager gradually reduces contact, but remains involved by working with the mother on long-term plans to finish high school and develop an education/training plan.

CONCLUSION

Homelessness is a condition that imposes severe mental, physical, and social deprivation on a significant number of children in the United States today. The extreme poverty of homeless families leaves them vulnerable in many areas and at high risk for negative consequences to the physical and mental health of the children. Despite the vulnerability and stress experienced by homeless families, many have developed unique ways of negotiating their environments, which provide strengths that health care professionals should seek to identify and build on in their treatment strategies.

Timely interventions may help homeless children deal effectively with the depression that can follow a catastrophic life event, such as losing a permanent residence, and may prevent them from developing a pattern of lifelong psychopathology. Efforts at crisis intervention and case management are vital steps from the outset: providing a combination of supports, assistance in navigating the welfare system and securing stability, and counseling focused on increased comprehension and sense of control.

A healthy resolution of a crisis may inoculate children against the effects of future crises. Combining intervention modalities such as case management, primary health care, crisis intervention, and counseling/psychotherapy for children and families who are homeless has been an effective strategy when planning care for this vulnerable and underserved population.

REFERENCES

Akiskal, H. S. (1979). A biobehavioral approach to depression. In R. A. Depue (Ed.), *The psychobiology of depressive disorders* (pp. 409–437). New York: Academic Press.

American Psychiatric Association. (1994). *Diagnostic and statistical manual of mental disorders* (4th ed.). Washington, DC: Author.

Bassuk, E., & Rubin, L. (1987). Homeless children: A neglected population. *American Journal of Orthopsychiatry, 57*, 279–286.

Beck, S., & Rosenberg, R. (1986). Frequency, quality, and impact of life events in self-rated depressed, behavioral-problem, and normal children. *Journal of Consulting and Clinical Psychology, 54*, 863–864.

Boxill, N., & Beaty, A. (1990). An exploration of mother/child interaction among homeless women and their children in a public night shelter in Atlanta, Georgia. In N. Boxill & A. Beaty (Eds.), *The waiters and the watchers: American homeless children* (pp. 49–64). New York: Hawthorne.

Brantly, D., & Takacs, D. (1991). Anxiety and depression in preschool and school-age children. In P. Clunn (Ed.), *Child psychiatric nursing,* (pp. 351–365). St. Louis, MO: Mosby.

Bufe, G. M. (1991, April 27–30). *Guided imagery with depressed children.* Poster session presentation at Ethical Issues in Nursing Research, 15th Annual Midwest Nursing Research Society Conference, Oklahoma City, OK.

Carlson, G. A. (1983). Depression and suicidal behavior in children and adolescents. In D. P. Cantwell & G. A. Carlson (Eds.), *Affective disorders in childhood and adolescence: An update* (pp. 335–352). Jamaica, NY: Spectrum.

Casey, R. J., & Berman, J. S. (1985). The outcome of psychotherapy with children. *Psychological Bulletin, 98*, 388–400.

Castaneda, A., McCandless, B., & Palermo, D. (1956). The children's form of the Manifest Anxiety Scale. *Child Development, 27*, 317–326.

Children's Defense Fund. (1995). Children's hardships intensify. *CDF Reports, 16*(6), 1–2, 12.

The crisis in homelessness: Effects on children and families. (1987). Hearing before the House Select Committee on Children, Youth, and Families. *House of Representatives,* 100th Congress, 1st Session.

Fristad, M. A., Weller, E. B., Weller, R. A., & Teare, M. (1988). Self-report vs. biological markers in assessment of childhood depression. *Journal of Affective Disorders, 15,* 339–345.

Garmezy, N. (1981). Children under stress: Perspectives on antecedents and correlates of vulnerability and resistance to psychopathology. In A. I. Robin, J. Aranoff, A. M. Barclay, & R. A. Zucker (Eds.), *Further explorations in personality* (pp. 196–296). New York: Wiley.

Gerwirtzman, R., & Fodor, I. (1987). The homeless child at school: From welfare hotel to classroom. *Child Welfare, 66,* 237–245.

Hall, J., & Maza, P. (1990). No fixed address: The effects of homelessness on families and children. *Child and Youth Services, 13,* 35–46.

Helsel, W., & Matson, J. (1984). Assessment of depression in children: The internal structure of the Child Depression Inventory. *Behavior Research and Therapy, 22,* 289–298.

Institute of Medicine. (1989). *Research on children and adolescents with mental, behavioral, and developmental disorders.* Rockville, MD: U.S. Department of Health and Human Services, Public Health Service, National Institute of Mental Health.

Kanter, J. (1989). Clinical case management: Definition, principles, components. *Hospital and Community Psychiatry, 40*(4), 361–367.

Kazdin, A. (1988). Childhood depression. In E. Mash & L. Tedral (Eds.), *Behavior assessment of childhood disorders* (pp. 157–195). New York: Guilford Press.

Kazdin, A. (1989). Childhood depression. In E. Mash & R. A. Barkley (Eds.), *Treatment of childhood disorders* (pp. 135–166). New York: Guilford Press.

Kovacs, M. (1985). The Children's Depression Inventory (CDI). *Psychopharmacology Bulletin, 21,* 995–998.

Lazarus, R., & Folkman, S. (1984). *Stress, appraisal, and coping.* New York: Springer.

Marchesano, D. R. (1993). *The triangulated, symptomatic child: A study of the relationship between marital adjustment, childhood depression, and academic under achievement.* Unpublished doctoral dissertation, University of Pennsylvania, Philadelphia.

Mihaly, L. (1989, April). *Beyond the numbers: Homeless families with children.* Paper presented at Homeless Children and Youth: Coping with a National Tragedy, Washington, DC.

Mills, C., & Ota, H. (1989). Homeless women with minor children in the Detroit metropolitan area. *Social Work, 34,* 485–489.

Paykel, E. (1969). Life events and depression. *Archives of General Psychiatry, 21,* 753–776.

Puig-Antich, J., & Gittleman, R. (1982). Depression in childhood and adolescence. In E. S. Paykel (Ed.), *Handbook of affective disorders* (pp. 379–392). New York: Guilford Press.

Puig-Antich, J., Lukens, E., Davies, M., Goetz, D., Brennan-Quattrock, J., & Todak, G. (1985). Psychosocial functioning in prepubertal major depressive disorders: Interpersonal relationships during the depressive episode. *Archives of General Psychiatry, 42,* 500–507.

Reynolds, C. R. (1980). Concurrent validity of 'What I Think and Feel': The Revised Children's Manifest Anxiety Scale. *Journal of Consulting and Clinical Psychology, 48,* 774–775.

Reynolds, C. R., & Richmond, B. O. (1979). Factor structure and construct validity of 'What I Think and Feel': The Revised Children's Manifest Anxiety Scale. *Journal of Personality Assessment, 43,* 281–283.

Reynolds, C. R., & Richmond, B. O. (1985). *Revised Children's Manifest Anxiety Scale.* Los Angeles: Western Psychological Services.

Roth, D., Dean, J., Lust, N., & Saveanu, T. (1985). *Homelessness in Ohio: A study of people in need.* Columbus, OH: Ohio Department of Mental Health.

Rutter, M. (1990). Psychosocial resilience and protective mechanisms. In J. Rolf, A. Masten, D. Cicchetti, K. Nuechterlein, & S. Weintraub (Eds.), *Risk and protective factors in the development of psychopathology* (pp. 181–215). Cambridge, England: Cambridge University Press.

Schmitz, C. L. (1993). Children at risk: Ex post facto research examining relationships among poverty, housing stability, anxiety, attitudes, locus of control, academic performance, and behavior. *Dissertation Abstracts International, 54,* 1097A.

Schmitz, C. L., Wagner, J. D., & Menke, E. M. (in press). Homelessness as one component of housing instability and its impact on the development of children in poverty. *Journal of Social Distress and the Homeless.*

Stark, K., Reynolds, W., & Kaslow, J. (1987). A comparison of the relative efficacy of self-control therapy and a behavioral problem-solving therapy for depression in children. *Journal of Abnormal Child Psychology, 15,* 91–113.

Tongue, R. (1990). Depression in children. *Australian Family Physician, 19,* 1388–1396.

Tuma, J. M. (1989). Mental health services for children: The state of the art. *American Psychologist, 44,* 188–199.

Wagner, J., & Menke, E. (1991a). *Homeless children and their mothers.* Final report to the the Ohio Department of Mental Health. Columbus, OH: Ohio State University.

Wagner, J., & Menke, E. (1991b). *Homeless children and their mothers.* Final report to the Ohio Department of Mental Health. Columbus, OH: Ohio State University.

Wagner, J., & Menke, E. (1991c). Stressor and coping behavior of homeless, poor, and low income mothers. *Journal of Community Health Nursing, 8*(2), 75–84.

Wagner, J., & Menke, E. (1992). Case management of homeless families. *Clinical Nurse Specialist: The Journal for Professional Nursing Practice, 6*(2), 65–70.

Wagner, J., & Menke, E. (1993). The health of homelessness and domiciled poor school-age children: Final report. Bethesda, MD: National Center for Nursing Research.

Wagner, J., Menke, E., & Schmitz, C. (1992). [The health and mental health of homeless and domiciled families with children in poverty]. Unpublished raw data.

Wisniewski, J. J., Mulick, J. A., Genshaft, J. L., & Coury, D. L. (1987). Test-retest reliability of the Revised Children's Manifest Anxiety Scale. *Perceptual and Motor Skills, 65,* 67–70.

5

Adoption Psychopathology and the "Adopted Child Syndrome"

David Kirschner, PhD

Dr. Kirschner is in private practice in Merrick, NY, and Woodbury, NY.

KEY POINTS

- Adopted children and adolescents exhibit proportionally more extreme antisocial behavior and conduct disorders than do young nonadoptees. Genetics may partially account for this pattern; however, research also indicates that adoptees encounter psychological problems during childhood and adolescence unique to being adopted.

- The "adopted child syndrome" refers to an extreme form of adoption-related psychopathology including provocative, antisocial behaviors and associated personality disturbances.

- The adopted child syndrome is an extreme outcome of minimizing or ignoring the adopted child's quest to understand his or her origins. Therefore, it may be mitigated to some degree by fostering honesty. However, even full disclosure of the identity of the birth parents and the reasons for adoption may not entirely alleviate pathogenic conditions.

- Adopted children are often curious about their birth parents, yet feel abandoned and rejected by them. This may lead to powerful feelings of ambivalence, causing children to act out against the adoptive parents as well as therapists, teachers, and other authority figures.

- The current emphasis on anonymity in adoption proceedings encourages the denial of feelings and distorts understanding of the true complexities involved in this process.

INTRODUCTION

For some time, mental health professionals have noted a large proportion of conduct disorders and extreme antisocial behavior among clinically referred adopted children and adolescents as compared with their nonadopted counterparts (Menlove, 1965; Offord, Aponte, & Cross, 1969; Sabalis & Burch, 1980; Schechter, Carlson, Simmons, & Work, 1964; Weiss, 1985). Although the influence of genetics may partially account for this pattern (Graham & Stevenson, 1985; Herrnstein & Wilson, 1985; Mednick, Gabrielli, & Hutchings, 1984), a growing body of clinical literature (Brinich, 1980; Easson, 1973; Kirschner, 1990, 1992; Kirschner & Nagel, 1988; Nickman, 1985; Toussieng, 1962) as well as first-person accounts by adult adoptees (Lifton, 1988, 1994a, 1994b) have identified unique psychological problems encountered by adoptees during childhood and adolescence. Complications in identity formation and adoption-related psychopathology, fantasies, and behavior are the most commonly cited examples. Especially in cases involving a genetic predisposition for behavioral disorders, such psychological complications are seen as critical factors in the etiology of antisocial psychopathology in adoptees.

The renewed focus on psychopathology among adoptees has fostered controversy. Some parties have argued against the delineation of adoption-specific psychiatric or psychological disturbances, warning that adoptees and adoptive parents might be stigmatized and that prospective adoptive parents might be discouraged from adopting (Bartholet, 1993; Feigelman, 1986; Klagsbrun, 1986). Nonetheless, the adoption community increasingly acknowledges emotional problems that may be engendered by traditional, "closed" adoptions (in which the identities of the birth parents are kept from the adoptive parents and child, and vice versa). As a result of this new awareness, proponents of "open" adoptions (arrangements in which all parties are known to each other [Chapman, Dorner, Silber, & Winterberg, 1987a, 1987b; Lifton, 1988, 1994a]) and advocates of disclosing closed adoption records are challenging the adoption establishment. Indeed, most observed cases of the "adopted child syndrome" have occurred in children who were adopted during infancy through closed adoptions.

The "adopted child syndrome" refers to an extreme form of adoption-related psychopathology, including provocative, antisocial behaviors as well as associated personality disturbances that are superficially similar to those found under the *Diagnostic and Statistical Manual of Mental Disorders* (DSM-IV) (American Psychiatric Association, 1994) diagnosis of conduct disorder. The adopted child syndrome can be differentiated from conduct disorder by underlying adoption-specific psychodynamics, greater emotional vulnerability, accessibility to and motivation for therapy, and better prognosis (Table 5.1).

Although the prevalence of acting-out disorders among clinically referred adoptees is widely reported in the literature, the term *adopted child syndrome* remains controversial. Furthermore, although many unique issues and related clinical problems are not uncommon among adopted children, it has not been established whether serious emotional and behavioral problems occur more frequently among adoptees than nonadoptees in the general population. Adoption *per se* does not necessarily give rise to psychopathology; however, it must be considered a risk factor — perhaps a precipitating one — in some families deemed dysfunctional in terms of key adoption issues and parent-child interactions.

DESCRIPTIVE CHARACTERISTICS

Acting-out behaviors, specific personality and interpersonal relationships, ideational content, and psychodynamics characterize the adopted child syndrome.

Behavioral Patterns:

By assessing only the behavioral patterns of an adopted child, it is all too easy to misdiagnose the adopted child syndrome as

Table 5.1
DIFFERENTIATING THE ADOPTED CHILD SYNDROME FROM CONDUCT DISORDER

Diagnostic Feature	Adopted Child Syndrome	Conduct Disorder
Behavior disturbance	Antisocial behavior often directed at parental figures, especially deceitfulness, theft, violation of rules, promiscuity, problems in school, and acting out of anger	*Aggressive conduct* directed at people/animals; conduct causes property loss or damage, deceitfulness, theft, or serious violations of rules
Personality traits	Impulsive; poor frustration tolerance; little empathy; superficial charm but little intimacy	Same
Underlying affect, ideation, and fantasy material	Preoccupied with identity quest; idealizes or demonizes birth and adoptive parents; feels empty, depressed, sensitive to rejection. *Problem conduct* triggered by real or perceived rejection.	Impoverished fantasy life; callous affect
Family characteristics and environment	Antisocial behavior not modeled by adoptive family	Antisocial behavior frequently modeled in family and social environments
Treatment approach	Express and work through adoption-related questions, beliefs, feelings; parental education regarding identity quest and normalcy of adoption-related concerns	Treatment often ineffective due to lack of motivation; residential placement may be indicated
Prognosis	Often excellent with psychotherapy	Poor

conduct disorder. Like conduct disorder, the adopted child syndrome is characterized by various forms of antisocial acting out, primarily directed against parental and authority figures. Pathologic lying, stealing, fire setting, promiscuity, substance abuse, and running away (or threats to do so) are typical; assaultiveness occurs in severe cases. The child socializes with "street-wise" delinquents, antisocial children or adults, often of a lower socioeconomic class than that of the adoptive family. School problems frequently include truancy, academic under-achievement, and specific learning problems.

If unresolved, these behavioral problems usually escalate with age, leading the child into conflicts with school and legal authorities. In some cases, after several failed attempts to reason with and discipline the child, and even have him or her clinically treated, the adoptive parents may finally submit a petition for court custody or seek placement of the child in a hospital or other residential treatment facility.

Adoptees who display signs of the syndrome typically have been raised in a middle-class environment, where antisocial behavior is not widely modeled by adults or sanctioned by most of their peers.

Personality and Interpersonal Relationships:

The personality profile of the child with the adopted child syndrome resembles that of a person with conduct disorder. More specifically, the impulsiveness and low frustration toler-ance typically associated with conduct disorders are present in the adopted child syndrome. The child may display a superficial charm, shamelessly prevaricate to and manipulate others, and show little guilt or remorse for hateful acts or transgressions committed. The child may lack deeply felt, meaningful relationships. Interactions with parents and au-thority figures are marked by frequent provocative and dis-ruptive limit-testing behavior. Finally, the child seems to expect or invite rejection by parents and other authority figures.

Ideational Content:

As the adoptee shares private adoption-related thoughts, fantasies, and dreams, the vulnerable side of the child's per-sonality emerges. This accessible vulnerability distinguishes the adopted child syndrome from conduct disorder and is crucial to the differential diagnosis and treatment planning. Typically, the child reveals an elaborate preoccupation with his or her origins and the circumstances of the adoption as well as a hypersensitivity to rejection of any kind.

In projective test responses, play therapy, or interviews, the child reveals privately held questions, fantasies, and beliefs about his or her origins. This ideation is often distorted, unrealistic, and obsessive—especially with regard to having two sets of parents. The child often demonstrates elaborate images of the unknown birth parents, who are believed to be either evil, immoral, and rejecting, or idealized, loving, generous, and powerful. The child often believes that the birth mother was promiscuous, even a prostitute. These fantasies may be understood as attempts to cope with the injury of the imagined rejection. Because the child partially identifies with the birth parents as they are idealized, such fantasies invariably distort the child's self-image.

The child also struggles with feelings of anger toward the adoptive parents that are aroused by these fantasies. Their role in the adoption may be construed as theft in the child's mind, as well as an aggression against both the birth parents and the child. The adoptive parents' failure to recognize the child's urgent curiosity about the original parents may be taken as a rejection of the birth parents and, by extension, a rejection of the genetic heritage of the child. The child tends to construe their failure to discuss adoption candidly as a form of lying. Paradoxically, children may feel the need to protect their adoptive parents from their interest in their birth parents but also resent feeling obligated to them for "the rescue" (Lifton, 1988).

THE CHILD'S QUEST FOR IDENTITY

Information about one's beginnings and ancestors is an essential building block in identity formation during childhood and adolescence. An adopted child usually learns little about his or her origins, perhaps a few details (often fictional) about his or her birth parents and an idealized version of the adoption (the "chosen-child" story). With maturity, the child reworks and reinterprets this story, which is poorly understood during early childhood (Brodzinsky, Schecter, & Henig, 1992). In addition to whatever is imparted by the adoptive parents, the child also gleans cultural clues. For instance, children become aware that, in many adoptions, the birth parents are not married.

Starting with this sketchy and ambiguous information, the child will develop many questions and seize on many answers in the quest for identity.

> Did my birth parents love me as a baby? If so, why did they relinquish me? Maybe they disliked me. Was there something wrong with me? How would they feel about me today? Was I given up willingly or taken away by force? Were my parents cruel, immoral, criminal, or defective and so unfit to be parents? If so, does that make me the same way? Was my birth mother a prostitute? How would my adoptive parents feel about my birth parents? Would they disapprove of them? Who are my real parents? What makes my adoptive parents my parents? Would they really love me if they knew I cared about my birth parents? If I really am like my birth parents, will my adoptive parents still love me? Might they change their minds and "unadopt" me if they decided they didn't love me?

These questions emerge gradually as the child's conceptual abilities develop.

It is hoped that the child will openly discuss these questions and the emotions attached to them (which may include grief, anger, mistrust, identity confusion, and separation anxiety). Unfortunately, a number of cultural and parental factors make the topic of adoption taboo in many adoptive families. The atmosphere within an adoptive family often discourages curiosity about adoption, enticing the child to conclude that something painful and bad (pertaining to his or her own character) is being kept a secret. Meanwhile, the child's questions remain relegated to the private domain of the imagination, where they inspire unhealthy, immature, and distorted fantasies unmoderated by reality testing or feedback from others.

In an atmosphere of denial and secrecy, even normal emotions in a growing child assume a toxic quality. For instance, all feelings of rejection may reverberate with the fantasized primal rejection by the birth parents. The child is also likely to feel powerless, frustrated, humiliated, and angry at the idea of having been passed along without any control over his or her own fate. If the child is inhibited from venting these thoughts and feelings as well as from obtaining any clarification or reassurance, he or she suffers an intense ambivalence toward his or her birth parents; a sense of longing, grief, anger, and mistrust often accompanies such ambivalence (Lifton, 1988).

In many adoptive families, parental love is implicitly conditional:

> The child is being asked to collude in the fiction that these are his only parents and to accept that his birth heritage is disposable.... Only if adopted children commit themselves fully to the identity of the adoptive clan can they have the adoptive parents' love. Already abandoned by the birth mother, the adoptive child feels no choice but to abandon her and, by so doing, to abandon his real self. This early, potential self that is still attached to the birth mother is unacceptable to the adoptive parents and, therefore, must become unacceptable to the child (Lifton, 1994a, pp. 50–51).

Severely disturbed adoptees, as well as apparently well-functioning adoptees, may suffer from the implied pressure to pretend that their adoption is unimportant in defining who they are.

PSYCHODYNAMICS

With normal development, the adopted child's positive and

negative images of self and others, especially parents, are gradually integrated into more realistic images. This crucial development is linked to the capacity for empathy and conscience. In less ideal circumstances, adoptees may lack the opportunity to interact with or even talk about their birth parents; their view of their birth parents cultivated in the context of their adoptive family would be constricted, secretive, and two dimensional. For these adoptees, good and bad images remain split, often with one set of parents identified as "all good" and the other as "all bad" (Brinich, 1980; Eiduson & Livermore, 1952; Schechter, 1960; Simon & Senturia, 1966) or with each mother split into discontinuous good and bad images (Lifton, 1994a). The superego is impaired, resulting in poor impulse control, acting out, and conduct-disordered behavior.

Although provocative and antisocial behavior is evident to the casual observer, the disturbed ideation and psychodynamics of the adopted child syndrome are usually hidden from view and manifest only through careful, informed clinical evaluation.

CULTURAL AND FAMILY COMPONENTS

The Institutional Context of Secrecy:

Closed adoption remains the standard practice in our society. When a child is adopted through an agency, the adoptive parents are advised by the agency to tell the child he or she is "special" and was "chosen." At the same time, the adoptive parents may have been advised to minimize the importance of the adoption and to communicate that the adoptee is no different from a genetic child.

Because most adoption records are sealed, any questions the growing child may have about the birth parents' character, motives, and feelings, as well as their physical appearance and other hereditary traits, cannot be definitively answered. This policy of secrecy thwarts even those adoptive parents who support and understand their child's natural curiosity.

The Family Context of Denial:

Parents of most children with the adopted child syndrome exhibit tension and denial surrounding the issue of adoption. During the initial interview with a therapist, they may dismiss all suggestions that adoption could be an issue for the child or might in any way be related to the behavioral problem(s). It soon becomes apparent that serious discussions of feelings about the adoption is taboo.

Although instructions from an adoption agency and the practice of closed adoption may facilitate parental denial, a pathogenic situation may arise when these external influences interact with the parents' own psychology. Some adoptive parents overreact to a child's normal sexual and aggressive behavior, especially given the specter of a genetic predisposition to such behavior. Temperamental differences between adopted parents and their child will exacerbate these tensions. Parents may warn and discipline their child excessively, and the child may respond with defiance.

Adoptive parents may also project their own unintegrated, unaccepted impulses onto their child, unconsciously provoking the child to act out their wishes while consciously rejecting the inappropriate behavior (Eiduson & Livermore, 1952). An adopted child is a particularly likely target for repressed parental impulses because the parents can disown all responsibility for the behavior, often unconsciously blaming it on someone else's "bad seed." In this extreme case, the fantasized birth parents also embody the repressed impulses of the adoptive parents (Brinich, 1980; Easson, 1973).

Parents may accept and identify with their child only when he or she is well-behaved, and figuratively disown the child whenever he or she does not behave properly. By failing to accept the child's positive and negative aspects as parts of a whole, parents ultimately hamper the development of an integrated self-image and a mature superego or conscience.

Parents may avoid thinking about or discussing their child's feelings about adoption because they are avoiding their own uncomfortable adoption-related feelings, such as guilt (toward the birth parents and child) and grief (for the natural child they never had). When they resist their adoption-related feelings, parents cannot empathize with the child's intense emotions and curiosity, nor can they accept or embrace those aspects of the child's emerging identity that they sense may derive from the birth parents.

THE SPECTRUM OF ADOPTION-RELATED PSYCHOPATHOLOGY

Lifton (1994a) stated that adoptees undergo a *cumulative adoption trauma*, which

> begins when they are separated from the mother at birth; builds when they learn that they were not born to the people they call mother and father; and is further compounded when they are denied knowledge of the mother and father to whom they were born (p. 7).

Lifton added that even well-functioning adoptees suffer from the unmet, often unacknowledged, need to know their birth parents as well as from the experience of growing up deprived of vital elements of their identity. In essence, virtually all adoptees "struggle with issues pertaining to self-esteem, lack of trust, and fear of abandonment" (p. 93).

The "Good" Adoptee and the "False Self":

One form of adoption psychopathology may be the "good adoptee" or "artificial self" (Lifton, 1994a) — compliant, nonrebellious, afraid to express real feelings, dedicated to preserving the relationship with the adoptive parents, even at the cost of thoughts and behaviors that might betray a connection to another family. Other adoptees are aware of having two selves: one is the culturally accepted "artificial" self; the other, which they may believe to be the "true" self, is linked to the imagined birth parents and feels alienated from the adoptive family. This "other" self may acquire a growing sense of urgency and frustration during adolescence or at times of family crisis.

In this connection, Pine (1980, p. 179) described a subgroup of children with borderline personality disorder, the characteristics of whom he first discovered in an adult adoptee "suffering from irreconcilable love-hate images toward her adoptive parents." They. . .

> show an omnipresent splitting of good and bad images of self and other. Such children, often "sweet" or "good" on the surface, will reveal an absorbing inner preoccupation with hate and violence, often with homicidal or world-destruction fantasies, equally often with scant and precarious control over them. The splitting is evidenced in the lack of connection between the "good" and the "bad" self and other. Hate, unmodified by affectionate images, becomes icy or fiery, devouring of the self or the other (in mental life), and frightening — to the parent and to the therapist who discovers it.

At the most malignant extreme of the range of adoption psychopathology are adoptees who murder their adoptive parents or others in a breakthrough of dissociated rage. These murders, committed under the sway of delusional notions about the adopted child's birth parents and adoptive parents, are always committed after a rejection crisis (Kirschner, 1978, 1992).

IMPLICATIONS FOR CLINICAL PRACTICE

A skillful, sensitive interviewer can penetrate the tough façade of a person exhibiting features of the adopted child syndrome.

This is achieved by conveying awareness of and interest in the patient's adoption-related concerns. Once the child believes it is safe to discuss these matters with a therapist — that they will be met with full respect and attention — he or she typically responds with gratitude and relief, readily confiding a great deal of enlightening material.

In most cases, the persistent hostility aimed at the adoptive parents and other authorities should be understood as anger toward the birth parents, which has been displaced onto available parental figures. Feeling abandoned and rejected by the birth parents and transcendently connected to them at the same time, the child deals with potent feelings of ambivalence by acting out against the adoptive parents as well as therapists, teachers, or other authority figures.

A fear or expectation of rejection underlies the provocative behavior of a child with the adopted child syndrome. This behavior may be understood as a counterphobic reaction (Glatzer, 1955; Kirschner, 1990), unconsciously designed to provoke rejection to prove that it will not occur and that the child will be accepted despite his or her unlikable qualities (Clothier, 1943).

All too often, this strategy of defensive provocation proves self-fulfilling. Adoptive parents may reach the limits of their tolerance and refer the child to the courts, a residential program, a hospital, or foster care. In this scenario, the provocative behavior still has a slightly adaptive function: the child retains some sense of control (and, hence, feels protected from utter humiliation) by virtue of sensing that he or she actively invited the rejection.

Diagnostic Techniques:

During the interviewing and testing processes of adopted children, it often helps to draw out adoption-related material by devising appropriate queries that may be used to adapt standard tests and materials. Sentence-completion, figure-drawing, and thematic apperception questions and responses may be modified. For instance, the child may be asked to specify whether parents and children in the projective responses are adopted or biologic. The Gardner Adoption Story Cards (Gardner, 1978) and the "Blacky" Pictures Test (Blum, 1950) have been especially useful with adopted children and adolescents.

Children may require assurance that discussions will not be repeated to their adoptive parents unless they so desire. Parents should be advised of this possible confidentiality, and their cooperation should be enlisted during the first consultation.

Treatment:

Children with the adopted child syndrome are usually responsive to a therapist's expression of interest in the topic of adoption, responding with a rush of adoption-related concerns and fantasy material. Children who are more inhibited or inarticulate sometimes may be reached through discussions of the many popular and classic stories whose themes relate to adoption, such as *Hansel and Gretel*, *Cinderella*, and *Pinocchio*. Several books written for adopted children and adolescents may facilitate a clinical dialogue as well (Table 5.2).

Interpretation of acting-out behaviors may provide an avenue for discussion of adoption. Children may respond positively to interpretations; for example, "Perhaps you lie because you feel you haven't been told the truth about your adoption" or, "Are you stealing because you sometimes feel *you* were stolen—or that your birth family was stolen from you?" Children who are especially sensitive to money issues may acknowledge a suspicion that they were sold for money by their birth parents to their adoptive parents. Running away may indicate an impulse to search for the birth parents (Lifton, 1994a).

Dreams, daydreams, obsessions, play themes, and other mental content should be interpreted in light of adoption

---

Table 5.2
SUGGESTED READING AND VIEWING FOR
ADOPTED CHILDREN AND ADOLESCENTS

Books
Duprau, J. (1990). *Adoption: The facts, feelings, and issues of a double heritage.* New York: Julian Messner.
Gravelle, K., & Fischer, B. (1993). *Where are my birth parents? A guide for teenage adoptees.* New York: Walker.
Krementz, J. (1982). *How it feels to be adopted.* New York: Knopf.
Lifton, B. J. (1981). *I'm still me.* New York: Knopf.
Lifton, B. J. (1994). *Tell me a real adoption story.* New York: Knopf.

Movies, TV, Folklore, and Popular Culture
"Greystoke: The Legend of Tarzan"
"Free Willy"
"The Emerald Forest"
"The Incredible Journey"
"Superman"
"Hansel and Gretel"
"Cinderella"
"Pinocchio"

---

issues. For instance, a common theme in the dreams or daydreams of adoptees is being followed or kidnapped by a stranger (symbolizing the birth parents).

If children feel guilty that curiosity about their birth parents is a betrayal of their adoptive parents, it is best to emphasize that the real issues are curiosity and identity, not loyalty or love.

Therapists are also a potential resource for patients who decide to search for their birth parents. However, when minors are involved, permission from the adoptive parents should be obtained before helping patients in this manner.

Family Therapy and Collateral Sessions

Family therapy is usually contraindicated because it is essential for the child to form a bond with the therapist, usually a transference to the birth parents, so the relationship can be reworked in therapy. However adoptive parents should be seen periodically by the child's therapist in separate parental sessions or by another therapist for their own individual or couples therapy — *if indicated.*

Parents should be sensitized to their child's continuing need for acceptance and help in assimilating the implications of adoption, in gradually understanding the motives and feelings of both sets of parents, and in integrating both sets of parents into a coherent sense of self and a complete identity. Moreover, parents should be educated to accept as normal their child's curiosity about the birth parents (Nickman, 1985). Reassurance that the child's interest in the birth parents is *not* a rejection of them, but rather a natural and healthy curiosity about essential aspects of heritage and identity, usually mitigates adoptive parents' anxieties. Because of the danger of fueling fears and anger when the child senses dishonesty, therapists should advise parents against lying to the child. Concerns about the inheritance of antisocial behavior should be brought to light, misconceptions about age-appropriate behavior corrected, and support given for acceptable degrees and types of discipline. Adoptive parents' feelings of guilt, anger, and insecurity toward their child and the birth parents should be ventilated. Referrals can be made to support groups or professional treatment.

With respect to the confidentiality of a child's sessions, the therapist should share with parents only what the child has agreed may be revealed to them. Parents should be clearly advised of the clinical importance of respecting their child's wish for confidentiality.

A significant number of support groups for adoptive families is emerging at the local level; referral to such groups is often indicated. (Up-to-date information on local groups can be obtained through the National Adoption Information Clearinghouse in Rockville, Maryland.) Table 5.3 provides suggested readings for adoptive parents. Appendix 5A contains a list of adoption-related organizations.

Table 5.3
SUGGESTED READING FOR ADOPTIVE
PARENTS AND ADULT ADOPTEES

Brodzinsky, D. M., Schecter, M. D., & Henig, R. M. (1992). *Being
    adopted: The lifelong search for self.* New York: Doubleday.
Kirk, H. D. (1964). *Shared fate.* Glencoe, IL: The Free Press.
Kirk, H. D. (1981). *Adoptive kinship: A modern institution in need of
    reform.* Toronto: Butterworth.
Lifton, B. J. (1977). *Twice born: Memoirs of an adopted daughter.* New
    York: Penguin Books.
Lifton, B. J. (1988). *Lost and found* (2nd ed.). New York:
    HarperCollins.
Lifton, B. J. (1994). *Journey of the adopted self: A quest for wholeness.*
    New York: Basic Books.

Denial and the Therapist:

Therapists may be easily misled by the adoptive parents'
insistence that adoption has no relevance to their child's
psychopathology. Therapists must look beyond the family
taboo and help parents acknowledge the importance of adoption to themselves as well as their child.

In the transference of the adoptive parents, therapists may
come to represent the birth parents. Unfortunately, once the
child begins to form a bond with the therapist, adoptive
parents may feel threatened by their child's potential attachment and even pull their child out of therapy. It is advisable to
address these feelings early, when they may still be managed.

THE VALUE OF HONESTY IN ADOPTION

What is known about the adopted child syndrome suggests
the advisability of opening sealed adoption records and revis-

ing current adoption practices to foster honesty and openness. The syndrome is an extreme outcome of the practice of minimizing or ignoring the adopted child's quest to understand his or her origins. The current emphasis on anonymity in adoption encourages the denial of feelings and distorts understanding of the true complexities involved in the adoption process (Chapman et al., 1987a, 1987b). However, even full disclosure of the identity of the birth parents and the reasons for adoption may not fully correct the pathogenic conditions. In such cases, it is also necessary for parents and therapists to acknowledge — and work through — the child's intense, ambivalent attachment to both sets of parents and identifications with both.

These findings also have relevance in the screening of prospective adoptive parents. A genuine acceptance of normal, age-appropriate aggressive and sexual behavior as well as the ability to identify unacceptable behavior are particularly important qualities in prospective adoptive parents. Above all, they should possess a willingness to acknowledge and discuss openly and honestly the potentially difficult, conflict-laden issue of adoption.

REFERENCES

American Psychiatric Association. (1994). *Diagnostic and statistical manual of mental disorders* (4th ed.). Washington, DC: Author.

Bartholet, E. (1993). *Family bonds: Adoption and the politics of parenting.* Boston: Houghton Mifflin.

Blum, G. S. (1950). *"Blacky" picture test* [Test]. Ann Arbor, MI: Psychodynamic Instruments.

Brinich, P. M. (1980). Some potential effects of adoption on self and object representations. *Psychoanalytic Study of the Child, 35,* 107–133.

Brodzinsky, D. M., Schecter, M. D., & Henig, R. M. (1992). *Being adopted: The lifelong search for self.* New York: Doubleday.

Chapman, C., Dorner, P., Silber, K., & Winterberg, T. S. (1987a). Meeting the needs of the adoption triangle through open adoptions: The adoptive parent. *Child and Adolescent Social Work, 4,* 3–12.

Chapman, C., Dorner, P., Silber, K., & Winterberg, T. S. (1987b). Meeting the needs of the adoption triangle through open adoption: The adoptee. *Child and Adolescent Social Work, 4,* 7–91.

Clothier, F. (1943). The psychology of the adopted child. *Mental Hygiene, 27,* 222–230.

Easson, W. M. (1973). Special sexual problems of the adopted adolescent. *Medical Aspects of Human Sexuality, 17,* 92–105.

Eiduson, B. N., & Livermore, J. B. (1952). Complications in therapy with adopted children. *American Journal of Orthopsychiatry, 23,* 795–802.

Feigelman, W. (1986, March 11). Don't stigmatize the adopted [Letter to the editor]. *The New York Times,* p. A26.

Gardner, R. A. (1978). *The Gardner adoption story cards* [Cards]. (Available from Creative Therapeutics, 155 County Road, Cresskill, NJ 07626)

Glatzer, H. T. (1955). Adoption and delinquency. *Nervous Child, 11,* 52–56.

Graham, P., & Stevenson, J. (1985). A twin study of genetic influences on behavioral deviance. *Journal of the American Academy of Child Psychiatry, 24,* 33–41.

Herrnstein, R. J., & Wilson, J. Q. (1985). *Crime and human nature.* New York: Simon & Schuster.

Kirschner, D. (1978, June). Son of Sam and the search for identity. *Adelphi Society for Psychoanalysis and Psychotherapy Newsletter,* pp. 7–9.

Kirschner, D. (1987, May). *Is there a pathological adoption syndrome?* Paper presented at the American Adoption Congress National Conference, Boston, MA.

Kirschner, D. (1990). The adopted child syndrome: Considerations for psychotherapy. *Psychotherapy in Private Practice, 8,* 93–100.

Kirschner, D. (1992). Understanding adoptees who kill: Dissociation, patricide, and the psychodynamics of adoption. *International Journal of Offender Therapy and Comparative Criminology, 36,* 323–333.

Kirschner, D., & Nagel, L. S. (1988). Antisocial behavior in adoptees: Patterns and dynamics. *Child and Adolescent Social Work, 5,* 300–314.

Klagsbrun, F. (1986, October). Debunking the 'adopted child syndrome.' [Letter to the editor]. *Ms. Magazine,* 102.

Lifton, B. J. (1988). *Lost and found* (2nd ed.). New York: Harper & Row.

Lifton, B. J. (1994a). *Journey of the adopted self: A quest for wholeness.* New York: Basic Books.

Lifton, B. J. (1994b). *Tell me a real adoption story.* New York: Knopf.

Mednick, S. A., Gabrielli, W. F., & Hutchings, B. (1984). Genetic influences in criminal convictions: Evidence from an adoption cohort. *Science, 224,* 891–894.

Menlove, F. L. (1965). Aggressive symptoms in emotionally disturbed adopted children. *Child Development, 36,* 519–532.

Nickman, S. (1985). Losses in adoption: The need for dialogue. *Psychoanalytic Study of the Child, 40,* 365–398.

Offord, D. R., Aponte, J. F., & Cross, L. A. (1969). Presenting symptomatology of adopted children. *Archives of General Psychiatry, 20,* 110–116.

Pine, F. (1980). On phase-characteristic pathology of the school-age child: Disturbances of personality development and organization (borderline conditions), of learning, and of behavior. In S. I. Greenspan & G. H. Pollock (Eds.), *The course of life: Psychoanalytic contributions toward understanding personality development: Latency, adolescence, and youth* (Vol. 2, pp. 165–183). Bethesda, MD: National Institute of Mental Health.

Sabalis, R. F., & Burch, E. A., Jr. (1980). Comparisons of psychiatric problems of adopted and nonadopted patients. *Southern Medical Journal, 73,* 867–869.

Schechter, M. D. (1960). Observations on adopted children. *Archives of General Psychiatry, 3,* 21–32.

Schechter, M. D., Carlson, P. V., Simmons, J. Q., III, & Work, H. H. (1964). Emotional problems in the adoptee. *Archives of General Psychiatry, 10,* 109–118.

Simon, N. M., & Senturia, A. G. (1966). Adoption and psychiatric illness. *American Journal of Psychiatry, 122,* 858–868.

Toussieng, P. W. (1962). Thoughts regarding the etiology of psychological difficulties in adopted children. *Child Welfare, 41,* 59–71.

Weiss, A. (1985). Symptomatology of adopted and nonadopted adolescents in a psychiatric hospital. *Adolescence, 20,* 763–774.

Appendix 5A
NATIONAL UMBRELLA NETWORK OF THE ADOPTION REFORM MOVEMENT

Call these organizations for a chapter near you, conference schedules, speakers, and newsletters.

Adoptees Liberty Movement Associates (ALMA)
P. O. Box 727
Radio City Station
New York, NY 10101-0727
(212) 581-1568

American Adoption Congress (AAC)
1000 Connecticut Avenue NW, #9
Washington, DC 20036
(202) 483-3399

Concerned United Birthparents (CUB)
200 Walker Street
Des Moines, IA 50317
(515) 263-9558

Council for Equal Rights in Adoption (CERA)
401 East 74th Street
Suite 17D
New York, NY 10021
(212) 988-0110

Orphan Voyage
601 South Birtchtree
Harrison, AR 72601

National Adoption Information Clearinghouse
5640 Nicholson Lane
Suite 300
Rockville, MD 20852
(30) 231-6512

The adoptive parent support groups listed here conduct pre-adoption and postadoption workshops, hold annual conferences, publish newsletters, and work for legislative reform.

Adoptive Families of America
3333 Highway 100 North
Minneapolis, MN 55422
(612) 535-4829

The Adoptive Parents Committee
P. O. Box 3525
Church Street Station
New York , NY 10008
(212) 304-8479

Adoptive Parents for Open Records
P. O. Box 193
Long Valley, NJ 07853
(908) 850-1706

Families Adopting Children Everywhere (FACE)
P. O. Box 28058
Baltimore, MD 21239
(410) 488-2656

New Jersey Coalition for Openness in Adoption
189 Cosmar Avenue
Washington Township, NJ 07675
(201) 358-0976
(includes adoptees and birth parents)

The North American Council on Adoptable Children (NACAC)
970 Raymond Ave.
Suite 106
St. Paul, MN 55114
(612) 644-3036

Resolve, Inc.
1310 Broadway
Somerville, MA 02144-1731
(617) 623-0744
(support organization on infertility)

Resources for Adoptive Parents
3381 Gorham Ave.
Suite 212
St. Louis Park, MN 55426
(612) 926-6959
(postadoption services)

Several states are home to birth parent support groups.

California
Bay Area Birthmothers Association
1546 Great Highway, #44
San Francisco, CA 94122

Birthparent Connection
P. O. Box 230643
Encinitas, CA 92023

Florida
National Organization for Birthfathers and Adoption Reform (NOBAR)
P. O. Box 50
Punta Gorda, FL 33951

Appendix 5A
NATIONAL UMBRELLA NETWORK OF THE ADOPTION REFORM MOVEMENT
(CONTINUED)

Iowa
Concerned United Birthparents
2000 Walker Street
Des Moines, IA 50317

New Jersey
Origins
Box 556
Whippany, NJ 07981

New York
Birthparent Support Network (BSN)
P. O. Box 120
North White Plains, NY 10603

Birthparent Support Network for Triad
93 Main Street
Queenbury, NY 12804

Various periodicals on adoption have been published.

Adoptalk
North American Council on Adoptable Children
970 Raymond Ave., Suite 106
Saint Paul, MN 55114

Adopted Child
P. O. Box 9362
Moscow, ID 83843

Adoption Therapist
House of Tomorrow Productions
c/o Hope Cottage, Financial Office
4209 McKinney Avenue, Suite 200
Dallas, TX 75205

AdoptNet Magazine
P. O. Box 50514
Palo Alto, CA 94303-0514

American Journal of Adoption Reform
1139 Bal Harbor Boulevard
P. O. Box 184
Punta Gorda, FL 33950
(monthly newsletter on family preservation)

Chain of Life
Box 8081
Berkeley, CA 94707

CUB Communicator
Concerned United Birth Parents
2000 Walker Street
Des Moines, IA 50317

The Decree
American Adoption Congress
1000 Connecticut Avenue NW, #9
Washington, DC 20036

Geborener Deutscher
805 Alvaredo Dr. N. E.
Albuquerque, NM 87108
(newsletter for German-born adoptees and their birth/adopted families)

Adoptive Families
Adoptive Families of America
3333 Highway 100 North
Minneapolis, MN 55422

People Searching News
P. O. Box 11044
Palm Bay, FL 3290-0444

Roots and Wings
P. O. Box 638
Chester, NJ 07930

Adapted from: Lifton, B. J. (1994). *Journey of the adopted self: A quest for wholeness.* New York: Basic Books.

6

Cognitive-Behavioral Play Therapy

Susan M. Knell, PhD

Dr. Knell is Adjunct Assistant Professor, Cleveland State University; and Lecturer, Case Western Reserve University, Cleveland, OH.

KEY POINTS

- Cognitive-behavioral play therapy with children addresses issues of control, self-mastery, and responsibility for one's own change in behavior.

- Although ample evidence suggests young children can understand complex problems if aided with concrete examples, many have challenged the use of cognitive therapy techniques with children, claiming that they are too sophisticated.

- Cognitive-behavioral therapy involves engaging the child in treatment via play; focusing on the child's thoughts, feelings, fantasies, and environment; pro-viding a strategy for developing more adaptive thoughts and behaviors; orienting treatment toward achieving goals; incorporating empirically demonstrated techniques; and allowing for an empirical examination of treatment.

- *Behavioral* techniques used in play therapy with children include systematic desensitization, contingency management, self-monitoring, and activity scheduling. *Cognitive* techniques include recording dysfunctional thoughts, cognitive change strategies, coping self-statements, and bibliotherapy.

INTRODUCTION: THEORY

Cognitive-behavioral play therapy is based on behavioral and cognitive theories of emotional development and psychopathology as well as the interventions derived from these theories. Cognitive therapy is a structured, focused approach that helps a person make changes in thinking, perceptions, and, ultimately, behavior (Beck, 1963, 1964, 1972, 1976; Beck, Rush, Shaw, & Emery, 1979; Ellis, 1958, 1962, 1971).

Cognitive-behavioral play therapy, which is designed specifically for preschool- and school-age children, emphasizes the child's involvement in treatment, by addressing issues of control, mastery, and responsibility for one's own change in behavior. By incorporating the cognitive components, the child may become an active participant in change. Children who are able to identify and modify potentially maladaptive beliefs have an increased capacity to experience a sense of personal understanding and empowerment. Integrating cognitive and behavioral interventions may offer combined properties of all approaches, which might not be available otherwise.

USE OF COGNITIVE-BEHAVIORAL PLAY THERAPY WITH YOUNG CHILDREN

Some authors have questioned the applicability and appropriateness of using cognitive-behavioral therapy with preschool children (Campbell, 1990). Frequently cited are developmental issues that might preclude the young child from understanding and benefiting from such interventions because cognitive-behavioral approaches often rely on fairly sophisticated cognitive abilities (e.g., abstract thinking, hypothesis testing).

However, ample data suggest that a young child's ability to understand complex problems may be enhanced by specific techniques, such as providing concrete examples and using fewer open-ended questions (Bierman, 1983). Rather than assume a lack of cognitive abilities to engage in cognitive-behavioral therapy, we must consider ways to make interventions more developmentally appropriate and therefore accessible to young children. To facilitate this, a match between the developmental level of the child and the level of complexity of the intervention chosen should be made. Therapists must capitalize on the child's strengths and abilities rather than weaknesses. Experiential therapies that incorporate play and deemphasize complex cognitive and verbal capabilities are likely to be the most useful for young children.

PRINCIPLES OF COGNITIVE THERAPY

Beck and Emery (1985) delineated 10 principles of cognitive therapy. Knell (1993) contends that, with minor modifications, most of these principles can be applied to cognitive-behavioral play therapy with young children.

Principles That Apply to Young Children:

Principle 1—Cognitive Therapy Is Based on the Cognitive Model of Emotional Disorders

The cognitive model of emotional disorders is based on the interplay among cognition, emotions, behavior, and physiology. Behavior is mediated through verbal processes, with disturbed behavior considered an expression of irrational thinking. Therapy is focused on cognitive change, which is comprised partly of altering irrational, maladaptive, or illogical thinking. A wide range of techniques has been developed to modify cognitions.

For children, the role of cognition must be viewed within a developmental context. The preoperational and concrete operational stages of a child's thinking can be illogical, irrational, and impulsive, with little verbal mediation of behavior. Cognitive therapy does not try to make children think like adults; rather, it attempts to help the child behave most adaptively.

Principle 2—*Cognitive Therapy Is Brief and Time Limited*

Cognitive therapy is task oriented, problem focused, and time limited, typically lasting less than 6 months. Brief therapy encourages the client to be self-sufficient and discourages dependency on the therapist. Strategies for keeping treatment brief include making interventions simple, specific, and concrete; keeping sessions task-related; and focusing on manageable problems (Beck & Emery, 1985). This approach makes sense for children because many of the more common childhood difficulties are transient and not indicative of serious psychopathology.

Principle 3—*A Sound Therapeutic Relationship Is a Necessary Condition for Effective Cognitive Therapy*

Cognitive therapy for persons of all ages relies on the establishment of a warm, therapeutic relationship based on trust and acceptance, which is the best predictor of positive treatment outcome (Brady et al., 1980; Rogers, Gendlin, Kiesler, & Truax, 1967).

Principle 4—*Therapy Is a Collaborative Effort Between Therapist and Patient*

Cognitive therapy uses a "team approach" to solve an individual's problems; the client supplies information and the therapist provides structure and expertise in problem solving. Together they work to develop strategies and plans to help the client deal with difficulties. Such a "collaborative environment" (Beck & Emery, 1985) is somewhat limited with children, although not impossible. A balance between imposing structure on the child and not interfering with the child's wishes and spontaneous behavior must be found, usually by following the child's lead. Moreover, some of the collaboration may be supplemented by work between the parent and therapist, rather than directly between the child and therapist.

Principle 5—*Cognitive Therapy Primarily Uses the Socratic Method*

The cognitive therapist uses the question as a lead and avoids direct suggestions and explanations. Direct questions are usually not effective with children, although the use of open-ended questions, if phrased in statement format, can be helpful.

Principle 6—Cognitive Therapy Is Structured and Directive

Cognitive therapy provides a structured, directive format, both for individual therapy sessions and therapy as a whole. Structure is determined by individual needs, but with children may involve the child's spontaneous material that is incorporated into more structured interventions.

Principle 7—Cognitive Therapy Is Problem Oriented

Cognitive therapy is focused on solving current problems although focusing on past and future concerns may be useful as well. By conceptualizing problems, choosing strategies and techniques, and assessing the effectiveness of the technique, the therapy remains problem oriented (Beck & Emery, 1985).

Principle 8—Cognitive Therapy Is Based on an Educational Model

The therapist helps the client learn more appropriate ways to deal with life situations by working with the client to change coping styles. Moreover, the therapist functions as a teacher who imparts positive coping skills and alternative behaviors. One aspect of this is teaching the client to learn from experiences so that coping skills can be applied on an ongoing basis. Beck and Emery (1985, p. 186) refer to this as "learning to learn." With children, the therapist often provides, through example, alternative coping skills that can be communicated via modeling with puppets and other toys.

Principles That Apply, With Modification, to Young Children:

Principle 9—The Theory and Techniques of Cognitive Therapy Rely on the Inductive Method

In cognitive therapy, clients are taught a scientific approach to their problems, with beliefs viewed as hypotheses, which can be revised based on new data. Both the therapist

and client conduct "experiments" to test hypotheses and re-
vise them accordingly. The choice of therapeutic techniques is
also driven by the inductive method; various techniques are
tested until a suitable one is found. The inductive method
cannot be used effectively with young children because it is
beyond their cognitive capabilities. However, the therapist
can still test hypotheses about the child and treatment techniques with case conceptualization and treatment plans
adapted accordingly.

Principles That Do Not Apply to Young Children:

Principle 10—Homework Is a Central Feature of Cognitive Therapy

With adults, between-session assignments are a critical
component of treatment. These are rarely used with young
children unless they are completed by the parent or by the
child with significant help from an adult.

PROPERTIES OF COGNITIVE-BEHAVIORAL PLAY THERAPY

The potential efficacy of cognitive-behavioral play therapy
may be related to the following six specific properties:

- *Engaging the child in treatment through play.* With the
  child as an active participant in therapy, the issues
  can be dealt with directly rather than through a
  parent or another significant adult (e.g., a guardian).

- *Focusing on the child's thoughts, feelings, fantasies, and
  environment.* Treatment focus is on situation-spe-
  cific factors as well as the child's feelings about the
  problem.

- *Providing a strategy for developing more adaptive
  thoughts and behaviors.* Through cognitive-behav-

ioral play therapy, the child is taught new, more adaptive strategies for coping with situations.

- *Orienting treatment toward achieving goals.*

- *Incorporating empirically demonstrated techniques.* Cognitive-behavioral play therapy draws heavily from the behavioral and cognitive traditions of using empirically based intervention. Further, it uses empirically demonstrated interventions. One of the most commonly used, well-documented, and perhaps most powerful techniques used is *modeling* (Bandura, 1977), which is the primary basis of cognitive-behavioral play therapy due to the need to demonstrate concretely, nonverbally, and specifically for young children.

- Allowing for an empirical examination of treatment: Cognitive-behavioral play therapy offers the opportunity to study the specific effects of well-defined interventions for well-delineated problems. Cognitive-behavioral play therapy can be set up in a way that maximizes empirical study of therapy outcome.

COGNITIVE-BEHAVIORAL PLAY THERAPY VERSUS TRADITIONAL PLAY THERAPIES

Cognitive-behavioral play therapy shares both similarities and differences with traditional play interventions with regard to basic assumptions and philosophy. These similarities and differences between cognitive-behavioral play therapy and traditional therapies (e.g., Axline, 1947), delineated by Knell (1993, 1994), are briefly described below and summarized in Tables 6.1 and 6.2.

Cognitive-behavioral play therapy is similar to other play

Table 6.1
SIMILARITIES BETWEEN COGNITIVE-BEHAVIORAL PLAY THERAPY
AND TRADITIONAL PLAY THERAPIES

- *Therapeutic relationship* — establish contact with child, engage child in treatment, engender child's trust

- *Communication via play* — play is a treatment modality as well as a means by which child and therapist communicate

- *Therapy as a safe place* — play therapy provides the child with a sense of security and safety

- *Obtaining clues to understand the child* — how child views self and others, conflicts and fantasies, problem-solving approaches

---

therapies in its reliance on a positive therapeutic relationship based on rapport and trust, the use of play activities as a means of communicating between therapist and child, and the message that therapy is a safe place.

It differs from other play therapies with regard to the establishment of goals. Unlike traditional play therapies, cognitive-behavioral play therapy provides specific direction toward established goals; encourages both the cognitive-behavioral play therapist and child to select toys and materials; uses therapy to educate, especially in a psychoeducational sense; and uses praise and interpretations. Moreover, the cognitive-behavioral play therapist uses interpretations or connections to help the child understand and grow from his or her behavior.

METHODS

Cognitive-behavioral interventions with children are typically delivered through modeling, role playing, and use of

Table 6.2 DIFFERENCES BETWEEN COGNITIVE-BEHAVIORAL PLAY THERAPY AND TRADITIONAL PLAY THERAPIES		
Psychoanalytic	*Nondirective (Axline)*	*Cognitive-Behavioral*
Directions and Goals		
Direction does not come from therapist	Direction is not accepted because it imposes on child; does not accept child as he or she is	Therapeutic goals are established; direction toward goals is basis of intervention
Play Materials and Activities		
Therapist is "participant observer," not playmate; therapist does not suggest any materials or activity	Play materials, activities, direction of play *always* selected by child	Both child and therapist select materials and activities
Play as Educational		
Play is not used to educate	Education is not appropriate because it is a form of direction	Play is used to teach skills and alternative behaviors
Interpretations/ Connections		
Interpretation as ultimate tool	Not made by therapist unless child introduces them first; therapist communicates unconditional acceptance, *not* interpretation of symbolic play	Introduced by therapist, who brings conflict into verbal expression for child
Praise		
Not considered appropriate	Praise should not be used by therapist; it communicates to child that therapist does not accept child, but rather wants child to be a certain way	Praise is crucial component, communicates to child which behaviors are appropriate, and reinforces these behaviors

behavioral contingencies (Braswell & Kendall, 1988). For very young children, modeling may be the most important method because reliance on verbal means is extremely limited. It is used to demonstrate adaptive coping and problem-solving skills.

Role playing is useful in that the child practices skills with the therapist and receives continuous feedback regarding progress. Role playing may be more effective with school-age, rather than preschool, children. Behavioral contingencies, which involve reinforcement or reward for children when they acquire new skills, are also useful for teaching new skills.

BEHAVIORAL AND COGNITIVE TECHNIQUES

A wide array of behavioral and cognitive techniques may be used in cognitive-behavioral play therapy, and many can be adapted for children as young as 4 or 5 years of age (Tables 6.3 and 6.4). Some of the techniques may require more adult/ parental assistance than others.

Behavioral Techniques:

Some of the more commonly used behavioral techniques are systematic desensitization, contingency management (which includes positive reinforcement, shaping, stimulus fading, extinction and differential reinforcement of other behavior, and time-out), self-monitoring, and activity scheduling.

Systematic Desensitization

In systematic desensitization, anxiety or fear can be reduced by replacing a maladaptive response with an adaptive one (Wolpe, 1958, 1982). This is accomplished by breaking the association between a particular stimulus and the anxiety or fear response that it usually elicits by presenting the stimulus and preventing the anxiety from occurring.

Table 6.3
EXAMPLES OF BEHAVIORAL TECHNIQUES IN COGNITIVE-BEHAVIORAL PLAY THERAPY

Behavioral technique modeled via puppet	*Vignette*
Systematic desensitization	Sexually abused child depicts abuse through drawings or play, beginning with least threatening material and gradually dealing with most threatening issues.
Shaping/positive reinforcement	Child is afraid to go to school. Therapist helps puppet go near the school building, visit the school, and gradually stay in the classroom (shaping). The puppet receives encouragement and positive feedback (reinforcement) from therapist as it gets closer and closer to school.
Extinction/differential reinforcement of other behavior	Child makes the puppet slap another puppet. Therapist knows that the nursery school teacher is concerned that the child deals with her anger by hitting other children. The puppet's slapping is ignored (extinction). When appropriate behavior (e.g., shaking hands) is shown, the puppet is praised (differential reinforcement of other behavior).
Self-monitoring	Child monitors feelings by marking picture of "happy, sad, or neutral" on chart.

With adults, systematic desensitization is usually accomplished through teaching muscle relaxation, which is incompatible with anxiety (Jacobson, 1938). For children, if muscle relaxation is not used, other enjoyable alternatives that counter anxiety may be taught. A viable alternative for very young children is facilitation of play activities that do not provoke anxiety.

Contingency Management

Contingency management describes techniques that modify a behavior by controlling its consequences. These management programs can be set up for the child in the natural environment or in the play therapy session. Common forms of contingency management are positive reinforcement, shaping, extinction, differential reinforcement of other behavior, and time-out.

Positive Reinforcement

Positive reinforcement often involves social reinforcers (such as praise) or material reinforcers (such as stickers). It is often used in combination with other procedures and may be direct (e.g., praise for playing appropriately) or more subtle (e.g., encouraging the child to explore certain topics as opposed to others). Praising a child for gaining mastery over a problem is a common example of positive reinforcement.

Shaping

When a child is lacking certain skills necessary to behave in a particular way, the child can be reinforced through successive approximations to the desired response. This is called shaping because positive reinforcement is given along the way as steps to the desired behavior are achieved.

Stimulus Fading

If a child possesses some of the requisite skills for a behavior but only exhibits the behavior in certain circumstances or with certain people, stimulus fading may be used. In such

Table 6.4 EXAMPLES OF COGNITIVE TECHNIQUES IN COGNITIVE-BEHAVIORAL PLAY THERAPY	
Cognitive technique	*Vignette*
Cognitive change strategies (identifying and correcting beliefs)	Child draws picture of a nightmare in which child was being scared by a man. Therapist draws a similar picture but includes the mother protecting the child.
Positive coping self-statement	Child afraid of being in closed room learns to make self-statements like, "I am OK; I can stay here."
Bibliotherapy	Therapist reads stories to child depicting children in similar circumstances and how they deal with them (e.g., divorce).

situations, the therapist may become a discriminative stimulus for behaving. The child might learn to use some of these positive skills in a setting with the therapist and then transfer the skills to other settings.

Extinction and Differential Reinforcement of Other Behavior

Behaviors can be extinguished by withholding reinforcement. Extinction itself does not teach new behaviors, so it is frequently used in conjunction with a reinforcement program. This way, a child can be reinforced for learning a new behavior at the same time that another behavior is being extinguished. This is often done through differential reinforcement of other behavior, through which behaviors that are different from or incompatible with the maladaptive behavior are reinforced. The main idea is that the unacceptable behavior cannot occur if a competing, more desirable behavior is taking place (e.g., reinforcing a child for appropriately playing with a toy, while extinguishing the child's efforts to break toys).

Time-out

Children sometimes need to be removed from whatever is reinforcing their behavior. This literally may demand removal of the child from the immediate environment. One technique for this is *time-out*, which is more frequently used in the natural environment, such as school or home, but may be used within the play therapy session as well. Although time-out technically calls for time away from reinforcement, it has come to mean removing children from what they perceive as a desirable environment to a less attractive one.

Self-Monitoring

In self-monitoring, clients observe and record information about their activities and moods. Self-monitoring can be used accurately by children as young as 4 or 5 years of age (Fixsen, Phillips, & Wolf, 1972; Risley & Hart, 1968). It is especially useful if the child is asked to monitor activities or events rather than mood. Young children usually need parental help with this task. However, if it is explained carefully and simply, the child can be expected to understand the task and complete it with supervision.

If mood is to be monitored, simple, concrete scales should be used. Whereas older children can understand a 10-point scale (e.g., 0 is "the worst you ever felt in your whole life"; 10 is "the best you ever felt in your whole life" [Emery, Bedrosian, & Garber, 1983]), younger children need scales that are even more concrete (e.g., with three faces representing mad, happy, and sad). Parents can monitor the accuracy of these perceptions by helping to clarify the child's feeling (e.g., "How did you feel when you hurt yourself? You were crying. Which picture looks like how you felt?").

Activity Scheduling

With activity scheduling, specific tasks are planned and

then implemented by the client. Planned activities for children and adolescents may reduce time spent in passive or ruminative activities. This can be particularly useful for depressed, withdrawn, or very anxious children, who may avoid activities because they do not expect to enjoy them or because they perceive themselves as failures when they try. When pressure is removed and children are encouraged to attempt the activity, many realize that they can have fun, despite any negative expectations. Even if they do not enjoy the activity, they can still be reinforced for their efforts to try.

Parental involvement is critical, although the child should have an active sense of control in activities planned. Providing the child with choices and control can be useful, particularly for the preschooler who is struggling with issues of autonomy and control (e.g., regarding eating and toileting).

Offering the child something he or she can control can be done by providing a limited range of *acceptable* options (e.g., "Would you rather play with your truck or with your blocks?"). The choice must be left up to the child, and the child should be allowed to feel a sense of competence at the assigned tasks and receive positive feedback for activities. Reinforcement should be based on the child's efforts and perseverance, not just on the final product.

Cognitive Techniques:

Cognitive methods, which can be incorporated into play activities, deal with changes in cognition—as opposed to behavior. This is an important distinction because cognitive theories suggest that changes in affect *and* behavior occur as a result of changes in thinking.

Recording Dysfunctional Thoughts

Cognitive therapists frequently ask clients to monitor and record their thoughts (e.g., in written or oral form). Although older children can be encouraged to record their thoughts, this is difficult—if not impossible to do with very young children.

Many times, this may be accomplished indirectly by having a parent monitor the child's activities and statements. Although this is the parent's perception of the child's statements, it is possible to obtain a recording of dysfunctional statements made by the child, rather than the child's self-recording of thoughts. The astute parent will listen for such comments through direct communication with the child *and* through the child's play. Although overheard and repeated by the parent as opposed to being directly reported by the child, these comments can be invaluable in providing clues to the youngster's perceptions.

Cognitive Change Strategies

With adults, hypothesis testing is used to change faulty cognitions. Thoughts, beliefs, assumptions, and expectations are treated as hypotheses to be tested scientifically. Problem areas are identified, and "experiments" are designed to test these thoughts. This examination typically involves a three-pronged approach: look at the evidence, explore the alternatives, and examine the consequences.

These strategies are difficult to use with children whose cognitive abilities are more limited than those of adolescents and adults. Children may have difficulty testing hypotheses, exploring situations, providing alternative explanations, and understanding consequences. Although children have the capacity to misinterpret and distort reality, their inferences may be consistent with *their* perceptions of reality – perceptions that are not necessarily accurate.

Therefore, helping children to change cognitions dictates that the child will need assistance from adults in generating alternative explanations, testing them, and altering beliefs (Emery et al., 1983). To challenge one's beliefs, it is necessary to distance oneself from those beliefs, something that is difficult for young children to do. In addition, the child needs an accumulated history of events to understand the ramifications of certain situations (Kendall, 1991). Learning occurs in part from experience and the very young child still has limited experiences on which to build. For young children, thought and reality are not always separate. Play can provide an arena to help the child bridge the gap between beliefs and reality and to build experiences that may help the child.

Play also allows the child to reenact problem situations and potentially gain mastery over events and circumstances. The therapist can assist in this endeavor by providing the "experiments" in the play situations and by helping the child look at the evidence, explore the alternatives, and examine the consequences. For example, the therapist may structure some of the play with the child to reflect alternative scenarios because the child then experiences different reactions and consequences for the same situation.

Coping Self-Statements

The way a person interprets events — rather than the events *per se* — affects the person's ability to cope. When one believes negative self-thoughts, maladaptive physiologic reactions may follow. These negative experiences may then prompt continued negative self-statements, which may lead to poor decisions. This feedback loop is illustrated by the school-age child who predicts he or she will do poorly on a test, supported by negative self-statements (e.g., "I did not study; I will fail; I do not understand this."), which may lead to physiologic reactions, such as an upset stomach or sweaty palms.

Persons of all ages can be helped to develop adaptive coping self-statements (Meichenbaum, 1985). Teaching coping self-statements must be modified based on the age and cognitive level of the child. Children in the preoperational stage of cognitive development may benefit most from learning simple statements about themselves. Often in the form of self-affirmation, these modified self-statements can be used with children as young as 2½–3 years of age. At this age, the self-statements are simple, both linguistically and conceptually (e.g., "good sitting"). Such self-statements should contain a component of self-reward (e.g., the message: "I am doing a good job.").

Positive self-statements can be modeled by the parent for the child. For example, young children enjoy hearing praise for accomplishments. Praise such as "good girl" or clapping one's hands for the child are often effective, but even more helpful is specific verbal labeling of what the child has done well (e.g., "Good boy, you did the entire puzzle."). Turning these into self-statements does not always occur spontaneously; parents must learn to prompt positive self-affirmative comments from their children. Moreover, children's positive self-comments often are short lived and situation specific. Thus, it is important to teach generalization and to ensure that parents reinforce the positive message for the child. For some parents, this concept is difficult because they *expect* good behavior from their child(ren) and do not feel that such behavior needs to be praised. Parents should understand that children will not internalize positive feelings unless taught the value of their actions. One way children learn the positive value of what they do is through specific labeling with positive feedback.

Bibliotherapy

Although not technically a cognitive intervention, bibliotherapy is used increasingly as an adjunct to cognitive therapy. Many self-help books for adults are based on cognitive theory (Burns, 1980) and provide an arena to help clients question their irrational beliefs and consider alternative options.

The use of bibliotherapy with children may have a somewhat different focus. Rather than specifically teaching concepts and suggesting ways of using these in one's life, children's books provide more of a storytelling approach. Although children's literature has always contained messages and morals, only recently has there been a proliferation of stories about children who have experienced particular stressors or traumas (e.g., divorce, death, moving). Such stories may model a child's reaction to a particular situation with the hope that the listener will learn something. When published materials are not available or appropriate, they may be created specifically for a child.

SPECIAL ISSUES

Therapy is focused on assisting the child to learn adaptive responses for dealing with individual situations, problems, or stressors. As gains are made, the therapist must also focus on helping the child generalize what is learned in therapy and help him or her avoid relapses after treatment is terminated. Dealing with the child and the family's feelings about termination is also an important issue in cognitive-behavioral play therapy.

Generalization Across Settings:

One obvious goal of treatment is for the child to maintain the adaptive behaviors learned in therapy in the natural environment. The maintenance of newly acquired skills may depend partly on the attitudes and behaviors of significant adults in the child's life. Therapy should be designed to promote and facilitate generalization rather than assuming it will occur naturally. Incorporating generalization skills into treatment involves interventions that mirror reality as much as possible; involvement of significant persons in the child's natural environment who are a source of reinforcement of the child's adaptive behavior; procedures that promote self-control of behavior; and interventions that continue past the initial acquisition of the skill to ensure that adequate learning has occurred.

Relapse Prevention:

Part of the original treatment must be geared toward the possibility of setbacks. This may involve preparing the parent and child for situations that may lead to a relapse. It can be useful to identify high-risk situations as those that might present a threat to the child's sense of control and ability to manage situations.

Termination:

Termination is usually a gradual process as the child and therapist talk about ending therapy. Children (as well as parents and therapists) often approach termination with mixed feelings. It is often helpful to remind the child, with very concrete references, of the number of sessions remaining until the final appointment. Termination may mean intermittent appointments until the therapy is eventually ended. These appointments may be scheduled over a period of time with a particular event in mind (e.g., beginning of school year, re-marriage of a parent). By spacing the final appointments several weeks apart, the therapist communicates a message that the child can manage without the therapist. It is important that children not believe that "bad" behavior will ensure that they will return to the therapist. Reassurances (e.g., the parent helps the child send a card to the therapist, the parent calls the therapist occasionally) may be useful. It is important in cogni-tive-behavioral play therapy to have an "open door" policy. Knowing that one can return to treatment can be important, regardless of whether or not the child ever needs to return.

SUMMARY

The application of cognitive-behavioral interventions with very young children is still in its early stages, largely because many do not believe that such work can be accomplished. Cognitive-behavioral play therapy incorporates behavioral and cognitive interventions into a play therapy paradigm and integrates them in a developmentally sensitive way. It places a strong emphasis on the child's active participation in treat-ment. The basic principles of cognitive therapy apply to children with minor modifications. Although similar to other play therapies, cognitive-behavioral play therapy is different in a number of ways. Most significantly, cognitive-behavioral play therapy is based on the establishment of treatment goals and is directive in nature.

REFERENCES

Axline, V. (1947). *Play therapy*. Boston: Houghton-Mifflin.

Bandura, A. (1977). *Social learning theory*. Englewood Cliffs, NJ: Prentice-Hall.

Beck, A. T. (1963). Thinking and depression. *Archives of General Psychiatry, 9*, 324–333.

Beck, A. T. (1964). Thinking and depression, II: Theory and therapy. *Archives of General Psychiatry, 10*, 561–571.

Beck, A. T. (1972). *Depression: Causes and treatment*. Philadelphia: University of Pennsylvania Press.

Beck, A. T. (1976). *Cognitive therapy and the emotional disorders*. New York: International Universities Press.

Beck, A. T., & Emery, G. (1985). *Anxiety disorders and phobias: A cognitive perspective*. New York: Basic Books.

Beck, A. T., Rush, A. J., Shaw, B. F., & Emery, G. (1979). *Cognitive therapy of depression*. New York: Guilford Press.

Bierman, K. L. (1983). Cognitive development and clinical interviews with children. In B. B. Lahey & A. Kazdin (Eds.), *Advances in clinical child psychology* (Vol. 6, pp. 217–250). New York: Plenum Press.

Brady, J. P., Davison, G. C., Dewald, P. A., Egan, G., Fad-mina, J., Frank, J. D., Gill, M. M., Hoffman, I., Kempler, W., Lazarus, A. A., Raimy, V., Rotter, J. B., & Strupp, H. H. (1980). Some views on effective principles of psychotherapy. *Cognitive Therapy and Research, 4*, 269–306.

Braswell, L., & Kendall, P. C. (1988). Cognitive-behavioral methods with children. In K. S. Dobson (Ed.), *Handbook of cognitive behavior therapy* (pp. 167–213). New York: Guilford Press.

Burns, D. (1980). *Feeling good.* New York: New American Library.

Campbell, S. (1990). *Behavior problems in preschool children.* New York: Guilford Press.

Ellis, A. (1958). Rational psychotherapy. *Journal of General Psychology, 59,* 35–49.

Ellis, A. (1962). *Reason and emotion in psychotherapy.* New York: Lyle Stuart.

Ellis, A. (1971). *Growth through reason: Verbatim cases in rational-emotive therapy and cognitive-behavior therapy.* New York: Lyle Stuart.

Emery, G., Bedrosian, R., & Garber, J. (1983). Cognitive therapy with depressed children and adolescents. In D. P. Cantwell & G. A. Carlson (Eds.), *Affective disorders in childhood and adolescence – An update* (pp. 445–471). New York: Spectrum Publications.

Fixsen, D. L., Phillips, E. L., & Wolf, M. M. (1972). Achievement place: The reliability of self-reporting and peer-reporting and their effects on behavior. *Journal of Applied Behavior Analysis, 5,* 19–30.

Jacobson, E. (1938). *Progressive relaxation.* Chicago: University of Chicago Press.

Kendall, P. C. (1991). *Child and adolescent therapy.* New York: Guilford.

Knell, S. M. (1993). *Cognitive-behavioral play therapy.* Montvale, NJ: Jason Aronson.

Knell, S. M. (1994). Cognitive-behavioral play therapy. In K. O'Connor & C. Schaefer (Eds.), *Handbook of play therapy* (Vol. 2, pp. 111-142). New York: Wiley.

Meichenbaum, D. (1985). *Stress inoculation training.* New York: Pergamon Press.

Risley, T. R., & Hart, B. (1968). Developing correspondence between the nonverbal and verbal behavior of school children. *Journal of Applied Behavior Analysis, 1,* 267–281.

Rogers, C. R., Gendlin, G. T., Kiesler, D. V., & Truax, C. B. (1967). *The therapeutic relationship and its impact: A study of psychotherapy with schizophrenics.* Madison, WI: University of Wisconsin Press.

Wolpe, J. (1958). *Psychotherapy by reciprocal inhibition.* Stanford, CA: Stanford University Press.

Wolpe, J. (1982). *The practice of behavior therapy* (3rd ed.). Oxford, UK: Pergamon Press.

7

Diagnosis and Management of Depression in Adolescents

Barry Sarvet, MD

Dr. Sarvet is Director of Training at the Division of Child and Adolescent Psychiatry, University of New Mexico School of Medicine, Albuquerque, NM.

KEY POINTS

- Depressive disorders are common in adolescents. Depression in this age group is associated with increased risk of depression during adulthood; it may also set the stage for excessive dependency, inhibition, anxiety, low self-esteem, interpersonal problems, and dropping out of school.

- The recognition of depression as a clinical syndrome in teenagers is a relatively recent historical development. It was previously thought that depression was merely excessive emotional turmoil associated with normal development in adolescence.

- The diagnostic criteria are essentially the same as those for adults. However, in teenagers, increased sleep, irritability, and mood reactivity tend to be more pronounced or common. Also, depressed adolescents may not be persistently anhedonic.

- Whereas antidepressant medications have constituted a mainstay of treatment for adult depression, their efficacy has not as yet been proved in adolescents. Nevertheless, pharmacotherapy is frequently used for adolescents with some depressive disorders.

- Various psychotherapeutic approaches may be used, including individual, group, and family therapy based on cognitive, behavioral, family systems, and psychodynamic models. A treatment plan incorporating a combination of these models would be optimal.

INTRODUCTION

The recognition of depression as a clinical syndrome in adolescence is a relatively recent historical development. The previously held notion that excessive emotional turmoil was a condition expected during normal development has been overturned in favor of a widespread recognition that specific types of adolescent turmoil are, in fact, depressive disorders.

Depressive disorders are common in adolescents. They may be associated with severe impairment in interpersonal relationships, substantial comorbidity, chronicity, and catastrophic outcome. Several lines of evidence — genetic studies, studies of longitudinal course, and psychobiologic studies — suggest a continuity between adolescent and adult manifestations of depression (Carlson & Garber, 1986). An awareness of developmental issues is critical to the diagnosis and management of adolescent depression.

CLINICAL FEATURES

Primary mood disorders, as defined in the fourth edition of the *Diagnostic and Statistical Manual of Mental Disorders* (DSM-IV) (American Psychiatric Association, 1994), include major depression, dysthymia, bipolar disorder, cyclothymia, mood disorder due to a general medical condition, and substance-induced mood disorder. Adolescents may suffer from any of these disorders. In general, the same diagnostic criteria are used in children and adolescents as in adults. Typical depressive symptoms include sadness, anhedonia, hopelessness, difficulty concentrating, feelings of worthlessness, thoughts of death, suicidality, sleep disturbance, weight changes or growth disturbance, decreased energy, agitation, and psychomotor retardation. Specific mood disorders are identified by chronicity, severity, and associated features in relation to these symptoms.

The following case example illustrates the presentation of major depression in an adolescent.

Steven, a 16-year-old was referred for evaluation by his father and stepmother. The father had previously enjoyed a warm relationship with his son and had been the adolescent's primary object of admiration and identification. However, for the past several months, Steven had been uncommunicative, isolating himself in his room, spending time with delinquent peers, and defying parental limits. He was ignoring previous interests in sports and academics and his grades in school were falling.

Steven's parents had grown mistrustful of him, and the more they attempted to set limits, the more he withdrew. They attributed most of his problems to manipulation by his peers. Although somewhat sympathetic, they harbored intense anger toward him for his defiance. While meeting with parents, Steven was quiet and withdrawn. Although he appeared defeated and hopeless, he did not express any of his personal feelings. During a private individual interview, Steven reported hopelessness and suicidal feelings. He felt helpless and unsure of himself with peers and family.

Steven also was preoccupied with losses, including abandonment by his mother 7 years before and the death of a devoted aunt. He was waking up three or four times a night, and he had lost approximately 10 pounds. During the several weeks prior to his evaluation, he was increasingly demoralized by conflicts with parents, teachers, and friends. Steven had shared his feelings with a friend who had been hospitalized for a suicide attempt. An extensive family history of unipolar depression was reported on the maternal side.

Depression in adolescents is commonly misconstrued as a disruptive behavioral disorder. Depressed symptoms are often accompanied by impaired interpersonal functioning. Parents and adults may become frustrated and threatened by the depressed adolescent's angry and rejecting attitudes, and their responses may accelerate a vicious downward spiral in which the adolescent feels increasingly misunderstood.

Depressed adolescents may differ from depressed adults in the following ways:

- Increased sleep is more likely

- Irritability may be a more accurate description of mood than sadness

- Mood reactivity tends to be more common in adolescents

- Depressed adolescents may not be persistently anhedonic

Adolescent depression—which is characterized by sudden onset, mood-congruent psychotic features, neurovegetative features, and a positive family history of bipolar disorder— carries with it the risk for bipolar disorder (Strober & Carlson, 1982). Rates of comorbidity are higher among depressed adolescents than among depressed adults. The most common comorbid diagnoses include anxiety disorders (30%–75%) and conduct/oppositional defiant disorders (32%–83%) (Angold, Weissman, John, Wickramaratne, & Prusoff, 1991; Kashani et al., 1987; McGee et al., 1990). Although pathologies (such as eating disorders, substance abuse disorders, learning disorders, and attention-deficit/hyperactivity disorder) commonly are associated with depressive symptoms, the precise relationship among these comorbid disorders remains speculative.

DEVELOPMENTAL CONSIDERATIONS

Adolescence often represents a turbulent phase of life, characterized by stormy interpersonal relationships and internal conflict. Unprecedented physical and cognitive changes— sexual maturation and the development of a capacity for increasingly abstract thinking—as well as evolving societal expectations and escalating social pressures pose formidable adaptive challenges to the adolescent. Landmark studies (Offer, 1969; Rutter, Graham, Chadwick, & Yule (1976) dispute the commonly held notion that alienation and interpersonal turmoil are normal during adolescence. Indeed, depressive symptoms are common among adolescents; however, these symptoms are usually fleeting and not pervasive. These studies suggest that severe symptoms of depression, especially those including impairments in functioning and interpersonal relationships, are not normal. In fact, most adolescents do *not* experience symptoms of alienation and conflict, severe mood disturbances, and behavioral instability with regard to their parents. Even though it continues to be reasonable to consider adolescence as a period of developmental challenge and heightened stress, the notion of severe adolescent depression as a benign phase-related phenomenon has been discarded.

EPIDEMIOLOGY

General population studies have revealed that depressive *symptoms* are relatively common during adolescence. The best known is the Isle of Wight study by Rutter and colleagues (1976), in which more than 40% of adolescents reported feelings of "misery." This was a sharp increase from the approximately 10% of 10- to 11-year-old children reporting similar symptoms. Parent-child alienation was somewhat less common but was more likely associated with psychiatric disorders. Similarly high prevalence rates have been replicated more recently (Kaplan, Hong, & Weinhold, 1984).

In many studies of depressive disorders (including major depression and dysthymia) in nonclinical samples, the prevalence rate ranged between 3% and 12% (Fleming, Boyle, & Offord, 1993; Kashani et al., 1987; McGee et al., 1990; Whitaker et al., 1990). The prevalence of depressive disorders increased dramatically from childhood to adolescence. A significant change in sex ratio is also apparent; among prepubertal children, the male/female ratio is roughly equal, whereas a definite female preponderance is evident among adolescents

(Angold & Costello, 1993). Among depressed adolescents, an earlier age of onset appears to correlate with longer duration of symptoms and suicidal ideation (Lewinsohn, Clarke, Seeley, & Rohde, 1994).

SUICIDALITY IN ADOLESCENTS

Depressed adolescents often come to psychiatric attention as a result of issues of suicidality. Although certainly not limited to depressed persons, an intimate association exists between suicidal phenomena and depressive disorders (Carlson & Cantwell, 1982; Levy & Deykin, 1989). Suicidal phenomena include ideation, threats, gestures, attempts, and completed suicide. Among depressed adolescents, approximately 60% demonstrated suicidality, ranging from occasional suicidal thoughts to attempts with high lethality (Myers et al., 1991). Depression is the most frequent diagnosis among adolescent suicide attempters.

Suicide among adolescents has become a serious public health concern. The suicide rate among adolescents has approximately tripled in the past 30 years (Sulik & Garfinkel, 1992), and suicide is currently one of the leading causes of adolescent mortality. The incidence of completed suicide is four times higher in boys than girls (Hoberman & Garfinkel, 1988). On the other hand, suicide *attempts* are more common among girls. The most frequently used method in completed suicide overall is the use of firearms; among girls, drug ingestion is the most frequently used method (Hoberman & Garfinkel, 1988).

Although suicidal acts are frequently preceded by expressions of severe hopelessness, suicidal ideation, and distress, a causal relationship between the presence of suicidal ideation and suicidal acts has not been established. On the other hand, suicide in adolescents is more commonly impulsive rather than premeditated (Brown, Overholser, Spirito, & Fritz, 1991). In addition to depression, highly significant risk factors in-

clude substance abuse (Levy & Deykin, 1989), disruptive behavior disorders (Myers et al., 1991), depressive cognitive
distortions (Brent, Kolko, Allan, & Brown, 1990), positive
family history of suicide (Brent et al., 1990; Weissman, Fendrich,
Warner, & Wickramaratne, 1990), stressful life events (Brent,
et al., 1990), and family discord (Brent, Kolko, Allan, & Brown,
1990). Longer duration of depressive symptoms is correlated
with risk of suicidality (Ryan et al., 1990). Among depressed
persons, separation anxiety exerts a protective effect (Myers et
al., 1991).

The phenomenon of suicidality underscores the importance of early detection and intervention in adolescent depression. A careful evaluation of risk factors and detailed exploration of the nature of suicidal ideation, the concept of death, and
degree of impulsivity are essential to the assessment of depressed adolescents.

COURSE AND OUTCOME

In addition to supporting the theory of continuity between
adolescent and adult depression, recent evidence suggests
that adolescent depressive disorders represent especially stub-
born and recurrent disorders. In an inpatient sample, Strober,
Lampert, Schmidt, and Morrell (1993) found that the mean
duration of depressive symptoms after admission was 34
weeks. Fleming and colleagues (1993) reported that among
adolescents with major depressive disorder, on follow-up 4
years later, 25% had suffered a recurrence within the prior 6
months. In a study of children and adolescents with major
depression and dysthymic disorder, 70% had experienced
recurrence within 5 years (Kovacs et al. , 1984).

A short-term outcome study among depressed adolescents
revealed evidence of "psychological scarring," including internalizing behavior problems (such as inhibition, anxiety,
and social withdrawal) and excessive dependence (Rohde,
Lewinsohn, & Seeley, 1994). Another study revealed problems

such as low self-esteem, interpersonal problems, and school dropout at follow-up (Fleming et al., 1993). A study of long-term outcome highlights the substantially increased risk of depression and psychiatric hospitalization during adulthood (Harrington, Fudge, Rutter, Pickles, & Hill, 1990).

Combined depression and conduct disorder has a prognosis somewhat distinct from depression without conduct disorder, with an elevated risk of subsequent adult criminality, substance abuse, and a lower risk of subsequent depression (Harrington, Fudge, Rutter, Pickles, & Hill, 1991). Depression combined with conduct disorder, representing approximately 25% of a general sample of depressed adolescents, may be a distinct entity more closely related to conduct disorder than to depression (Harrington et al., 1991).

In an inpatient sample of adolescents with major depression, 20% developed bipolar disorder within 3 to 4 years (Strober & Carlson, 1982). Factors associated with a bipolar outcome included rapid onset of symptoms, psychomotor retardation, mood-congruent psychotic features, family history of bipolar disorder, and a history of pharmacologically induced hypomania. In a later study of adolescents with psychotic depression, 28% developed bipolar disorder (Strober et al., 1993). Psychotic depression in adolescents is believed to be more closely linked to bipolar disorder than to adult-onset psychotic depression (Strober et al., 1993).

ASSESSMENT

The assessment of an adolescent with symptoms of depression should include a thorough exploration of history provided by both the adolescent and the parents. Parents tend to underreport depression, and adolescents may underreport behavioral problems. Information should be obtained from collateral sources, such as the school and pediatrician, to gain a more comprehensive appreciation of the adolescent's functioning.

The evaluating clinician must carefully consider issues of privacy and confidentiality when gathering clinical historical information because adolescents are often acutely sensitive in this regard. Questioning collateral sources of information may invade the adolescent's privacy. Therefore, in cases when collateral sources must be questioned, the clinician must discuss *beforehand* his or her plan with the adolescent. Gaining the trust of the adolescent is more readily accomplished by the use of a consistently honest, straightforward clinical style than by mere reassurances about confidentiality. Moreover, it is helpful to inform the adolescent patient that he or she is entitled to confidentiality *except with regard to issues of potential danger.*

Every evaluation should include an exploration of suicidality, substance abuse, and symptoms of impulsivity to assess risk of dangerous complications. Family history is an important area that may bolster diagnostic impressions as well as suggest significant patterns of psychosocial stress. A thorough review of pediatric history, as well as physical, neurologic, and laboratory tests, is necessary to identify any contributing medical or organic factors. Developmental history may yield information regarding chronicity of symptoms, relationship of symptoms to early life events, and any developmental adaptive vulnerabilities that may contribute to the current presentation. (In ordinary circumstances, most of this information can be gathered through detailed questioning of the parents.)

Differential Diagnosis:

Before assigning a diagnosis of depression in an adolescent, it is necessary to consider other psychiatric and medical conditions that may underlie the symptoms. Symptoms of apathy, emotional withdrawal, and psychomotor retardation may reflect a schizophrenic disorder. Weight loss and constriction of interests may be related to anorexia nervosa. Avoidance, hopelessness, and irritability may be symptoms of a posttraumatic stress disorder. Interpersonal turmoil and mood reactivity may reflect an emerging borderline personality disorder. Any depressive presentation during adolescence could be a manifestation of bipolar disorder. Depressive symptoms could also be related to a substance abuse disorder. With the exception of schizophrenia and bipolar disorder, these psychiatric conditions may represent comorbid rather than alternative diagnoses.

Medical conditions that may cause signs and symptoms of depression include various endocrine diseases (such as diabetes mellitus, hypothyroidism, hyperthyroidism, Addison's disease, and Cushing's disease), infections (such as central nervous system infections, acquired immunodeficiency syndrome [AIDS], chronic viral illnesses, and tuberculosis), and neurologic disorders (such as multiple sclerosis and epilepsy). Practically any systemic disease or malignancy can be initially confused with depression, especially those with insidious onset. One must also consider medications as a possible cause of depressive presentation. Common examples are antihypertensives, including clonidine (Catapres), central nervous system depressants, oral contraceptives, corticosteroids, and theophylline derivatives.

TREATMENT

Treatment of a depressed adolescent must be individualized according to the range and severity of symptoms, the family and social context, and the available resources. The assessment of dangerousness to self is pivotal in determining the intensity and setting of treatment. A thorough exploration of the details of any suicidal thinking or behavior allows one to judge aspects of lethality. The clinician must consider factors that might affect impulsivity, such as substance abuse, and temperament. Hospitalization is often necessary for acutely suicidal adolescents and may be strongly considered for adolescents with psychotic depression, and severe, disabling depressive symptoms, or for severe cases that have been refractory to less restrictive treatment modalities.

Treatment objectives extend well beyond the direct resolution of depressive symptoms. They usually address a variety of factors that are associated with the depression. These may include comorbid psychiatric disorders such as substance abuse, anxiety disorders, and conduct disorders. Treatment planning often addresses patterns of family communication, school performance, peer relationships, health issues, and occupational functioning.

The involvement of the parents is an essential but consistently problematic aspect of treating an adolescent patient. Because of the transitional nature of the adolescent developmental period, it is often unclear to therapists how to involve parents adequately without failing to respect the adolescent's wish for autonomy. Factors to be considered include the age, degree of psychological and practical emancipation, degree of family enmeshment, severity of problems, and degree to which family environment influences expression of symptoms. The clinician often must strike a careful balance between satisfying the parents' need to be involved and the adolescent's need to be treated as an autonomous person. Wherever that balance is found, it is usually worthwhile to inform all parties of their role in the treatment process and to explore feelings and concerns about confidentiality. Ensuring that parents are being educated about the therapeutic process and about relevant mental health issues is important. It is especially crucial to lead parents away from the notion that they are "to blame."

Because depression in adolescence is a recurrent syndrome, treatment strategies should include a long-term component that addresses relapse prevention. Although not systematically studied, multimodal treatment often addresses the multiple depressive symptoms and associated factors that are usually present. Whatever varied treatment approaches are applied over a period of several years, continuity of care is enormously beneficial in the face of complex developmental variables and differential response to treatment.

Biologic Treatments:

Although antidepressant medications have constituted the

mainstay of treatment for adult depression, their role in adolescent depression remains somewhat controversial. Despite cogent evidence based on outcome and genetic studies (Beardslee, Bemporad, Keller, & Klerman, 1983; Kutcher & Marton, 1991) that adolescent depression is integrally related to adult depression, studies of clinical response to antidepressant medications in adolescents have failed to prove their efficacy.

Over the past 12 years, systematic clinical studies have been conducted testing imipramine (Tofranil) (Ryan et al., 1985; Strober, Freeman, & Rigali, 1990), nortriptyline (Aventyl, Pamelor) (Geller, Cooper, Graham, Marstellar, & Bryant, 1990), desipramine (Norpramin, Pertofrane) (Kutcher et al., 1994), fluoxetine (Prozac) (Simeon, Dinicola, Ferguson, & Copping, 1990), and other antidepressants in depressed adolescents. Researchers have concluded that current empirical data do not support the efficacy of antidepressants in children and adolescents. Nonetheless, antidepressant pharmacotherapy has become routine for adolescents with moderate to severe depression. This practice is based on positive results from earlier open clinical trials and widespread clinical impression of beneficial response. Rather than doubting efficacy, some researchers and clinicians suspect that methodologic problems with heterogeneous samples (including subgroups of adolescent depressives who have bipolar disorder or comorbid conduct disorder) and high placebo response have precipitated the failure to demonstrate efficacy. Others believe that antidepressants are less effective in adolescents because of factors such as incomplete maturation of the central nervous system or the different hormonal milieu of adolescents. Studies also have failed to demonstrate relationships between plasma levels and clinical responses, which are so widely appreciated in adults. Nonetheless, adult guidelines on plasma levels continue to influence clinical practice. Research attempting to further clarify the question of the efficacy of antidepressant medication continues with increasingly sophisticated methodology. Lithium augmentation has been recommended to increase efficacy (Ambrosini, Bianchi, Rabinovich, & Elia, 1993; Strober, Freeman, Rigali, Schmidt, & Diamond, 1992). Although modest, beneficial results were demonstrated in a study of adolescent imipramine nonresponders (Strober et al., 1992).

Despite the lack of definitive proof of efficacy, it is standard practice for antidepressant medication to be included in the treatment plan for adolescent patients with major depressive disorder or dysthymia. For mild cases, it is reasonable to rely on psychotherapeutic intervention alone; however, pharmacotherapy should be considered if progress in treatment is sluggish. Early use of medication is warranted in the presence of neurovegetative symptoms, psychiatric symptoms, or severely compromised adaptive functioning.

In addition to questions about efficacy, a safety concern has recently emerged with respect to tricyclic antidepressants in children and adolescents; these agents have been associated with several cases of sudden death in children and adolescents (Riddle et al., 1991). Recent research has convincingly linked these deaths to underlying subclinical or clinical cardiac conduction abnormalities, most notably the prolonged QT interval syndrome. Persons with this syndrome are at increased risk for sudden death caused by malignant cardiac arrhythmias, which may be induced by exercise and potentiated by the quinidine-like effect of the tricyclics. Current recommendations include: (a) screening child and adolescent candidates for tricyclics with careful gathering of history on cardiac-related symptoms that suggest arrhythmias, syncope, family history of sudden death or cardiac arrhythmias; (b) monitoring electrocardiograms (ECGs) before and after initiation of treatment; and (c) monitoring blood levels and side effects to prevent cardiotoxicity. Discontinuation or avoidance of tricyclic therapy should be strongly considered if patients show evidence of excessive conduction delays leading to QTc greater than 450 msec (Riddle et al., 1991; Tingelstad, 1991). Because of these considerations, some clinicians prefer a selective serotonin reuptake inhibitor as a first-line treatment option.

Indeed, despite failure to demonstrate efficacy in clinical trials, a wide variety of antidepressants should be considered in the treatment of moderate to severe depression in adolescents. With the exception of tricyclics, dosing may be guided by clinical and laboratory measurements of therapeutic and adverse effects rather than on guidelines for adult plasma levels. Patients at increased risk for bipolar disorder should be treated with caution; adjunctive therapy with a mood-stabilizing agent such as lithium, carbamazepine (Tegretol), or valproate (Depakote) may also be effective.

Psychotherapeutic Modalities:

Psychotherapeutic approaches to adolescent depression include individual, group, and family therapy based on cognitive, behavioral, family systems, and psychodynamic models, as well as suitable combinations of these. Even though clinicians tend to favor the approaches with which they are most familiar, some effort toward deriving an approach from a comprehensive clinical formulation would be optimal. An individualized therapeutic approach should be flexible enough to address diverse problems that include, but are not limited to, depressive symptoms. For example, in the previously described case of Steven, issues of guilt and loss, negative cognitions, oppositionality, interpersonal problems, and parental reactions could all be appropriate foci for therapy. The clinician must select one or a combination of approaches based on clinical urgency and feasibility.

Few therapeutic techniques have been tested in adolescent depression using controlled systematic trials. A recent trial of a group-based, cognitive-behavioral therapy demonstrated a beneficial effect that was maintained at 2-year follow-up (Lewinsohn, Clarke, Hops, & Andrews, 1990). A comparison study of other group therapy approaches found that a therapeutic support group and a social skills group had equally beneficial effects after 9 months (Fine, Forth, Gilbert, & Haley, 1991). Preliminary studies of an individually based therapy, interpersonal psychotherapy, which was modified for adolescents (IPT-A), has also shown promising results (Mufson et al., 1994; Mufson, Moreau, Weissman, & Klerman, 1993). Increasingly, researchers are endeavoring to generate data on psychotherapy that may guide clinicians. Unfortunately, the manual-based therapies being studied represent only a small fraction of the therapeutic approaches in common practice.

Cognitive and behavioral treatment strategies for depressed adolescents directly address phenomena such as negative irrational thoughts, avoidant or self-defeating behaviors, poor social skills, management of emotional stress, psychobiologic stress response, and problem solving. These therapies usually are time-limited and include psychoeducation. Cognitive therapy is often presented in a practical kind of tone and style that may be reassuring to certain adolescents who would fear feelings of exposure in more intimate therapeutic approaches.

Interpersonal psychotherapy (Mufson et al., 1993) is a specific form of individual therapy that addresses maladaptive patterns of interpersonal processes in relationships. This is especially relevant for depressed adolescents, who often experience turmoil or alienation in their relationships with family and peers. It involves a time-limited treatment with the goal of modifying styles of communication and typical reactions to other people through the examination of interpersonal phenomena in the patient's life.

Psychodynamic approaches are widely varied and may be combined with other approaches. Psychodynamic therapies for depressed adolescents can be based on a model of depression as a response to the loss of the comfort and security of childhood status and relationships (anaclitic). It is also possible that depression will be framed as a consequence of guilt or anger turned inward (introjective) (Bemporad, 1988). In either case, it is critical to approach depressed adolescents in a supportive manner, respectful of their need for defenses against powerful anxieties related to potential threats from within (such as increasing sexual and aggressive impulses) and challenges from the outside world. Psychodynamic therapies generally have avoided a specific focus, allowing a natural unfolding of the therapy with the goal of long-term symptom resolution and internal change. And yet, an appreciation of psychodynamic aspects may enrich a more focal treatment, if the latter is found to be more feasible or relevant.

Therapy directed toward the family may be central or adjunctive in the treatment of adolescent depression. Family issues that may be a focus of treatment include excessive enmeshment, unclear roles, excessive or misdirected conflict, and poor communication. Issues of parental loss commonly are exacerbated in response to the withdrawal or alienation of the depressed adolescent. Parent guidance therapy or parent skills training may alleviate the alienation and maintain safety.

CONCLUSION

Depression is one of the more common disorders of adolescence. Although considered closely related to adult depression, its clinical presentation and associated features are influenced strongly by developmental factors. There are high rates of comorbidity, and long-term outcome suggests that it is a chronic, recurrent disorder. Adolescent depression is a contributing factor in the alarmingly high rates of suicide among adolescents in recent years. These issues underscore the importance of early detection, effective treatment, and long-term management. Treatment strategies involving multimodal and additional research efforts are needed to establish the efficacy of the most commonly applied treatments.

REFERENCES

Ambrosini, P. J., Bianchi, M. D., Rabinovich, H., & Elia, J. (1993). Antidepressant treatments in children and adolescents, I: Affective disorders. *Journal of the American Academy of Child and Adolescent Psychiatry, 32*, 1–6.

American Psychiatric Association. (1994). *Diagnostic and statistical manual of mental disorders.* (4th ed.) Washington, DC: Author.

Angold, A., & Costello, E. J. (1993). Depressive comorbidity in children and adolescents: Empirical, theoretical, and methodological issues. *American Journal of Psychiatry, 150*, 1779–1791.

Angold, A., Weissman, M. M., John, K., Wickramaratne, P., & Prusoff, B. (1991). The effects of age and sex on depression ratings in children and adolescents. *Journal of the American Academy of Child and Adolescent Psychiatry, 30*, 67–74.

Beardslee, W. R., Bemporad, J., Keller, M. B., & Klerman, G. L. (1983). Children of parents with major affective disorder: A review. *American Journal of Psychiatry, 140*, 825–832.

Bemporad, J. R. (1988). Psychodynamic treatment of depressed adolescents. *Journal of Clinical Psychiatry, 49*(9, Suppl.), 26–31.

Brent, D. A., Kolko, D. J., Allan, M. J., & Brown, R. V. (1990). Suicidality in affectively disordered adolescent inpatients. *Journal of the American Academy of Child and Adolescent Psychiatry, 29*, 586–593.

Brown, L. K., Overholser, J., Spirito, A., & Fritz, G. K. (1991). The correlates of planning in adolescent suicide attempts. *Journal of the American Academy of Child and Adolescent Psychiatry, 30*, 95–99.

Carlson, G. A., & Cantwell, D. P. (1982). Suicidal behavior and depression in children and adolescents. *Journal of the American Academy of Child and Adolescent Psychiatry, 21*, 361–368.

Carlson, G. A., & Garber, J. (1986). Developmental issues in the classification of depression in children. In M. Rutter, C. Izard, & P. Read (Eds.), *Depression in young people* (pp. 399–434). New York, NY: Guilford Press.

Fine, S., Forth, A., Gilbert, M., & Haley, G. (1991). Group therapy for adolescent depressive disorder: A comparison of social skills and therapeutic support. *Journal of the American Academy of Child and Adolescent Psychiatry, 30,* 79–85.

Fleming, J. E., Boyle, M. H., & Offord, D. R. (1993). The outcome of adolescent depression in the Ontario Child Health Study follow-up. *Journal of the American Academy of Child and Adolescent Psychiatry, 32,* 28–33.

Geller, B., Cooper, T. B., Graham, D. L., Marstellar, F. A., & Bryant, D. M. (1990). Double-blind, placebo-controlled study of nortriptyline in depressed adolescents using a 'fixed plasma level' design. *Psychopharmocology Bulletin, 26*(1), 85–90.

Harrington, R., Fudge, H., Rutter, M., Pickles, A., & Hill, J. (1990). Adult outcomes of childhood and adolescent depression. *Archives of General Psychiatry, 47,* 465–473.

Harrington, R., Fudge, H., Rutter, M., Pickles, A., & Hill, J. (1991). Adult outcomes of childhood and adolescent depression, II: Links with antisocial disorders. *Journal of the American Academy of Child and Adolescent Psychiatry, 30,* 434–439.

Hoberman, H. M., & Garfinkel, B. D. (1988). Completed suicide in children and adolescents. *Journal of the American Academy of Child and Adolescent Psychiatry, 27,* 689–695.

Kaplan, S. L., Hong, G. K., & Weinhold, C. (1984). Epidemiology of depressive symptomatology in adolescents. *Journal of the American Academy of Child and Adolescent Psychiatry, 23,* 91–98.

Kashani, J. H., Beck, N., Hoeper, E. W., Fallahi, C., Corcoran, C., McAllister, J., Rosenberg, T., & Reid, J. (1987). Psychiatric disorders in a community sample of adolescents. *American Journal of Psychiatry, 144,* 584–588.

Kovacs, M., Feinberg, T. L., Crouse-Novak, M., Paulauskas, S. L., Pollock, M., & Finkelstein, R. (1984). Depressive disorders in childhood, II: A longitudinal study of the risk for a subsequent major depression. *Archives of General Psychiatry, 41,* 643–649.

Kutcher, S., Boulos, C., Ward, B., Marton, P., Simeon, J., Fergeson, H. B., Szalai, J., Katic, M., Roberts, N., Dubois, C., & Reed, K. (1994). Response to desipramine treatment in adolescent depression: A fixed-dose, placebo-controlled trial. *Journal of the American Academy of Child and Adolescent Psychiatry, 33,* 686–694.

Kutcher, S., & Marton, P. (1991). Affective disorders in first-degree relatives of adolescent onset bipolars, unipolars, and normal controls. *Journal of the American Academy of Child and Adolescent Psychiatry, 30,* 75–78.

Levy, J. C., & Deykin, E. Y. (1989). Suicidality, depression, and substance abuse in adolescents. *American Journal of Psychiatry, 146,* 1462–1467.

Lewinsohn, P., Clarke, G., Hops, H., & Andrews, J. (1990). Cognitive-behavioral treatment for depressed adolescents. *Behavior Therapy, 21,* 385–401.

Lewinsohn, P. M., Clarke, G. N., Seeley, J. R., & Rohde, P. (1994). Major depression in community adolescents: Age at onset, episode duration, and time to recurrence. *Journal of the American Academy of Child and Adolescent Psychiatry, 33,* 809–818.

McGee, R., Feehan, M., Williams, S., Partridge, F., Silva, P. A., & Kelly, J. (1990) . DSM-III disorders in a large sample of adolescents. *Journal of the American Academy of Child and Adolescent Psychiatry, 29,* 611–619.

Mufson, L., Moreau, D., Weissman, M., & Klerman, G. (1993). *Interpersonal psychotherapy for depressed adolescents.* New York: Guilford Press.

Mufson, L., Moreau, D., Weissman, M. M., Wickramaratne, P., Martin, J., & Samoilov, A. (1994). Modification of interpersonal psychotherapy with depressed adolescents (IPT-A): Phase I and II studies. *Journal of the American Academy of Child and Adolescent Psychiatry, 33,* 695–705.

Myers, K., McCauley, E., Calderon, R., Mitchell, J., Burke, P., & Schloredt, K. (1991). Risks for suicidality in major depressive disorder. *Journal of the American Academy of Child and Adolescent Psychiatry, 30,* 86–94.

Offer, D. (1969). *The psychological world of the teenager: A study of normal adolescent boys.* London, England: Basic Books.

Riddle, M., Nelson, J. C., Kleinman, C., Rasmusson, A., Leckman, J., King, R., & Cohen, D. J. (1991). Sudden death in children receiving Norpramin: A review of three reported cases and commentary. *Journal of the American Academy of Child and Adolescent Psychiatry, 30,* 104–108.

Rohde, P., Lewinsohn, P. M., & Seeley, J. R. (1994). Are adolescents changed by an episode of major depression? *Journal of the American Academy of Child and Adolescent Psychiatry, 33,* 1289–1298.

Rutter, M., Graham, P., Chadwick, O. F. D., & Yule, W. (1976). Adolescent turmoil: Fact or fiction? *Journal of Child Psychology and Psychiatry and Allied Disciplines, 17,* 35–56.

Ryan, N., Puig-Antich, J., Cooper, T., Rabinovich, H., Ambrosini, P., Davies, M., King, J., Torres, D., & Fried, J. (1985). Imipramine in adolescent major depression: Plasma level and clinical response. *Acta Psychiatrica Scandinavica, 73,* 275–288.

Ryan, N., Puig-Antich, J., Ambrosini, P., Rabinovich, H., Robinson, D., Nelson, B., Iyengar, S., & Tuomey, J. (1990). The clinical picture of major depression in children and adolescents. *Archives of General Psychiatry, 44,* 854-861.

Simeon, J. G., Dinicola, V. F., Ferguson, H. B., & Copping, W. (1990). Adolescent depression: A placebo-controlled fluoxetine treatment study and follow-up. *Progress in Neuropsychopharmacology and Biological Psychiatry, 14,* 791–795.

Strober, M.,& Carlson, G. (1982). Bipolar illness in adolescents with major depression. *Archives of General Psychiatry, 39,* 549–555.

Strober, M., Freeman, R., & Rigali, J. (1990). The pharmacotherapy of depressive illness in adolescence, I: An open label trial of imipramine. *Psychopharmocology Bulletin, 26,* 80–84.

Strober, M., Freeman, R., Rigali, J., Schmidt, S., & Diamond, R. (1992). The pharmacotherapy of depressive illness in adolescence, II: Effects of lithium augmentation in nonresponders to imipramine. *Journal of the American Academy of Child and Adolescent Psychiatry, 31,* 16–20.

Strober, M., Lampert, C., Schmidt, S., & Morrell, W. (1993). The course of major depressive disorder in adolescents, I: Recovery and risk of manic switching in a follow-up of psychotic and nonpsychotic subtypes. *Journal of the American Academy of Child and Adolescent Psychiatry, 32*, 34-42.

Sulik, L., & Garfinkel, B. (1992). Adolescent suicidal behavior: Understanding the breadth of the problem. *Child and Adolescent Psychiatric Clinics of North America, 1*, 197-228.

Tingelstad, J. (1991). The cardiotoxicity of the tricyclics. *Journal of the American Academy of Child and Adolescent Psychiatry, 30*, 845-846.

Weissman, M. M., Fendrich, M., Warner, V., & Wickramaratne, P. (1990). Incidence of psychiatric disorder in offspring at high and low risk for depression. *Journal of the American Academy of Child and Adolescent Psychiatry, 31*, 640-648.

Whitaker, A., Johnson, J., Shaffer, D., Rappoport, J., Kalikow, K., Walsh, B. T., Davies, M., Braiman, S., & Dolinski, A. (1990). Uncommon troubles in young people. *Archives of General Psychiatry, 47*, 487-496.

8

Group Therapy for Adolescents

Seth Aronson, PsyD, and Saul Scheidlinger, PhD

Dr. Aronson is Assistant Director, Child/Adolescent Psychiatry, Bronx Municipal Hospital Center/Albert Einstein College of Medicine, Bronx, NY. Dr. Scheidlinger is Professor Emeritus of Psychiatry (Child Psychology), Albert Einstein College of Medicine, Bronx, NY.

KEY POINTS

- Group therapy is often viewed as a more economical way to deal with mental and emotional disorders.

- The group can provide many forms of learning, such as peer support, self-esteem enhancement, and interpersonal learning; for adolescents, group therapy can also help to facilitate separation from the family.

- Four basic types of group approaches exist for adolescents: group psychotherapy; therapeutic groups, such as occupational therapies; human development and training groups; and self-help groups.

- If a careful balancing of the group

structure is achieved, group psychotherapy can be the treatment of choice for most adolescents. One way to achieve such a balance is to conduct interviews with group therapy candidates.

- Adolescents tend to function best in homogeneous groups with explicit limits and rules. Counselors working with such groups must demonstrate honesty, directness, and authenticity and be willing to enforce the group structure.

- Common themes that develop in group therapy include identity formation, separation-individuation, conflicts over dependency and independence, and sexuality.

INTRODUCTION

Adolescence and the concept of group life are inextricably woven together. A typical high school comprises a number of defined groups, each bound by its own rules and structure. In addition, informal groups, such as clubs, street-corner cliques, and sports teams have key functions in psychological and social development.

Peer groupings play an important role in normative personality development. They represent an arena for self-esteem enhancement, the development of a moral code, interpersonal learning, and, ultimately, the psychological separation from the family. The concept of *universalization* — that everyone else in the group is "in the same boat" — provides comfort and reassurance at a time of rapid bodily and intellectual changes that are fraught with much anxiety.

In fact, the group provides an ideal forum in which the developmental tasks of this phase can be addressed. Peers are sought out to fill the void created by attempts to separate from parents. Steps toward identity consolidation can be achieved by listening and speaking to others, thereby developing new interests, opinions, and ideas, while concurrently refining interpersonal skills. Learning to create intimate, emotional relationships outside the family occurs as the adolescent begins to identify with new figures. The propensity of adolescents to form group relationships can be channeled successfully in a practical intervention measure to promote change and growth — group therapy.

DIFFERENT GROUP MODALITIES

Group work with adolescents can be performed in a variety of contexts. Scheidlinger (1985) has described four distinct, yet related, types of group structure designed to help adolescents work through problems and achieve various developmental milestones.

Group Psychotherapy:

The first type of group therapy structure is *group psychotherapy proper*. It has been defined as

> ... a specific clinical modality lodged in the broader field of the psychotherapies. A trained mental health professional uses the emotional interaction among participants in a small, carefully balanced group to effectuate amelioration of personality difficulties in individuals specifically selected for this purpose. Each group member has a diagnosed problem and views the group experience as a means of modifying his or her psychological functioning. (Scheidlinger & Aronson, 1991, p. 104)

The key factors include trained group therapists, a carefully balanced group, and a membership specifically chosen from those in need of this treatment modality. Group psychotherapy may take place in a variety of settings, such as inpatient psychiatric facilities, outpatient clinics, and residential treatment centers.

Therapeutic Groups:

The second category, *therapeutic groups*, encompasses all group approaches, other than group psychotherapy *per se*, that are being used by human services personnel in inpatient and outpatient settings. Examples include therapeutic community meetings and art, dance, and occupational therapies. Informal therapeutic groups are also used in special education settings and in residential treatment facilities. Short-term groups such as diagnostic groups, groups for those on a waiting list for services, and groups for adolescents with chronic illnesses also fall in this category.

Human Development and Training Groups:

The third group intervention category is comprised of

human development and training groups, which stress cognitive and affective education over therapeutics. Examples include consciousness-raising and sensitivity-training groups, as well as the mushrooming school-based education groups, which aim to prevent acquired immunodeficiency syndrome (AIDS), substance abuse, teen pregnancy, and other specific problems facing adolescents.

Self-Help and Mutual-Help Groups:

The fourth category consists of *self-help and mutual-help groups*. Generally formed on a voluntary basis, these groups are designed to provide mutual aid and to accomplish specific, defined goals. Examples of institutions that use this model are Alcoholics Anonymous and Narcotics Anonymous.

Although the boundaries between the four categories can be blurred, it is generally useful for counselors to be able to distinguish among them. This chapter focuses on the first category, group psychotherapy.

PURPOSE OF GROUP THERAPY

Despite methodologic differences, the groups in each category are designed to bring about behavioral change. In distinguishing between the categories, four variables should be considered: (a) the leader-change agent variable, which includes the latter's training and theoretical orientation; (b) the patient/client variable, which refers to the identifying characteristics of the group members such as age, sex, and sociocultural background; (c) the methodology variable, which encompasses the group leader's techniques (generally related to his or her theoretical orientation) used to promote behavioral change and growth; and (d) the process variable, which reflects what the leader believes to be occurring within the group experience.

BEGINNING A GROUP: INDICATIONS AND CONTRAINDICATIONS

To achieve a group balance, selection of group members requires careful consideration (Slavson, 1950). Variables to consider include age, sex, level of psychological sophistication, sociocultural and educational background, and degree and type of psychopathology. For example, a severely impaired schizophrenic adolescent included in a group of higher-functioning adolescents may be easily made a scapegoat and ultimately excluded. Therefore, the group therapist must not only consider whether the adolescent can benefit from the group but also whether this particular group represents the right fit for the adolescent. Careful balancing may at times allow for the inclusion of some youths who might otherwise be inappropriate members. Gardner (1988) included a few antisocial patients in some of his groups. Because they were selectively chosen and in the minority, the group experience helped them recognize the self-defeating quality of their behavior without their constituting a threat to the others.

A permissive, psychoanalytically informed group structure is usually contraindicated because adolescents are generally prone to contagious, provocative behavior and are sensitive to emotional disclosures. Young people tend to function best in homogeneous groups with explicit limits and rules. With careful balancing and implementation of structure, group psychotherapy emerges as the treatment of choice for most adolescents.

One practice designed to help establish the group's foundation is to provide individual preparatory sessions for the group therapy candidates. These sessions are conducted by the group therapists to initiate a working alliance with the patient. They also allow time to address the inevitable concerns and anxieties connected with joining a group. In these interviews, potential members often have questions regarding the degree of confidentiality, who the other members will be, and what the expectations are. These interviews also offer a means to assess the suitability of the adolescent for the particular group.

Some counselors prefer to see their adolescent patients concurrently in individual and group therapy; some adolescents are in individual treatment with one counselor and in group therapy with another. This "combined therapy" often can be used in a complementary fashion, allowing the patient to "work through" and process the vicissitudes of treatment (Bromfield & Pfeiffer, 1988; Scheidlinger, 1982).

Other "nuts and bolts" issues involve the number of members in the group. Ideally, eight to ten teenagers provide enough points of view to foster meaningful interaction. It is especially important to consider the census of outpatient groups, because absences and missed appointments (a common outpatient occurrence) can deplete the group's numbers.

The length of group sessions varies. Many outpatient group therapists prefer to have group sessions that are 1½ to 2 hours in length. Inpatient group sessions may be shorter because of scheduling constraints.

The physical setting has a distinct influence on the interaction. An overly large room may trigger undesirable mobility, avoidance of interaction, and more physical activity. A smaller room may be too limiting, thus increasing tension. The type and quality of furniture can also influence the tone and mood of the group and should be considered carefully (Berkovitz, 1972).

YOUNGER AND OLDER ADOLESCENT GROUPS

Most mental health professionals can easily describe the unique difficulties involved in engaging younger adolescents in any treatment. Those aged 10 to 14 are exceedingly prone to denial and externalization; moreover, they may still manifest more concrete thinking and possess a pressing need toward immediate gratification. These elements combine to make attempts at self-awareness difficult. The group setting and structure for such youths should ideally combine snacks, discussion, and some allowance for free movement via activities. Younger adolescents are also extremely prone to self-consciousness. Group behavior is often characterized by squirming, teasing, whispering, and emotional lability. Further, girls at this developmental stage may be more physically and emotionally mature than boys and may complain about the boys' relative immaturity. For this reason, in addition to the high degree of anxiety and self-consciousness, it is usually preferable *not to mix sexes* in groups with younger adolescents.

Older adolescents are generally able to tolerate more anxiety. By the ages of 15 to 18, boys and girls have achieved some degree of developmental parity. It is more critical for older adolescents to learn to interact with the opposite sex. Consequently, coeducational groups can provide an important forum to learn about the nature of relationships and are preferable for this age group.

THE GROUP THERAPIST

Anyone working with adolescents can attest to the art, skill, and patience required for working with this challenging client population (Phelan, 1974). It is extremely difficult to avoid either being pushed into the role of an authority figure or, at the other end of the spectrum, identifying too much with the adolescent, thus becoming "one of the gang."

Counselors working with adolescents must demonstrate honesty, directness, and authenticity. An atmosphere of safety and trust is essential and an active stance is required; most adolescents cannot tolerate passivity on the part of their counselors. This active stance may entail the establishment in the first session of a group "contract," which must include rules, the purpose of the group, and expectations regarding attendance. Confidentiality must be addressed openly with the explicit understanding that content is not to be shared with anyone outside the group. (The counselor naturally will share health-threatening behaviors with parents or guardians. This caveat should be made clear to the group members from the start.) In coeducational groups, dating among group members should be discouraged.

The adolescent group therapist must be comfortable — and secure — in setting up these rules and be willing to withstand the groans and comments of protest that inevitably arise in response to them. At times, this level of activity on the part of the counselor may also call for personal disclosures that need to remain within the bounds of therapeutic propriety. It is important (and necessary) for the adolescents to feel that they are dealing with a "real" person with "real" thoughts, feelings, and experiences.

The group therapist must also be willing to stand the taunts, provocations, and defensive maneuvers at which adolescents are so adept (Maclennan & Felsenfeld, 1968; Redl, 1966; Rosenthal, 1971), without attacking their self-esteem.

Cotherapy:

A cotherapy model, as advocated by Davis and Lohr (1971), helps provide support for therapists and minimizes problems in a situation where one of the therapists is called away or is absent. The use of male and female cotherapists enhances the idea that the group is a corrective recapitulation of the family experience (Yalom, 1975). Moreover, a cotherapy model can be useful in the training of new practitioners.

Countertransference:

As in all therapeutic work, it is important to be watchful of countertransference reactions. Such reactions may be more frequent in work with the adolescent age group because of the large number of unresolved issues from this developmental stage that often remain with most adults. Thus, the group therapist may envy the adolescent's youth and vitality. Adolescent "crushes" call for extreme sensitivity and understanding. Cramer (1972) has outlined countertransferential phenomena, such as overidentification with the adolescent against his or her parents. Other potential pitfalls include the adolescent's need for an omnipotent counselor, particularly if the latter is one who encourages overdependence and entertains fantasies of being all powerful. Many of these manifestations are best handled in supervision or in discussion with colleagues.

PHASES OF GROUP DEVELOPMENT

Once the group members are chosen and the group begins, a series of group developmental phases can be discerned (Garland, Jones, & Kolodny, 1973; Siepker & Kandaras, 1985). During the early stages of "pre-affiliation" and of "power and control" (Garland et al., 1973), the group members begin to get acquainted with each other. Issues of trust arise as: the adolescents attempt to "size each other up" and decide whether or not they can risk self-disclosure. Questions of others' opinions of them and concerns over acceptance are paramount.

The power and control theme can be a difficult one for the group therapist to negotiate. The therapist must establish himself or herself as the leader and establish what behaviors will be tolerated. For example, teasing or scapegoating must be controlled so that the therapy room is perceived as a safe, secure setting. (The rules and expectations are clarified and a contract is established in the initial stages of the group.)

Working Phase:

Once the group has begun to coalesce, the working phase ensues. This occurs only after a working alliance has been established and an atmosphere of trust has taken hold. Corder, Whiteside, and Haizlip (1981) asked adolescents to rank the group-therapy curative factors of Yalom (1975) from "most helpful" to "least helpful." The adolescents' responses seem to indicate that expressions of feelings, assistance, and gentle confrontation from peers — as well as stimulation of new ways to deal with people and situations and lessening isolation — were most important to them. Thus, techniques that actively structure and provide opportunities for feedback — such as role playing — would appear to be useful in the working phase of adolescent groups. The study by Corder and colleagues (1981) also highlights how adolescents desire help in learning constructive ways to express emotions. Various techniques, such as role playing, can be used toward this end and can also increase self-awareness and insight. These interventions may be confrontational, clarifying, or interpretive and may focus on the here-and-now behavior or on material drawn from the past. Group members are often helpful in providing feedback and confronting others who deny or externalize because feedback from peers is usually more palatable, potent, and easily accepted than a comment made by an adult authority figure.

Termination:

The group's final phase is that of termination. Issues and images of separation are often evoked. Some regressions may occur in response to the impending termination. The therapist must prevent the adolescents from denying or minimizing their feelings at this juncture. Modeling how to deal with sadness and loss is useful. In this phase, the group may often discuss its history, reminiscing and reliving significant events. Assessments of each member's progress and gains are also appropriate at this milestone.

COMMON THEMES

The themes of adolescence have been discussed by many theorists (Blos, 1967; Erikson, 1968; Freud, 1958; Offer, Ostrov, & Howard, 1981). Psychoanalytic writers are particularly concerned with the second separation-individuation of adolescence as well as with a reactivation of oedipal and pre-oedipal conflicts. Identity formation also represents a major theme of this developmental stage.

The conflict over desiring independence while concurrently harboring latent dependency needs is common. This may be reflected in how teenagers relate to parental-authority figures. Adolescents are usually extremely sensitive to how others perceive them and look on any criticism as fuel for their self-doubts. The counselor must negotiate his or her role to avoid the pitfalls of this conflict.

As adolescents mature physically, concerns regarding sexuality arise. Questions about body changes, of sexual identity, of masturbation, and of sexual experimentation abound. Discussions of these themes may, in turn, lead to themes of coping with current new family configurations or wishes and hopes for families of their own in the future.

The inevitable alliances and conflicts within the group usually become the subjects of scrutiny. A nondefensive posture by the counselor is critical; group members must learn to recognize the differences and negotiate them in appropriate ways. Adolescents are all too ready to act on, rather than discuss, their feelings. The group therapist can model and encourage the members to discuss feelings rather than deny, project, or act on them impulsively.

SOME "PROBLEM" GROUP BEHAVIORS

The provocations of adolescents are well-known, and group therapists may find themselves in positions where they are openly confronted. For example, an adolescent may remark, "This group is boring." The counselor might best handle this by asking, "What would you like me to do differently?" This conveys a forthright, nondefensive stance as well as the idea that the question is being taken seriously.

The silence of some members of adolescent groups does not necessarily signify withdrawal. For example, some youths may be too shy or fearful to speak, but nevertheless they can gain a great deal from their careful observation of the group transactions. Some members may refuse to participate. Their reasons—such as not trusting the group or feeling as if they have nothing worthwhile to contribute—should be explored. Long group silences are not desirable because adolescents tend to become inordinately anxious. Counselors are advised to interrupt the silence in some way, either by relating information, encouraging someone to speak, or initiating conversation themselves.

Tangential storytelling may be a subtle and seductive defensive behavior, particularly if the storyteller is a good one. Some group members may weave rich, detailed, elaborate stories that are empty of affect and often unrelated to actual group discussion. They need to be directed back to the group theme and to the reasons for their defensive maneuver.

Some adolescents will attempt to monopolize the group by talking too much. It is best if other group members confront them early on. If not, the counselor might ask the group, "Why are you permitting him to take so much of the group's time?" or might firmly but gently limit the monopolizer's monologue.

Diversionary tactics are another common problem behavior. It is important to remember that although these resistances serve a need, they do not always require immediate handling. For example, clowning and joking may occur at a difficult, painful moment, requiring a direct confrontation. At other times, this same behavior may simply be addressed with the statement, "It seems as if the group is not yet ready to handle such an emotionally charged issue."

Scapegoating is an all-too-common occurrence and requires immediate handling. Scheidlinger (1982) wrote about the need for "psychological first-aid" for the victim. Afterward, the counselor must discuss with the group the *why* and the *how* of this event. A latent theme can often be uncovered. For example, scapegoating of an immature peer may be the result of the group's defending against their own unacceptable regressive wishes. Calling a group member "dumb" may mask the other members' fear of school/academic failure. Gay bashing is usually a projection of the other members' own homosexual concerns.

Negative transference manifestations can be especially trying for the adolescent group therapist. An explanation for the reasons behind a momentary display of anger and dissatisfaction can usually help restore some therapeutic alliance. The group can be enlisted through questions such as, "It feels to me as if I did something to get you angry. Can you tell me what it is?" More chronic negative transference is best handled in supervision or in consultation with peers.

A LOOK TOWARD THE FUTURE

As expanded mental health services for adolescents are created (Jemerin & Phillips, 1988), increased opportunities for group work with adolescents will occur. Pressure from third-party payers and managed care groups for the most cost-effective treatment modalities will also lead to more group work.

Shorter-term groups also seem to be growing in popularity in schools, departments of pediatrics, and clinics. The numbers of specialized groups targeted toward specific populations, including sexually abused adolescents, teenagers from alcoholic families, and youths with chronic medical conditions, have been growing.

Cramer-Azima and Dies (1989) reviewed current research in adolescent group work and suggested new directions. They advocate a careful combination of process and outcome variables to provide a research-phenomenology approach. Increased implementation of research will lead to a more refined understanding of how group process works and, ultimately, to more effective client care.

In today's society, with its weakened familial and community supports, adolescent groups can play a critical role in meeting developmental and restitutive needs while providing a favorable milieu to address the many concerns of young people.

REFERENCES

Berkovitz, I. (1972). On growing a group: Some thoughts on structure, process, and setting. In I. Berkovitz (Ed.), *Adolescent growth in groups: Experiences in adolescent group psychotherapy* (pp. 6–28). New York: Brunner/Mazel.

Blos, P. (1967). The second individuation process of adolescence. *Psychoanalytic Study of the Child, 22*, 162–186.

Bromfield, R., & Pfeiffer, G. (1988). Combining group and individual psychotherapy: Impact on the individual treatment experience. *Journal of the American Academy of Child and Adolescent Psychiatry, 27*, 220–225.

Corder, B., Whiteside, L., & Haizlip, T. (1981). A study of curative factors in group psychotherapy with adolescents. *International Journal of Group Psychotherapy, 21*, 943–958.

Cramer, F. (1972). Transference-countertransference issues in group psychotherapy for adolescents. *International Journal of Child Psychotherapy, 1*, 51–70.

Cramer-Azima, F., & Dies, K. (1989). Clinical research in adolescent group psychotherapy: Status, guidelines, and directions. In F. Cramer-Azima & L. Richmond (Eds.), *Adolescent group psychotherapy* (pp. 193–223). Madison, CT: International Universities Press.

Davis, F., & Lohr, N. (1971). Special problems with the use of cotherapists in group psychotherapy. *International Journal of Group Psychotherapy, 21*, 943–958.

Erikson, E. (1968). *Identity: Youth and crisis.* New York: Norton.

Freud, A. (1958). Adolescence. *Psychoanalytic Study of the Child, 13*, 225–278.

Gardner, R. (1988). *Psychotherapy with adolescents.* Cresskill, NJ: Creative Therapeutics.

Garland, J., Jones, H., & Kolodny, R. (1973). A model for stages in development in social work groups. In S. Bernstein (Ed.), *Explorations in group work: Essays in theory and practice* (pp. 21–30). Boston: Milford House.

Jemerin, J., & Phillips, I. (1988). Changes in inpatient psychiatry: Consequences and recommendations. *Journal of the American Academy of Child and Adolescent Psychiatry, 27*, 397–403.

Maclennan, B., & Felsenfeld, N. (1968). *Group counseling and psychotherapy with adolescents.* New York: Columbia University Press.

Offer, D., Ostrov, E., & Howard, K. I. (1981). *The adolescent: A psychological self-portrait.* New York: Basic Books.

Phelan, J. (1974). Parent, teacher, or analyst: The adolescent group therapist's trilemma. *International Journal of Group Psychotherapy, 24*, 238–244.

Redl, F. (1966). *When we deal with children.* Glencoe, IL: Free Press.

Rosenthal, L. (1971). Some dynamics of resistance and therapeutic management in adolescent group therapy. *Psychoanalytic Review, 58*, 353–366.

Scheidlinger, S. (1982). *Focus on group psychotherapy.* New York: International Universities Press.

Scheidlinger, S. (1985). Group treatment of adolescents: An overview. *American Journal of Orthopsychiatry, 55*, 110–111.

Scheidlinger, S., & Aronson, S. (1991). Group psychotherapy of adolescents. In M. Slomowitz (Ed.), *Adolescent psychotherapy* (pp. 103–119). Washington, DC: American Psychiatric Press.

Siepker, B., & Kandaras, C. (1985). *Group therapy with children and adolescents.* New York: Human Services Press.

Slavson, S. (1950). *Analytic group psychotherapy.* New York: Columbia University Press.

Yalom, I. (1975). *The theory and practice of group psychotherapy.* New York: Basic Books.

9

Aggression Replacement Training in Children and Adolescents

Barry Glick, PhD, NCC

Dr. Glick is a consultant at G & G Associates, Scotia, NY.

KEY POINTS

- Recent research has identified four primary traits as characteristic of aggressive youth: verbal and physical aggression, skill deficiency, immaturity, and withdrawal; a major part of aggression reflects psychological and social skill deficiencies.

- The author and his colleague have developed a unique program, Aggression Replacement Training (ART), which has been implemented in the therapeutic rehabilitation of aggressive youth.

- ART is a differential intervention program that seeks to reduce aggression among adolescents by addressing the primary factors contributing to the aggressive behavior.

- ART consists of three compo-

nents: Structured Learning Training (SLT), Anger Control Training (ACT), and Moral Education (ME). SLT is a 50-skill curriculum that teaches social skills through modeling, role playing, performance feedback, and transfer training. ACT teaches youth to internally monitor and control violent responses by identifying triggers and cues to anger and using reminders, reducers, and self-evaluation. ME, used in a discussion group context, is designed to increase the level of moral reasoning required when evaluating an aggression-provoking situation.

- The chapter introduces mental health professionals to ART and explains many of its methodologies so that they may be replicated and used in a variety of therapeutic settings.

INTRODUCTION

Aggression: Any action an individual takes against another person that results in injury; any action an individual takes against property that results in damage.

We live in an aggressive and violent society. Although most of us do not fancy ourselves as hostile or aggressive—certainly not violent—we do indeed exist in a basically hostile world. We teach aggression to our children at home, in school, in church. Aggression pays! Americans learn at an early age that aggression is immediately, richly, effectively, and efficiently rewarded. Furthermore, most of us experience various forms of aggression so frequently that we are desensitized to its effects on our own growth, perceptions, values, and attitudes. Table 9.1 summarizes conditions that promote aggression.

Table 9.1
CONDITIONS THAT PROMOTE AGGRESSION

- Weak familial or social bonding
- Being a frequent target of aggression
- Observation of successful acts of aggression
- Positive reinforcement of aggressive acts
- Deficiency in information processing skills (e.g., ability to identify means-ends relationships, ability to generate alternative solutions, and ability to generate consequences)
- Overattribution of hostile intentions
- Belief that aggression is legitimate behavior
- Belief that aggression increases self-esteem
- Belief that aggression yields positive tangible results for self and significant others
- Deficiency in moral reasoning (the capacity to view the world in terms of justice and fairness)
- Deficiency in identifying and using alternative prosocial skill competencies in anger-producing situations

---

THE SOCIOLOGY OF AGGRESSION

Aggression and hostility are so prevalent in our society that by the time a child reaches adolescence, chances are he or she will commit some act of delinquency within 2 years of the onset of puberty. The youth population and crime rate have been declining; however, juvenile delinquency is on the rise (Federal Bureau of Investigation, 1988-1994). From 1988-1992, the Violent Crime Index (which includes criminal homicide, forcible rape, robbery, and aggravated assault) increased 56%. The Property Crime Index increased as well, but only a mere 23%. As Table 9.2 indicates, delinquency cases by offense all increased over the same 5-year period, with the exception of stolen property offenses, drug law violations, liquor law violations, and other public order disturbances, which decreased from 7% to 26%.

According to crime statistics from the annual reports of the Chief Administrator of the courts, the most frequent violent crime committed by males is robbery; for females, it is aggravated assault (Office of Court Administration, 1995). The average age for a first arrest is 13 years. African-American youth are arrested five times more than white youth (violent crimes, 3:1; and theft, 11:1). Juvenile aggression is more likely to occur in urban rather than rural settings. Juveniles are more likely to act in groups, less likely to use a gun, and equally likely to use a knife or some other weapon. The victim of juvenile criminal aggression is more likely to be female rather than male, older rather than younger, a person of color rather than white, poor rather than wealthy, and an acquaintance rather than a stranger. In addition, the victim of a juvenile crime is seven times more likely to be another juvenile rather than an adult.

THE PSYCHOLOGY OF ADOLESCENT AGGRESSION

Research identifies four primary traits that are characteristic

Table 9.2
DELINQUENCY CASES BY OFFENSE, 1992

OFFENSE	NUMBER OF CASES	PERCENTAGE CHANGE 1991–1992	1988–1992
Total Delinquency	1,471,200	7%	26%
Person	301,000	13	56
Criminal Homicide	2,500	-9	55
Forcible Rape	5,400	10	27
Robbery	32,900	9	52
Aggravated Assault	77,900	16	80
Simple Assault	152,800	14	47
Other Violent Sex Offenses	9,900	13	60
Other Person Offenses	19,800	11	63
Property	842,200	3	23
Burglary	156,400	4	22
Larceny-Theft	361,600	1	16
Motor Vehicle Theft	73,000	2	34
Arson	8,300	10	24
Vandalism	127,700	12	50
Trespassing	58,500	2	17
Stolen Property Offenses	28,900	7	-7
Other Property Offenses	33,700	6	57
Drug Law Violations	72,100	15	-12
Public Order	255,900	11	68
Obstruction of Justice	87,100	8	10
Disorderly Conduct	69,300	13	50
Weapons Offenses	41,000	26	86
Liquor Law Violations	12,500	-7	-26
Nonviolent Sex Offenses	12,900	22	19
Other Public Order	33,000	3	-8

Source: Office of Juvenile Justice and Delinquency Prevention (1994). *Juvenile Justice Bulletin*. Washington, DC: Author.

of aggressive youth: verbal and physical aggression, skill deficiency, immaturity, and withdrawal.

Verbal and Physical Aggression:

Quay (1983) developed a classification for aggressive adolescents. He found that they could be identified by such behaviors as fighting, disruptiveness, profanity, irritability, quarrelsomeness, defiance of authority, irresponsibility, high levels of attention seeking, and low levels of guilt feelings. Quay observed active antisocial aggressiveness that resulted in conflict with parents, peers, and social institutions.

Skill Deficiency:

Most behaviorally disordered (aggressive) adolescents are skill deficient; that is, they have not developed the social skills necessary to successfully negotiate their environments.

Immaturity:

Aggressive youth frequently are immature; they exhibit such behaviors as a short attention span, clumsiness, preference for younger playmates, passivity, daydreaming, and incompetence. By definition, these behaviors represent patterns that may have been appropriate at earlier stages of development but are not acceptable for the adolescent. In the case of conduct disorders, immaturity leads to attacks on others or withdrawal (in the cases of personality disorders). Immaturity often leads to alienation from peers.

Withdrawal:

Persons with behaviors linked to withdrawal have been labeled as having a "personality problem" (Patterson, Reid, & Jones, 1975) or being "disturbed neurotic" (Quay, 1983) or "overinhibited." These behaviors are associated with depression, feelings of inferiority, self-consciousness, shyness, anxiety, hypersensitivity, seclusiveness, and timidity. Although withdrawal is not ordinarily associated with aggression, it certainly lends itself to the aggressive adolescent and is often clinically diagnosed as a component of the passive-aggressive personality.

AGGRESSION REPLACEMENT TRAINING (ART): A MULTIMODAL RESPONSE

Various approaches to mitigating aggressive adolescent behaviors have been developed. The central question that must be addressed in prescriptive programming is: Which types of youth, meeting with which types of change agents, for which types of interventions, will yield optimal outcomes?

Effective intervention is differential intervention. Differential interventions ensure that an array of services and programs are available to the aggressive child and adolescent. Once sufficient programming is available, this hypothesis states that different children and adolescents will respond to different counseling methods.

Glick and Goldstein (1987) developed a differential intervention called *Aggression Replacement Training* (ART), which aims to reduce aggression among adolescents by providing them with a multimodal program that addresses the primary factors contributing to the aggressive behavior. Although aggressive behavior has many other internal and external antecedents than those addressed in ART, it was predicted that much of the outcome variance associated with efforts to change such behavior would occur in the domains of enhanced prosocial skill proficiency, heightened anger control, and more advanced levels of moral reasoning.

ART RESEARCH AND EFFICACY EVALUATIONS

A series of program evaluations and research efficacy studies of ART are examined in this section. Some of these investigations were conducted by our own research group (Glick & Goldstein, 1987, 1995; Goldstein, Glick, Irwin, Pask-McCartney, & Rubama, 1989); a number were the efforts of others. We now have more than a decade of research and experience with ART as an intervention for aggressive and violent youth. We present these assessments for what they report about the impact of ART, its apparent strengths and weaknesses, as well as what may be gleaned for further research and development in this most critical area.

The Annsville Youth Center Project:

The first ART program evaluation was developed, designed, and implemented at the Annsville Youth Center, a noncommunity residential facility. In this facility, 60 young men (aged 14–17) were incarcerated for crimes such as burglary, robbery, assaults, and various drug offenses; 24 of these young men enrolled in the 10-week ART program.

Each resident attended three sessions per week, one each of Structured Learning Training (SLT), Anger Control Training (ACT), and Moral Education (ME). A second group of 24 young men were assigned to a no-ART, Brief Instruction control group. This condition was included in our research plan to control for any apparent ART-derived gains in skills that were not due to ART, but rather in case the youngsters already possessed the skills and were not using them, or simply were motivated to display already learned skills, or learned the skills just by maturation (i.e., they grew chronologically or emotionally and developmentally). A third, more traditional No-Treatment control group consisted of 12 young men who did not participate in ART or Brief Instructions procedures.

The evaluation goals of this project were to study the effectiveness of ART, specifically in reference to:

1. *Skill acquisition.* Do the youngsters learn the 10 Prosocial Skills in the ART curriculum?

2. *Minimal skill transfer.* Can the young people perform the skills in response to a new situation, similar in format to those on which they were trained.

3. *Extended skill transfer.* Can the young men perform the skills in response to new situations, dissimilar in format and more like real life than those on which they were trained?

4. *Anger control enhancement.* Do the youth actually demonstrate fewer altercations or other acting-out behaviors, as reflected in weekly behavior incident reports completed on all participating young men by the staff?

5. *Impulse reduction.* Are the youngsters rated to be less compulsive, more reflective, and more self-controlled in their interpersonal behavior?

Data analyses revealed that adolescents undergoing ART, compared to both control groups, significantly acquired and transferred (both minimal and extended), 4 of the 10 Social Skills: Expressing a Complaint, Preparing for a Stressful Conversation, Responding to Anger, and Dealing with Group Pressure. Additionally, we found significant differences when we compared ART to control groups on both the number and intensity of in-facility, acting-out behaviors as well as on staff-rated impulsiveness.

After we completed the posttesting of the entire population in week 11 of the project, new ART groups were formed for the 36 youths in the three control group units. This phase essentially replicated all the procedures that were done during the first 10 weeks. Sessions were held three times per week for 10 weeks.

Our research methodology in this second phase was an own-control test for the efficacy of ART, with particular atten-

by comparing for this second group of 36 youths, their incident reports during weeks 11–20 (while in ART) with their incidence reports from the first phase (weeks 1–10) when they served as the control group. Both statistical comparisons, for number and severity, conducted to test for replication effects yielded significant positive results.

During the Annsville project, 54 residents were released from the facility and returned to communities. Our hope was that ART might be a sufficiently powerful inoculation, such that moderate carryover of in-facility ART learning to the community would occur. Seventeen youth had received ART; 37 had not. We contacted each youth's aftercare worker (similar to a parole officer responsible for community supervision) throughout New York State, and without informing the worker whether the youth had or had not received ART, requested the worker to complete the global rating measure on each Annsville resident who was discharged during that time period. In four of the six areas rated (i.e., Home and Family, Peer, Legal, and Overall; not School or Work), ART youth were significantly superior in rated in-community functioning than were the young men who had not received ART.

The results of this informal assessment are intriguing. This population often has considerable difficulty with successfully transferring skill acquisition from the more protective institutional environment to community settings. Many times, the family and peers are reinforcers of antisocial behaviors, ignoring or even punishing constructive alternative actions. Such indifference or overt hostility from these real-world significant others served as information that would prove beneficial in some of our later community-based projects.

The MacCormick Youth Center Project:

The second efficacy evaluation of ART was conducted at the MacCormick Secure Center, a New York State Division for Youth maximum security facility that serves male juvenile offenders aged 13–21. Crimes committed by these young men included murder, manslaughter, rape, sodomy, attempted murder, armed assault, and armed robbery. Our second project sought both to replicate the exact procedures and findings of the Annsville project and to extend them to youths incarcerated for substantially more serious, heinous felonies. Fifty-one young men participated in this study, which used the same preparatory activities, materials, ART curriculum, testing, staff training, resident training, supervision, and data analysis methodology.

Data indicated significant acquisition or transfer of training skills on 5 of the 10 Prosocial Skills. These findings, as well as the skill deficits that were identified essentially replicated the Annsville SLT results. In contrast to the Annsville results, the MacCormick data also yielded a significant result on the Sociomoral Reflections Measure, which was used to assess levels of moral development. The adolescents who participated in ME sessions at MacCormick, in contrast to those at Annsville, grew significantly in the moral reasoning stage over the 10-week intervention period.

With respect to overt, in-facility behaviors, young persons who received ART, compared to those who did not, increased significantly over their base rates in constructive, prosocial behaviors they used (e.g., offering or accepting criticism appropriately, using self-control when provoked) and decreased significantly in their rated levels of impulsiveness. In contrast to the Annsville findings, MacCormick adolescents who received ART did not differ from controls in either the number or intensity of acting-out behaviors. These findings appear to be largely explained by the substantial differences in potential for such behaviors between the two institutions. Annsville is not a locked, closed facility. The 60 young offenders live in one dormitory, in contrast to the locked, single room sleeping quarters at MacCormick. MacCormick, a higher security facility, also had a staff of 2:1 over Annsville's. MacCormick operated under stricter regulations, sanctions, and controls.

Therefore, the opportunity for acting-out behaviors were lower across all conditions at MacCormick. At Annsville, acting-out behaviors were contextually more possible at base rate, and thus could and did decrease over the intervention period. At MacCormick, all young men started low and probably for these same contextual reasons (i.e., sanctions, controls, richer staffing), remained low. Their use of prosocial behaviors with regard to which no floor or ceiling effect influences are relevant, did increase differentially as a function of the ART intervention.

The Community-Based (Aftercare) Project:

The findings of our first two research efforts show that ART is a multimodal, habilitation intervention of considerable potency with incarcerated, aggressive, and violent adolescents. ART enhances prosocial skill competency and overt prosocial behaviors, reduces the level of rated impulsiveness, and in one of the two samples studied, decreases the frequency and the intensity of acting-out behaviors and enhances the participants' levels of moral reasoning. Furthermore, some moderately substantial evidence, provided independently, reveal it to lead to valuable changes in community functioning.

Our third efficacy study of ART sought to ascertain the value of ART when provided to youth on aftercare, living in their community. Eighty-four young people participated in this project. Because we were aware of the influence significant others had on this population, we not only attempted to offer ART to the youth, but also to their parents and other family members, whom we trained in reciprocal skills.

Table 9.3 depicts our experimental design for this research effort. Our design is essentially a three-way comparison of: providing ART to youths and to their parents or other family members, providing ART to youths only, and a no-ART control group.

Participating adolescents were assigned to research conditions on a random basis, with departures from randomization only to occasionally accommodate for the rigors of the multisite, time-extended nature of the project. The community-based

Table 9.3			
EVALUATION DESIGN FOR THE ART COMMUNITY PROJECT			
	Trainee	Evaluation	Condition
	I	II	III
ART for Delinquent Youth	X	X	– –
ART for Parents and Family	X		– –

ART program was designed to last 3 months, in which young people attended meetings twice per week, for a planned total of approximately 25 sessions. Each meeting lasted 1.5–2 hours and began with a discussion about current life events and experienced difficulties while on aftercare. Then the adolescents underwent SLT (usually a skill relevant to the life events or experienced difficulties); and, on an alternating session basis, either ACT or ME. An ART session was held for the parents and their family members each week to demonstrate the sample of skills offered to their youngsters. If family members were unable to attend the weekly meeting, they were provided ART in modified form via a weekly home visit or phone visit.

Because all of the adolescents previously had ART in the facility, the different groups that continued ART in the community each chose, in consultation with their trainers, which of the 50 skills that comprise the full Prosocial Skills Curriculum they wished to learn. Hence, different groups learned different, if not overlapping, sets of skills. We did not, therefore, examine in our statistical analyses, participant change on *individual* skills. Instead, we performed analyses on total skill change for the ART participating youths (conditions I and II) versus both each other and the other no-ART control group (condition III). Results indicated that while they did not differ significantly one from another, the two ART conditions each increased significantly in their overall interpersonal skill competencies, compared to condition III (no-ART). A significant outcome emerged (both ART groups versus no-ART) for decreases in self-reported anger levels in response to mild (i.e., seeing others abused, minor nuisance, unfair treatment) but not severe (i.e., betrayal of trust, control/coercion, physical abuse) anger-provoking situations.

Recidivism is considered by juvenile justice authorities to be a particularly critical evaluation criterion to indicate success within juvenile justice interventions. Research (Maltz, 1984) indicates that the vast majority of young people returning to their communities from incarceration and who recidivate will do so within the first 6 months of release. Thus, for the purposes of this effort, we defined recidivism as those young people who were rearrested within the first 6 months following their released to their communities. We tracked the young people for a 6-month period, during which they received ART for the first 3 months, and no-ART for the subsequent 3 months. Condition III youth, of course, received no-ART during the entire 6-month tracking period. Data analysis, which examined frequency of rearrest by condition, showed significant effect for youth who participated in ART. Both condition I and II youths were rearrested significantly less than were youths who did not receive ART.

Results from our community-based ART project are presented in Table 9.4. When the two ART conditions are compared, there is a substantial decrease in the percentage of rearrests when the youths' families participate simultaneously in their own ART groups. The family groups were taught reciprocal (to what the delinquent was learning) prosocial skills, as well as anger control techniques. We believe the latter may have provided for the delinquency youths a more responsive and prosocially reinforcing real-world environment (i.e.,

Table 9.4
FREQUENCY OF REARREST BY CONDITION

Condition	Total N	Rearrested N	Rearrested %
Youth ART+ Parent/Sibling ART	13	2	15
Youth ART Only	20	6	30
no-ART (Control)	32	14	43

providing a context in which the newly acquired skill—negotiating for example—was reinforced and praised rather than ridiculed).

The Prosocial Gang Project:

Our final effort to evaluate the efficacy of the ART intervention was based, in part, on our belief that aggressive and violent young people are most influenced by their own peers. We sought to find the peer groups that exerted the most control, power, and authority over their members. Our investigation studied 10 gangs (including two female gangs) in Brooklyn, New York over a 2-year period. We conducted the intervention at two private, not-for-profit, community-based organizations: The Brownsville Neighborhood Youth Action Center, which served young people in the Crown Heights and Brownsville neighborhoods, and Youth Dares, which served the youth of the Sheepshead Bay neighborhood. Crown Heights is predominantly African-American; Sheepshead Bay is predominantly white and Italian.

Managing this multisite, multigang project required diverse planning, training, supervision, data collection, data analysis, budget management, and resource coordination efforts. Our fundamental strategy to ensure that we accomplished our evaluation goals was *consultation* and *negotiation*. We conducted frequent, honest, and open communication with the agencies. Staff input was used in program design, planning, and implementation. We continued this participatory process throughout the project to its completion, providing training, supervision, and project monitoring on a frequent (at least weekly) and regular basis.

We conducted a quantitative appraisal of the project. As in our earlier three previous evaluations, both proximal and distal criteria were examined. The proximal queries included: Were the skills learned? Was anger reduced? The distal queries included participant-rated performance in a variety of areas of functioning in the community and whether the gang member was rearrested during the 8-month period (which consisted of 4 months of the ART sequence and 4 months of follow-up).

The assessment used for SLT was the Skill Checklist (Goldstein, Sprafkin, Gershaw, & Klein, 1980; Goldstein, Glick, Irwin, Pask-McCartney, & Rubama, 1989). It consists of brief descriptions of the 50 prosocial skills that comprise the SLT curriculum. The rater indicates the frequency with which they believe the youth uses each skill.

The assessment for the ACT component was the Anger Situations Inventory (Hoshmand, Austin, & Appell, 1981; Hoshmand & Austin, 1987). It is a 66-item questionnaire completed (as all of the assessments, on both a pre and post basis) by the youth. The instrument is designed to assess both the young person's overall level of self-reported anger arousal, as well as the degree of anger aroused in the individual as a function of several different types of potentially provocative situations. The 11 subscales include Seeing Others Abused, Intrusion, Personal Devaluation, Betrayal of Trust, Minor Nuisance, Control/Coercion, Verbal Abuse, Physical Abuse, Unfair Treatment, Goal Blocking, and Neutral.

The Community Adjustment Rating Scale, developed by Glick and Goldstein (1987), was used to measure postintervention community function. It affords the raters (the staff trainers in this project) the opportunity to rate each gang member on the following dimensions: Home and Family Adjustment, School Adjustment, Work Adjustment, Peer Adjustment, and Legal System Adjustment.

We selected *rearrest* as the criterion index of recidivism. Essentially all of the young people who participated in this project had been arrested at least once, and often several times. As described earlier, Maltz (1984) demonstrated that a large majority of previously incarcerated youth who recidivate, do so within the first 6 months after release. We tracked the gang members for 8 months, not unmindful of the weaknesses of using rearrest as the index of recidivism (Farrington, Ohlin, & Wilson, 1986).

Our results were encouraging. Repeated measures analysis of variance, crossing project condition (ART versus control) with time of measurement (pre versus post), revealed a significant interaction effect favoring ART participants for each of the seven skill categories: Beginning Social Skills, Advanced Social Skills, Feelings Relevant Skills, Aggression Management Skills, Stress Management Skills, and Planning Skills, as well as a Total Skills score.

None of the resultant ANOVA comparisons on the study's Anger Control measure of ART with control scores yielded significant differences. It is noteworthy, however, that on all subscales, those youth who received ART demonstrated greater gain in anger control than did control group youths. The magnitude of between-condition differences is not significant; however, its uniform direction may suggest a trend toward the impact of ART on participant anger control.

Of the five community functioning domains rated by group leaders using the Community Adjustment Rating Scale, only Work Adjustment approached significant difference (t = 2.14, p= .04). Peer Adjustment approached significant difference (t=1.86, p= .06). The direction of these results all favored ART over control group participants. For example, in the months immediately following their ART sequence, the majority of the participating Lo Lives (a Crown Heights gang) left their gang and took jobs in various retail businesses. At an analogous point in time, a substantial number of the Baby Wolfpack (another Crown Heights gang) obtained employment in the construction trades, rebuilding much of the neighborhood they had ravaged.

Arrest data for the youth who participated in our first two ART sequences and their respective control groups indicated that 5 of 38 ART participants (13%) and 14 of 27 control group members (52%) were rearrested during the 8-month tracking period (X^2 = 6.08., p= .01). Our primary rationale for working with intact gangs in this project was the opportunity afforded by such a strategy to attempt to capture a major feature of the adolescents' environment and turn it in prosocial directions. Once the teenagers learned given prosocial behaviors, they were able to transfer and maintain them (or be discouraged from using them) by the persons with whom they interacted regularly. Our favorable outcome, as indicated by rearrest rates, implies the possibility that such a more harmonious and prosocially conducive post-ART peer environment may have been created. Future research should examine this possibility more directly.

Other Efficacy Evaluations:

Our own research efforts provided a series of encouraging findings with respect to the effectiveness of ART, both proximal to the ART procedures (i.e., skill acquisition, anger control, enhanced moral reasoning), as well as to distal effects (i.e., reduced rearrest, enhanced community functioning, less hostility, violence, and volatility). We are pleased that others have also begun to investigate the efficacy of ART and include findings from other independent research.

Curulla (1990) evaluated a 14-week ART Program (a) versus ART without the ME component and (b) versus a no-ART control group. She used 67 young adult offenders in a Seattle, Washington community setting. She reports:

Tendency towards recidivism and actual recidivism were compared among the three groups. Tendency towards recidivism, as measured by the Weekly Activity Record, was significantly reduced in the dilemma group [Condition 1 above]. The nondilemma [Condition 2] and control [Condition 3] groups showed no significant reduction. The dilemma group also had the lowest frequency of subsequent offense. . . However, the difference in actual recidivism among the three groups did not reach statistical significance due to the low incidence of recorded changes during the 6-month follow-up. (pp. 1-2)

Curulla corroborated our own results in that overt acting-out behaviors were significantly reduced with ART participation. However, unlike our findings, post-ART recidivism was not reduced.

Jones (1990) compared ART to ME and a No-Treatment control group, using highly aggressive male students in a high school in Brisbane, Australia. Her results were positive and consistent to findings already cited:

Compared to the two control conditions, students completing the ART program: showed a significant decrease in aggressive incidents, a significant increase in coping incidents, and acquired more social skills. Students in Condition I [also] improved on. . . self-control and impulsivity. . . . ART appears to be an effective intervention for aggressive youth within a high school setting. (p. 1)

Coleman, Pfeiffer, and Oakland (1991) evaluated the effectiveness of a 10-week ART program used with behavioral disordered adolescents in a Texas residential treatment center. Results indicated improved participant skill knowledge, but not actual overt skill behaviors. Coleman and associates (1991) comment:

The current study thus provides additional support for the contention that although cognitive gains can be demonstrated, the link to actual behavior is tenuous, especially with disturbed populations. (p. 14)

As my own discussions have already suggested, however, I believe that the likelihood of overt behavioral expression (i.e., performance) of newly acquired skills is less a function of the degree of trainee emotional disturbance and more a matter of trainee motivation to perform and staff or other significant persons' perceived receptivity to and likely reward for such overt behaviors. Coleman and colleagues continue:

> Of the ten social skills that were taught, three accounted for the improvement in social skills knowledge: keeping out fights, dealing with group pressure, and expressing a complaint. The fact that Glick and Goldstein (1987) also found these same skills to be improved in two separate studies suggests that these skills may be the most responsive to intervention. One plausible explanation is that these three skills may be construed as contributing to self-preservation, especially within the context of residential or institutional living. (p. 15)

One final investigation we note here, also affirming the efficacy of ART, applies the intervention in yet another setting, and a new direction. Gibbs (1986) and co-workers in the Ohio Department of Youth Services had for some years used and evaluated a Positive Peer Culture treatment approach in their work with delinquents. This technique, which they described as an adult-guided, but youth-run, small group treatment approach, places most of the responsibility on the young people in a group setting for the management of its living environment, as well as for the change in their own behaviors. Gibbs and associates' rationale for this approach was based on their experience that while adolescents were highly motivated to conduct their own governance, they often lacked the skills and anger control to do so. As such, Gibbs and colleagues combined Positive Peer Culture with ART to yield a motivation-plus, skills-oriented intervention they named *EQUIP*. Leeman, Gibbs, & Fuller (1993) note:

> In EQUIP, moral discussions, anger management, or social skills sessions are designated as equipment meetings; that is,

meetings wherein the group gains equipment for helping group members. (pp. 5-6)

EQUIP is a program intervention at a medium security institution for juvenile felony offenders, the Buckeye Youth Center, in Ohio. Three conditions were constituted: EQUIP, a motivational control group, and a No-Treatment Control group. Outcome results were significant and supportive of the EQUIP intervention on both proximal and distal criteria. Gibbs and colleagues comment:

> Institutional conduct improvements were highly significant for the EQUIP relative to the control groups in terms of self-reported misconduct, staff-filed incident reports, and unexcused absences from school. (p. 18)

> Interestingly, whereas the recidivism rate of EQUIP subjects was low (15%) at both 6 and 12 months following release, the control group rates worsened from 6 to 12 months (25% to 35% for the motivational control; 30% to 40% for the simple passage of time control). This pattern suggests that the treatment result is maintained as a stable effect. (p. 19)

These other efficacy evaluations combine to suggest that ART is significant treatment intervention. With considerable reliability, it appears to promote skill acquisition and performance; improve anger control; and decrease the frequency of acting-out behaviors. Beyond institutional and residential walls, its effects persist; however, less fully perhaps than when the adolescent is in a controlled environment, with support and persistent reinforcement.

STRUCTURED LEARNING TRAINING

Structured Learning Training (SLT) is a psychoeducational intervention designed by Glick and Goldstein (1987) in which a 50-skill curriculum of prosocial behaviors is systematically taught to small groups of chronically aggressive adolescents (Table 9.5). The SLT curriculum is preferably implemented with six to eight adolescents in a group.

The techniques used to teach children and adolescents social skills training are founded on sound pedagogy that is used to teach any behavioral skill. If I wanted to teach my 17-year-old son how to drive, I would first take him into my car and *show* him (modeling) how to place the key in the ignition, ensure the car was in neutral, turn on the ignition, and coordinate the flow of gas with the raising of the clutch so as to properly engage the car into first gear, and so on. I would then ask him to *try* (role playing) what he was shown. I would then provide an opportunity for *discussion* (performance feedback), to give constructive criticism of his performance. Finally, I would give him an opportunity to *practice* (transfer training) what he had learned. Nothing more is done when facilitating both the skill training and anger control components of SLT.

Modeling:

Modeling exercises demonstrate examples of expert use of behaviors constituting the skills in which the youngsters are weak or lacking. During the modeling sequence, the facilitator ensures that the modeling display is presented to trainees in a clear and unambiguous manner. The display should depict the behavioral steps that constitute the skill being taught. All the steps that make up the skill should be modeled in their correct sequence. Modeling consists of live vignettes enacted by the trainers. Audio or visual tapes may be substituted as the modeling display although these are not as effective as live demonstrations. The trainers should always rehearse the vignettes before each session and ensure that all the steps are in proper sequence and enacted correctly. Modeling displays should incorporate at least two examples of different situations for each skill being demonstrated. If a given skill is taught in more than one group meeting, the facilitator should develop the corresponding number of modeling displays, taking care

Table 9.5
THE STRUCTURED LEARNING SKILL CURRICULUM

GROUP I: BEGINNING SOCIAL SKILLS

1. Listening	5. Saying "thank you"
2. Starting a conversation	6. Introducing yourself
3. Having a conversation	7. Introducing other people
4. Asking a question	8. Giving a complaint

GROUP II: ADVANCED SOCIAL SKILLS

9. Asking for help	12. Following instructions
10. Joining in	13. Apologizing
11. Giving instructions	14. Convincing others

GROUP III: SKILLS DEALING WITH FEELINGS

15. Knowing your feelings	19. Expressing affection
16. Expressing your feelings	20. Dealing with fear
17. Understanding the feelings of others	21. Rewarding yourself
18. Dealing with someone else's anger	

GROUP IV: SKILL ALTERNATIVES TO AGGRESSION

22. Asking permission	27. Standing up for your rights
23. Sharing something	
24. Helping others	28. Responding to teasing
25. Negotiation	29. Avoiding trouble with others
26. Using self-control	
	30. Keeping out of fights

GROUP V: SKILLS FOR DEALING WITH STRESS

31. Making a complaint
32. Answering a complaint
33. Sportsmanship after the game
34. Dealing with embarrassment
35. Dealing with being left out
36. Standing up for a friend

37. Responding to persuasion

38. Responding to failure
39. Dealing with contradictory messages
40. Dealing with an accusation
41. Getting ready for a difficult conversation
42. Dealing with group pressure

GROUP VI: PLANNING SKILLS

43. Deciding on something to do

44. Deciding what caused a problem
45. Setting a goal
46. Deciding on your abilities

47. Gathering information
48. Arranging problems by importance
49. Making a decision
50. Concentrating on a task

to select situations relevant to the trainees' real-life circumstances. The main actor (the person enacting the behavioral steps of the skill) should be portrayed as a person who is reasonably similar in age, socioeconomic background, verbal ability, and so on, to the participants in the structured learning group.

For clarity and ease of understanding, modeling displays should depict only one skill at a time and should depict all behavioral steps of the skill in the correct sequence; all extraneous content should be eliminated. All displays should depict positive outcomes. As the modeling display is performed by the trainers, "skill cards," (pocket-sized cards given to group members to carry with them during the week to refer to as they practice their assignments), which contain the name of the skill and its steps, are distributed before the modeling display. Trainees are told to watch and listen carefully as the models portray the skill. The trainer/facilitator tells the group that sometimes, to depict some of the behavioral steps in certain skills, the actors will occasionally engage in "thinking out loud" statements that would ordinarily be thought silently.

Role Playing:

Role playing provides several guided opportunities to practice and rehearse competent interpersonal behaviors. Role playing should immediately follow the modeling display, and should relate the modeled skill to the lives of the trainees. First, invite comments on the behavioral steps and how these steps might be useful in real-life situations that the trainees themselves might encounter. Second, focus on current and future skill use rather than only past events or general issues that involve the skill.

Once a trainee describes a situation in which the skill would be useful, that person is designated the "main actor." The trainee selects a second trainee as a "co-actor" to play the role of the other person in his or her life who is relevant to the situation (e.g., mother, peer, staff member, etc.). Be sure to encourage the trainee to choose someone who resembles the real-life person in as many ways as possible (e.g., physically, expressively). Next, solicit additional information to set the stage for the role playing such as a description of the physical setting, events immediately preceding the role play, a description of the manner that the co-actor should display, or any other information to increase a sense of reality.

The facilitator/trainer should review the steps of the skill with the actor and make sure the actor understands how the steps are to be applied to the role play. Tell the actor to refer to the skill card and assign other group members to watch the role playing and ensure that the steps are being completed. The trainer should ensure that the co-actor stays in his or her role, and also coaches the observers on the cues to watch by his or her posture, tone of voice, and content of speech. The facilitator may break the role playing and start again, giving the necessary instruction or reinstruction before restarting. (Remember, in ART, one is interested in *practice of perfect, not "practice makes perfect."*)

One facilitator/trainer should be positioned near the chalkboard pointing out each step as it is role played. A second facilitator/trainer should be strategically seated with the group to help the members with the tasks at hand or to maintain order. Role playing continues until all participants have an opportunity to be a main actor. Sound group role-playing techniques can be used, such as "role reversal" (where the actor and co-actor switch roles); with hesitant clients, the trainer may assume the role of the co-actor.

Performance Feedback:

Performance feedback is a discussion period that provides praise, reinstruction, and related feedback on how well the adolescent's role playing of the skill matched the expert model's portrayal of it. It also examines the psychological impact of the enactment on the co-actor and provides the main actor with encouragement to try out the role-played behaviors in real-life situations. The facilitator first should ask the co-actor about his or her reactions, and then have the observers comment on how well the behavioral steps were followed. Next, trainers should comment on how well the behavioral steps were followed and provide social reinforcement (praise, approval, encouragement). During this activity, the facilitator should follow sound reinforcement techniques as in any good behavioral feedback session. That is, provide reinforcement only after role plays that follow the behavioral steps, and, at the earliest appropriate opportunity, vary the specific content of the reinforcements. For example, praise particular aspects of the performance such as the tone of voice, posture, and phrasing; provide enough role playing activity for each group member to have sufficient opportunity to be reinforced; provide reinforcement in an amount consistent with the quality of the given role play; provide no reinforcement when the role playing departs significantly from the behavioral steps (except for "trying" in the first session or two); provide reinforcement for an individual trainee's improvement over previous performances; and always provide reinforcement to the co-actor for being helpful, cooperative, and willing to try. The trainer should focus on behavioral structured learning components. Comments should reflect concrete behaviors, not general evaluations. Negative comments should always be followed by a constructive comment as to how a skill or step should be improved. Poor performance may be reinforced simply by saying, "Good try." Trainees who fail to follow the behavioral steps of the skill should be given the opportunity to role play the same behavioral steps after receiving corrective feedback.

Transfer Training:

Transfer training, or practicing, encourages youth to engage in a series of activities designed to increase the chances that the skill learned in the training setting will endure and be available for use when needed in the environment, whether it be the institution, home, school, community, or other real setting. The general principles needed to implement transfer training begin with the trainer providing the trainees elementary understanding of basic stimulus-response relationships operating in the training and real-world environments. Thus, one should provide the trainees' information visually, verbally, and in writing. Three principles that are particularly useful in transfer training are: overlearning, identical elements, and positive transfer.

Overlearning
Overlearning involves training in a skill beyond what is necessary to produce initial changes in behavior. In both

structured learning and anger control groups, overlearning is substantial for each skill taught. Its behavioral steps are modeled several times, role played one or more times by the trainees, observed live by the trainee as every other group member role plays, read by the trainee from a chalkboard and a skill card, and practiced in real-life settings one or more times by the trainee as part of the formal homework assignments.

Identical Elements

Another principle involved in transfer training is what Glick and Goldstein (1987) call "identical elements." The greater the similarity of physical and interpersonal stimuli in the group setting, as well as the homework and community or other setting in which the skill is to be applied, the greater the likelihood of transfer. The trainer may ensure that the structured learning or anger control setting is more similar to real life settings by designing the live modeling displays to be highly similar to what trainees face in their daily lives through the representative, relevant, and realistic portrayal of the models, protagonists, and situations; designing the role playing to be similar to real-life situations through the use of props, the physical arrangement of the setting, and the choice of realistic co-actors; conducting the role play to be as responsive as possible to the real-life interpersonal stimuli to which the trainees must actually respond later with the given skill; rehearsing each skill in role plays as the trainees actually plan to use it; and assigning homework.

Positive Transfer

Positive transfer of skills is greater when a *variety* of relevant training stimuli are used; this is called "stimulus variability." To apply this principle to structured learning and anger control groups, one should rotate group leaders across groups, rotate trainees across groups, role play a given skill with several different co-actors, role play a given skill with trainees across several relevant settings, and complete multiple homework assignments for each given skill.

ANGER CONTROL TRAINING

Anger Control Training (ACT) was first developed by Feindler, Marriott, and Iwata (1984), and was partially based on the earlier anger control and stress inoculation research of Novaco (1975) and Meichenbaum (1977). The goal is to teach youngsters the inhibition of violent responses. In ACT, each young person is required to bring to each session a description of a recent anger-arousing experience (a hassle), which they record in a binder (their hassle log). For 10 weeks, the youngsters are trained to respond to their hassles with a chain of behaviors that include:

- identifying triggers (external events and internal self-statements that provoke anger responses)

- identifying cues (individual physical events such as tightened muscles, flushed face, and clenched fists that let the child or adolescent know that the emotion he or she is experiencing is anger)

- using reminders (self-statements such as "stay calm," "chill out," "cool down," or nonhostile explanations of others' behavior)

- using reducers (techniques that, like the use of reminders, are designed expressly to lower the individual's level of anger—such as deep breathing, counting backward, imagining a peaceful scene, or imagining the long-term consequences of one's behavior)

- using self-evaluation (reflecting on how well the hassle was responded to by identifying triggers, identifying cues, using reminders, and using reducers; and then praising or rewarding oneself for effective performance)

Young people who have participated in SLT and ACT are knowledgeable about what to do and what not to do in circumstances that instigate aggression. However, because aggressive behavior is so consistently rewarded in many of the real-world settings in which children and adolescents live, work, go to school, and interact, they may still consciously choose to behave aggressively. Thus, Glick and Goldstein (1987) believed it was important to add a values-oriented component to the intervention approach that Feindler and colleagues were developing and evaluating.

MORAL EDUCATION

The Moral Education (ME) component of ART is a set of procedures designed to raise the young person's level of fairness, justice, and concern with the needs and rights of others. In a long and pioneering series of investigations, Kohlberg (1969, 1973) demonstrated that exposing youngsters to a series of moral dilemmas (in a discussion group context in which youngsters reason at differing levels of moral thinking) arouses an experience of cognitive conflict, the resolution of which will frequently advance a youngster's reasoning in the group. Such advancement of moral reasoning is a reliable finding, but, as with other single-enhancing interventions, efforts to use it alone as a means of actual, overt moral behavior have resulted in only mixed success (Arbuthnot & Gordon, 1983; Zimmerman, 1983). Glick and Goldstein (1987) suggest a need for increasing adolescents' levels of moral reasoning because such youth did not have in their behavioral repertoires either the actual skills for acting prosocially or for successfully inhibiting antisocial or more aggressive behaviors. Thus, it was reasoned that Kohlberg's ME has marked potential to provide constructive direction toward sociability and away from antisocial behavior.

Two trainers meet with at least 12 youngsters in each ME group. Once the groups are formed, trainers must choose and prepare the moral dilemmas, create a proper environment and attitude, initiate the discussion, guide the discussion, and then end the discussion. Facilitators are trained to conduct each of these procedural steps so they may accomplish the following:

Choose and Prepare a Dilemma:

The trainer first should anticipate how the participants will reason at each stage. Second, the trainers should prepare elaborations to generate disagreements for each dilemma. Finally, the trainers should prepare at least two counterarguments for how to deal with the dilemma.

Create the Proper Environment and Attitude:

The facilitator should ensure that the group is physically and psychologically safe and secure so that the participants will share ideas and beliefs openly. The facilitator should then identify the goals of the group; that is, provide explanations for the purpose of ME groups, the group format and members' roles, the leader's role, and the group norms. Once the goals have been articulated, the trainer should establish group norms to be followed and invite group members to identify norms they wish to follow.

Initiate the Discussion:

The facilitator begins by passing out copies of a moral dilemma and reads or has a group member read the dilemma to the group. The major points of the dilemma are then summarized through brief group discussion. The trainer should encourage questions from the group that help make the dilemma more clear. The facilitator should then clarify questions, problems, or misconceptions about the dilemma.

Guide the Group Discussion:

The leader begins the moral education discussion by obtaining initial opinions from all residents and the rationale for their positions. (It is critical to keep this part brief.) The trainer then rephrases or paraphrases each participant's rationale, writes a short summary of initial rationales on newsprint or a chalkboard (the purpose for these procedures is to "stage" each participant so the leader may direct discussion), and conducts a "differing opinions debate."

End Discussion:

The facilitator should summarize debates for each pair of debaters or for each group and should present an argument at one stage higher than the most sophisticated or abstract argument presented. Again, keep in mind that *there are no right or wrong answers.* The objective for the ME sequence is to expose individuals to higher order or levels of moral reasoning.

PRACTICAL, ETHICAL, AND LEGAL CONSIDERATIONS

Aggression Replacement Training has been designed to be culturally and ethnically neutral. It may be used in any type of environment with homogeneous or heterogenous, culturally diverse clients. Language barriers may be overcome through translation.

When dealing with violent children and adolescents, the same precautions and ethical standards need to be applied as in any other counseling modality. Although confidentiality must be honored, participants must understand — and the group norms must reflect — that the group and its members are guaranteed their safety and security. Therefore, any information that would lead to harmful conditions to group members or others will not be held in confidence. For example, if through the group process the counselor obtains information that a client will commit an act that is in violation of the law, the counselor is obligated to inform the police. If a client threatens harm to himself or herself, the counselor is obligated to refer that information to the appropriate source (in the case of nonreferral, counselors may be held liable for aiding and abetting criminal activities of juvenile delinquents). Finally, as counselors deal with adjudicated youth, or others who are deemed a threat to society by their aggressive or violent nature, they need to be well versed in the laws within their jurisdictions that govern their clients.

SUMMARY

Aggression is a complex, multifaceted, learned, behavioral response. Children and adolescents have become more aggressive, with greater incidence and intensity over the last three decades. Counselors need to identify and implement appropriate multimodal treatment interventions to modify the attitudes and behaviors of their aggressive clients.

The purpose of this chapter is to give mental health professionals an opportunity to explore the nature of aggression in children and youth, identify the principles of aggressive behavior, and learn, in detail, about one intervention that has been successfully developed, implemented, and evaluated.

For mental health professionals, it is imperative to implement professional treatment skills to deal adequately with the growing problem of youth violence. It is equally important to take the time to evaluate new programs and treatment services offered so that further development and enhancement of the quality of professional tools available can occur.

REFERENCES

Arbuthnot, J., & Gordon, D. A. (1983). Moral reasoning development in correctional intervention. *Journal of Correctional Education, 34*, 133–138.

Coleman, M., Pfeiffer, S. & Oakland, T. (1991). *Aggression replacement training with behavior disordered adolescents*. Unpublished manuscript, University of Texas.

Curulla, V. L. (1990). *Aggression replacement training in the community for adult learning disabled offenders*. Unpublished manuscript, University of Washington.

Farrington, D. P., Ohlin, L. E., & Wilson, J. Q. (1986). *Understanding and controlling crime*. New York: Springer-Verlag.

Federal Bureau of Investigation. (1988-1994). *Uniform crime report*. Washington, DC: U.S. Government Printing Office.

Feindler, E. L., Marriott, S. A., & Iwata, M. (1984). Group anger control for junior high school delinquents. *Cognitive Therapy and Research, 8*, 299–311.

Gibbs, J. C. (1986). *Small group sociomoral treatment programs: Dilemmas for use with conduct-disordered or antisocial adolescents or preadolescents*. Unpublished manuscript, The Ohio State University.

Glick, B., & Goldstein, A. P. (1987). Aggression replacement training: An intervention for counselors. *Journal of Counseling and Development, 65*(7), 356–362.

Glick, B., & Goldstein A. P. (1995). *Managing delinquency programs that work*. Laurel, MD: American Correctional Association.

Goldstein, A. P., Glick, B., Irwin, M. J., Pask-McCartney, C., & Rubama, I. (1989). *Reducing delinquency: Interventions in the Community*. Elmsford, NY: Pergamon Press.

Goldstein, A. P., Sprafkin, R. P., Gershaw, N. J., & Klein, P. (1980). *Skillstreaming the adolescent*. Champaign, IL: Research Press.

Hoshman, L. T., & Austin, G. W. (1987). Validation studies of a multifactor cognitive-behavioral anger control inventory. *Journal of Personality Assessment, 51*(3), 417-432.

Hoshman, L. T., Austin, G. W., & Appell, J. (1981, August). *The diagnosis and assessment of anger control problems*. Paper presented to the American Psychological Association, Los Angeles.

Jones, Y. (1990). *Aggression replacement training in a high school setting*. Unpublished manuscript, Center for Learning and Adjustment Difficulties. Brisbane, Australia.

Kohlberg, L. (1969). Stage and sequence: The cognitive-development approach to socialization. In D. A. Goslin (Ed.), *Handbook of socialization theory and research*. Chicago: Rand McNally.

Kohlberg, L. (Ed.). (1973). *Collected papers on moral development and moral education*. Cambridge, MA: Center for Moral Education.

Leeman, L. W., Gibbs, J. C., & Fuller, D. (1993). Evaluation of a Multi-component group treatment program for juvenile delinquents. *Aggressive Behavior, 19*, 281-292.

Maltz, D. (1984). *Recidivism*. New York: Academic Press.

Meichenbaum, D. H. (1977). *Cognitive-behavioral modification: An integrative approach*. New York: Plenum Press.

Novaco, R. W. (1975). *Anger control: The development and evaluation of an experimental treatment*. Lexington, MA: D. C. Heath.

Office of Court Administration. (1995). *Crime Statistics 1982-1995: Annual report of the Chief Administrator of the Courts*. Washington, DC: Author.

Office of Juvenile Justice and Delinquency Prevention (1994). *Juvenile Justice Bulletin*. Washington, DC: Author.

Patterson, G. R., Reid, J. G., & Jones, R. R. (1975). *A social learning approach to family interventions* (Vol. 1). Eugene, OR: Castalia.

Quay, H. C. (1983). *Technical manual for the behavioral classification system for adult offenders* (Grant No. FB-6). Washington, DC: National Institute of Corrections.

Zimmerman, D. (1983). Moral education. In Center for Research on Aggression (Ed.), *Prevention and control of aggression.* Elmsford, NY: Pergamon Press.

FOR FURTHER READING

Alexander, R., Corbett, T., & Snigel, J. (1976). The effects of individual and group consequences on school attendance and curfew violators with predelinquent adolescents. *Journal of Applied Behavior Analysis, 9,* 221–226.

Bandura, A. (1973). *Aggression: A social learning analysis.* Englewood Cliffs, NJ: Prentice-Hall.

Blakely, C. H., & Davidson, W. S., III. (1984). Behavioral approaches to delinquency: A review. In P. Karoly & J. J. Steffen (Eds.), *Adolescent behavior disorders: Foundations and contemporary concerns.* Lexington, MA: Lexington Books/D. C. Heath.

Borenstein, P. H., Hamilton, S. B., & McFall, M. E. (1981). Modification of adult aggression: A critical review of theory, research, and practice. In M. Herson, R. M. Eisler, & P. M. Miller (Eds.), *Progress in behavior modification* (Vol. 12). New York: Academic Press.

Fehrenbach, P. A., & Thelen, M. H. (1982). Behavioral approaches to the treatment of aggressive disorders. *Behavior Modification, 6*(4), 465–467.

Goldstein, A. P., & Stein, N. (1976). *Prescriptive psychotherapies.* Elmsford, NY: Pergamon Press.

Hobbs, T. R., & Holt, M. M. (1976). The effects of token reinforcement on the behavior of delinquents in cottage settings. *Journal of Applied Behavior Analysis, 9,* 189–198.

Kaufman, K. F., & O'Leary, K. D. (1972). Reward, cost, and self-evaluation for disruptive adolescents in a psychiatric hospital school. *Journal of Applied Behavior Analysis, 5,* 293–309.

Lochman, J. E. (1984). Psychological characteristics and assessment of aggressive adolescents. In C. R. Keith (Ed.), *The aggressive adolescent: Clinical perspectives.* New York: The Free Press.

Martinson, R. (1974, Spring). What works? Questions and answers about prison reform. *Public Interest*, pp. 22–54.

Moss, G. R., & Rick, G. R. (1981). Application of a token economy for adolescents in a private psychiatric hospital. *Behavior Therapy, 12,* 585–590.

Novaco, R. W. (1979). The cognitive regulation of anger and stress. In P. C. Kendall & D. S. Hollon (Eds.), *Cognitive-behavioral interventions.* Orlando, FL: Academic Press.

Palmer, T. (1975). Martinson revisited. *Journal of Research in Crime and Delinquency, 12,* 133–152.

Patterson, G. R., & Anderson, D. (1964). Peers as social reinforcers. *Child Development, 35,* 951–960.

Phillips, J. S., & Ray, R. S. (1980). Behavioral approaches to childhood disorders. *Behavior Modification, 4,* 3–34.

Rule, B. G., & Nesdale A. R. (1976). Emotional arousal and aggressive behavior. *Psychologic Bulletin, 83,* 851-861.

Stumphauzer, J. (1981). Behavioral approaches to juvenile delinquency: Future perspectives. In L. Michelson, M. Hersen, & S. M. Turner (Eds.), *Future perspectives in behavior therapy.* New York: Plenum Press.

Varley, W. H. (1984). Behavior modification approaches to the aggressive adolescent. In C. R. Keith (Ed.), *The aggressive adolescent: Clinical perspectives.* New York: The Free Press.

Wood, R., & Flynn, J. M. (1978). A self-evaluation token system versus an external evaluation token system alone in a residential setting with predelinquent youth. *Journal of Applied Behavior Analysis, 11*(4), 503–512.

10

Evaluation and Treatment of the Substance-Abusing Adolescent

R. Jeremy A. Stowell, MD, FAPA

Dr. Stowell is former Director of Adolescent Programs, Virginia Beach Psychiatric Center. He is currently Medical Director with the Division of Substance Abuse, Norfolk Community Services Board, and is in private practice in Virginia Beach, VA.

KEY POINTS

- A thorough evaluation of the adolescent substance abuser should determine which problems are most central to the cause and perpetuation of the abuse, examine familial and biologic risk factors, prioritize treatment needs, and decide the appropriate level of care.

- The physiologic, behavioral, and psychological signs and symptoms of addiction that may be revealed in the evaluation are discussed. Interviews with the adolescent and his or her parents are both important parts of such an evaluation.

- Diagnosing substance abuse can follow from three criteria: objective use characteristics, symptomatic use behaviors, and areas of functional impairment associated with the abuse.

- Typical motivations for substance abuse may include alienation from parents, social ostracism, severely painful emotions, academic failure, and sexual abuse.

- The author discusses guidelines for – and limitations of – outpatient treatment. He describes the application of various diagnostic tools to the inpatient setting, discusses the role of laboratory testing in the evaluation, and suggests the use of a treatment contract among the adolescent, mental health professional, and the adolescent's family.

INTRODUCTION

The past 30 years have witnessed a geometric increase in substance abuse among adolescents and young adults in all parts of the United States (Martin, Arria, Mezzizh, & Bukstein, 1993). The dissemination of drugs has proceeded from adult users to child users as young as 7 and 8 years old. Although Bailey (1992) has reported a general decline in child and adolescent substance abuse, the high numbers of young substance abusers and the types of drugs used continue to have alarming consequences.

Psychoactive substance abuse must be placed in proper perspective with other major public health issues that affect children, adolescents, and their families. Alcohol and drug use is associated with accidents, suicides, and psychiatric illness. It is also associated with a wide range of problems including teenage pregnancy, infant morbidity and mortality, family dysfunction and violence, crime, rising health care costs, and general misery. Therefore, it is critical to make the diagnosis early to expedite the processes of treatment and recovery. This chapter addresses aspects of the evaluation and treatment of the substance-abusing adolescent.

DEVELOPMENTAL ISSUES

When evaluating the substance-abusing adolescent, it is important to consider the developmental issues — biologic, psychological, sociologic, and spiritual — that are involved for the adolescent and the family. Adolescent development is characterized by rapid growth and sexual maturation as well as cognitive development (beginning to think in abstract terms). A shift from dependence on adults (particularly parents) to peers occurs and is accompanied by a strong identification with the peer group. A key developmental issue in this period involves exploration of values and lifestyles; this phase is often characterized by intense confusion about central identity issues. The issues include:

- Adapting to physical growth and hormonal changes

- Separating and individuating from parents

- Attaining adult cognitive development and abstraction

- Developing a sexual identity and achieving aspects of intimacy; developing sexual relationships

- Further developing the ego, superego, and ego-ideal

- Preparing for further educational and vocational goals

Abuse of substances on a regular basis may produce a delay, disruption, or even arrest of these developmental tasks in adolescents. This perspective is critical in the overall evaluation of the substance-abusing adolescent.

OVERVIEW OF THE EVALUATION

Evaluation of the substance-abusing adolescent is often complicated by the fact that many psychopathologic and substance use disorders may be nonspecific and nondiagnostic (Estroff & Gold, 1984). One concern is that treatment could begin before all diagnoses are made, thereby leading to the lack of adequate treatment and relapse of both the substance abuse and the psychopathologic disorder (Worden, 1985). A thorough evaluation is important to determine which problems are most central to the cause of and perpetuation of the

substance abuse (Winters & Henley, 1988a). The heterogene-
ity of dual diagnosis clients is not surprising when one consid-
ers the multiple combinations of substance abuse disorders
and psychiatric illnesses (Stowell, 1991; Stowell & Estroff,
1992).

In the interview with the family, it is important to recognize
family risk factors (Clayton, 1992; Johnson , Sher, & Rolf, 1991;
Tarter, Blackson, Martin, Loeber, & Moss, 1993). It is also
useful to identify genetic or biologic risk factors; 25% of the
sons of alcoholics, whether they are reared by their biologic
parents or not, will develop alcoholism, as has been shown in
adoption and twin studies (Cloninger, Bodman, & Sigvardsson,
1981).

A thorough and structured evaluation of the adolescent
substance abuser reveals the treatment needs and determines
the treatment priorities. An excellent guideline in the diagnostic process of adolescents and their parents has been developed by Ayers (1992).

Evaluation also involves a decision about the appropriate
level of care. Special patient placement criteria for the treatment of psychoactive substance use disorders in adolescents
are available from the American Society of Addiction Medicine (12 West 21st Street, New York, NY 10010; telephone:
[212] 206-6770).

DIAGNOSIS OF ADOLESCENT SUBSTANCE ABUSE

No researched or validated classification system for adolescent substance abuse and dependence currently exists. One
can use criteria from the latest edition of the *Diagnostic and
Statistical Manual of Mental Disorders* (DSM-IV) (American
Psychiatric Association, 1994), but the particular value of
these criteria for *adolescent* substance abuse and dependence
has not been established. "The state of the art of adolescent
psychoactive substance use disorders does not support a
distinct adolescent-oriented category from the present DSM-

III-R/DSM-IV oriented terminology" (Kaminer, 1994, p. 14). It is not necessarily true that a valid diagnostic system for adult substance abuse would be equally useful for adolescents. Regarding the current operational definitions and diagnosis of adolescent substance *abuse*, Kaminer (1991) offers the following criteria:

- Objective use characteristics such as quantity and frequency as defined by the National Institute of Alcohol Abuse and Alcoholism. This includes drinking to the point of being drunk six or more times per year.

- Symptomatic use behaviors such as intoxication, blackouts, and the like.

- Areas of functional impairment presumed to be caused by substance abuse that occurs at least twice per year and are considered to be part of the substance abuse syndrome. These may include impaired relationships with family, peers, or teachers, and problems with school, police, or driving under the influence of alcohol.

OUTPATIENT EVALUATION

A structured clinical interview with the parents and a diagnostic interview of the adolescent are needed in most cases. The evaluator is charged with making an assessment of the substance use and the psychiatric diagnoses followed by appropriate recommendations. One of the first questions must be, "Is there a drug-abuse problem?" If the client has been using drugs only on an experimental basis and no indication of substance abuse is apparent, it is likely that some form of substance abuse education can be useful. It is important to look for elements of addiction such as:

- Compulsion

- Loss of control

- Continued use despite adverse consequences

SIGNS AND SYMPTOMS

The adolescent substance abuser displays numerous signs and symptoms indicative of substance abuse problems (Table 10.1). Physical evidence includes staggering, the smell of alcohol or marijuana, complaints of nausea or vomiting, glassy or bloodshot eyes, problems with coordination, slurred speech, or notable changes in appearance.

Use of depressants, such as alcohol, is often manifest in staggering, slurred speech, dilation of pupils, concentration difficulties, and sleepiness. Regular marijuana use often results in red eyes, time distortion, change in appetite, memory impairment (especially recent), chronic cough and chest pain, fatigue, sleep disturbance, menstrual irregularities, diminished hygiene, and a general decline of performance in most areas as the drug use progresses.

Stimulants such as cocaine and amphetamines generally provoke excessive activity, overexcitement, euphoria, talkativeness, aggression, and paranoia. Physical evidence includes pupil dilation, decreased appetite, and increased blood pressure and pulse rate.

Hallucinogens such as lysergic acid diethylamide (LSD) and phencyclidine hydrocholoride (PCP) tend to produce hypertension (elevated blood pressure) and tachycardia (rapid heart rate), irregular breathing, sweating, and tremulousness of the hands. The hallucinogen abuser may evidence changes in hearing, touching, smelling, and seeing.

Inhalants may produce notable physical changes such as the strong smell of the odor particular to the inhalant, excess nasal secretion, watering of the eyes, difficulty with stagger-

Table 10.1 EFFECTS OF PSYCHOACTIVE SUBSTANCES	
Drug	*Signs*
Depressants (e.g., alcohol)	Staggering, slurred speech, pupil dilation, concentration difficulties, sleepiness
Marijuana	Red eyes, time distortion, change in appetite, memory impairment, chronic cough/chest pain, fatigue, sleep disturbance, menstrual irregularities, diminished hygiene
Stimulants (e.g., cocaine, amphetamines)	Excessive activity, overexcitement, euphoria, loquaciousness, aggression, paranoia, pupil dilation, decreased appetite, increased blood pressure and heart rate, irregular breathing, sweating, tremulousness
Inhalants	Smell of the inhalant, excess nasal secretion, watering of eyes, staggering, drowsiness, altered cognitive abilities

ing or drowsiness, or slurred speech. These adolescents also generally demonstrate altered cognitive perceptions and abilities.

Adolescent substance abusers typically manifest marked disruptive behaviors, including refusal to follow rules and guidelines, disciplinary problems in school, outbursts of abusive language, irresponsibility in relationships at home and school, fighting, negative attention getting, and a dramatic increase in negative mood states (e.g., nervousness and depression). A social shift is common from family orientation to orientation with drug-using peers, accompanied by secrecy and dishonesty.

STAGES OF ADOLESCENT SUBSTANCE ABUSE

Adolescent substance abuse can be viewed as progressing through three stages: an early stage, a middle stage, and a late stage.

Early Stage:

The early stage is characterized by occasional drug use during weekends and with friends. Toward the end of this phase, preoccupation with drug use grows and peer pressure increases.

Middle Stage:

As the adolescent becomes more tolerant of the drug, physical and psychological dependence increases, preoccupation with drug use escalates, and socializing with drug-using friends occurs more often. This middle stage is often characterized by the onset of memory blackouts as well as the use of multiple types of drugs. During this phase, school and work performance decrease, and the adolescent may drop out of sports and nonessential activities. The youngster may begin to spend more money on drugs and may steal and lie to obtain them. An increase in psychiatric symptoms such as depression and suicidal ideation is not unusual during this stage. By this point, attempts to limit alcohol and other drug consumption — or to quit altogether — have been unsuccessful.

Late Stage:

In the late stage, the adolescent is completely absorbed in drugs. Participation in school and extracurricular activities is minimal, and the user is unable to be honest with himself or herself, or with others. The adolescent often experiences a notable worsening of the sleep process, accompanied by physical deterioration and increasing blackouts from use of alcohol or other drugs. During outpatient evaluation, it is useful to determine what level of care will be needed to treat the abuse problem. Clinical experience and use of specific placement criteria can lead to the correct decision.

INTERVIEWING THE PARENTS

As a routine part of the evaluation, the adolescent's parents should be interviewed because they can provide important information about their child's premorbid functioning and personality. Furthermore, this interview often presents an excellent opportunity to discuss behavioral issues and preexisting psychiatric disorders. Structured data collection in the following areas is essential:

- Developmental history

- Educational history

- Family history, including parental use of substances and extended family data on substance use and psychiatric disorders

- Marital history

- Medical history

- Social history

- Substance use history

Interestingly enough, parents are able to provide specific

information about their child's drug use—for example, the type of paraphernalia he or she is using. However, given that the illness is based on denial, secrets, and lies, parents may not be able to provide much information regarding the extent of the drug abuse.

It is useful to question the parents about symptoms such as violence, temper tantrums, oppositional behavior, severe mood swings, psychotic symptoms, suicidal statements, suicidal behaviors, and possible suicide attempts (including drug overdose). Should the interview with the parents reveal imminent danger to the adolescent (suicidal risk), inpatient treatment must be seriously considered.

A difficult area of exploration with parents is their own use of substances and substance use in their families of origin. This can be a delicate matter because the parental denial system may be powerful. Moreover, the parents may become so emotionally reactive that they pull themselves and their adolescent away from the evaluation process. Because the literature has indicated a strong correlation between family histories of drug abuse and adolescent problems (Bennett, Wolin, & Reiss, 1988), it is critical to uncover any history of family substance abuse.

In the parental interview, the evaluator should listen for other signs of substance abuse problems. For example, the parents may report that their son or daughter is failing in school, exhibits delinquent behavior, has few friends, is overtly aggressive toward siblings or peers, has withdrawn from peers, or has somatic symptoms such as stomach pain or headaches. These adolescents often are depressed, angry, confused, and anxious, and have significant problems in close relationships.

One area that is underevaluated and underreported is the frequent presence of psychiatric disorders in the parents. The parents should be asked about emotional and psychological disturbances that they may have been experiencing. The evaluator should also inquire about the extended family history of depression, substance abuse, and other psychiatric disorders.

The parents' responses may suggest the possibility of certain biogenetic disorders that could predispose the adolescent to substance abuse or comorbid psychopathologic disturbances.

Parents should be asked about any prior treatment approaches used by their son or daughter. This may include multiple clinical treatment efforts and their own efforts in the home setting, as well as possible court intervention. It is important to understand what leverage can be used to help the adolescent obtain treatment. By the end of the interview, it is absolutely essential for the evaluator to understand the degree of family support available so that treatment can be planned accordingly.

INTERVIEWING THE ADOLESCENT

Obtaining Material:

In the adolescent diagnostic interview, the first step is to establish rapport and initiate the therapeutic relationship. It may be useful to allow part of the interview to be unstructured so that the adolescent has the opportunity to present personal concerns and issues about himself or herself and the family. The mental health professional should then try to obtain specific material regarding:

- The relationship of the adolescent to each parent, stepparent, siblings, and others living in the home

- The adolescent's friends and social activities

- Problem behaviors such as stealing, running away, and truancy

- The emotional life of the adolescent — primary emotional states (anger, depression, and anxiety) associated with the present illness

- Information about painful traumatic memories such as being abused physically, emotionally, or sexually

- Developmental areas

- A detailed substance use history

- Detailed counseling experiences as well as efforts at substance abuse intervention

- Detailed information about peer associations (Oetting et al. [1989] have emphasized the significant role played by peer associations in adolescent substance abuse.)

- The spiritual and/or religious beliefs of the adolescent and family

An assessment of religious beliefs is an important part of a diagnostic interview because incorporating aspects of spirituality into the treatment plan often can play a critical role in the overall treatment. This is supported by a growing body of literature (e.g., Adlaf, 1985; Amoateng & Bahr, 1986; Gartner, Larson, & Allen, 1991; Larson & Larson, 1994; Muffler, Langrod, & Larson, 1992, Newcombe, Maddahian, & Bentlor, 1986). The positive results from integrating spirituality into the treatment process may include reduced relapsed rates and better quality of recovery (Adlaf, 1985; Gartner, Larson, & Allen, 1991); religious affiliation and commitment reduce alcohol and drug use in adolescents (Amoateng & Bahr, 1986; Newcombe, Maddahian, & Bentlor 1986). Further clinical research is needed to help develop better treatment strategies in this area; instruments to assess spirituality and methods to measure spiritual progress in substance-abusing adolescents need to be developed.

Areas of Motivation:

The adolescent's interview may reveal various possible areas of motivation for substance abuse based on the adolescent's own experience. These might include:

- Severely painful emotions, especially those associated with suicide

- School failure

- A negative drug experience

- Social ostracism

- Alienation from parents

In some cases, drug involvement may have become so severe that the adolescent has resorted to selling drugs, stealing, or prostitution. However, because the income from these sources may be insufficient to cover the expenses of a heavy drug habit, drug-abusing adolescents may owe significant amounts of money to their suppliers. Sometimes, an adolescent agrees to be evaluated and to enter treatment because he or she is receiving threats from drug dealers or other external sources of pressure. The adolescent is occasionally given the choice between going to court or receiving treatment.

LABORATORY TESTING

A thorough evaluation should include comprehensive laboratory data. This includes a complete blood count, blood chemistry, pregnancy test in young women, a urine or serum drug screen, and possibly a hepatitis B profile. Testing for human immunodeficiency virus (HIV) may also be advisable if exposure to the virus is suspected. The urine test should be supervised and observed. In addition, the counselor should have first-hand knowledge of the laboratory values and various cutoff points for the blood and urine specimens for the drugs in question.

LIMITS OF OUTPATIENT EVALUATION

Significant limitations in the outpatient evaluation and treatment of adolescent substance abusers may exist. For instance, clinical intervention may be frustrated by defensive denial on the part of the adolescent or the parent(s). Because of the limited number of cross-sectional evaluations that may be performed (usually no more than two per week), significant clinical issues may be hidden from the examiner and the parent(s). These may include ongoing drug use that is not detectable in the usual urine drug screen (e.g., LSD, anabolic steroids, inhalants), severe underlying depression, and suicidal risk.

Indications for Inpatient Treatment:

A primary consideration for using inpatient treatment is the failure of outpatient treatment to improve the clinical conditions of the adolescent. Admission criteria for inpatient treatment of adolescents involve the risk of withdrawal syndrome being present as evidenced by history of current severe alcohol abuse or other drug use. Moreover, impaired neuropsychiatric function may be present, as evidenced by severe depression, altered mental status (with or without delirium), hallucinations, toxic psychosis, extreme emotionality, volatility of behavior, and violence.

Inpatient treatment is also indicated when the adolescent has biomedical conditions and complications (e.g., diabetes, asthma, infections). Inpatient treatment should be considered if the substance abuse complicates or exacerbates a previously diagnosed medical condition.

Other considerations of inpatient treatment are emotional and behavioral conditions that require acute intervention. These conditions will reflect significant impairment in social, interpersonal, educational, and occupational functioning. Specifically, there is often a failure to maintain behavioral stability for more than a few hours at a time with associated poor impulse control and judgment. Recurrent suicidal ideation or risk of harm to others is often present in these adolescents.

Inpatient treatment should also be considered when the potential for relapse is severe and when the patient is experiencing intensification of addiction symptomatology despite use of current treatment interventions at that particular level of care. Naturally, inpatient treatment should be considered when the person is unable to remain alcohol- and drug-free long enough to benefit from treatment at the current level of care.

The recovery environment itself may be such that the severity of family conflicts precludes recovery for the patient. Physical, emotional, or sexual abuse may prohibit safe outpatient treatment. Further, at times, the parents or legal guardians are unable to provide consistent supervision or participation necessary to support treatment at the current level of care.

The real possibility of suicide among adolescent substance abusers is another indication for inpatient treatment. At least three separate studies (Crumley, 1990; Kaminer, 1992; Kandel, Ravels, & Davis, 1991) have concluded that loss of control over drug use was often a precipitant for a suicide attempt. A suicide attempt in a substance-abusing adolescent is much more likely to result in death than it would be for adolescents who suffer with depression or mania but who do not have a substance abuse disorder (Fowler et al., 1986). Inpatient treatment for substance abuse is used most often for adolescents who have displayed violent and antisocial behaviors.

Detoxification and withdrawal, though infrequent in adolescent patients, is still an important consideration for inpatient treatment. Drugs associated with a withdrawal syndrome may include alcohol, nicotine, opiates, and tranquilizers. Cocaine withdrawal frequently precipitates paranoia and depression during the intoxication and detoxification periods. Inpatient care is also indicated when the adolescent displays acute psychotic symptoms secondary to drug use, has been severely sexually traumatized, or is living in an environment with other substance abusers.

In the event that inpatient treatment is selected, a full explanation should be given to the adolescent about the nature of hospitalization and an agreement should be reached on how this will be accomplished. Some adolescents might be resistant to being hospitalized. In such cases, one or both parents and the mental health professional may have to exert appropriate pressure to have the adolescent enter the hospital environment. It is often useful to inform a hospital intake team of the adolescent's impending arrival and arrange to accompany the adolescent to the unit. Moreover, it is important to stress to the parents that strong measures are sometimes necessary to achieve hospitalization — but it may save the adolescent's life.

INPATIENT EVALUATION

Inpatient evaluation can lead to a complete diagnostic profile due to the added structure and resources available at this level of care. Increased level of safety is a major advantage of inpatient care. That is, risk of relapse and risk that consequences will be realized from suicidal or violent behaviors are decreased.

Although much information may have been gathered from the adolescent and parents in an outpatient evaluation, it is important to review the data in detail. Often, for instance, under the stress of initial outpatient evaluation, parents may omit important details. Careful medical and psychiatric reviews will often reveal illnesses that preceded the substance abuse and have contributed to it. At the inpatient level of care, it is possible to gather information rapidly from all sources in an effort to formulate the initial treatment plan. For example, the adolescent's school may report learning disabilities, disruptive behaviors, further evidence of substance abuse, peer difficulties, and other important information.

Assessment Tools:

Intensive interviewing of the adolescent in both the psychopathologic and substance use areas will help develop a complete treatment plan. Various instruments can be used to assess drug abuse and dependence; one such measure is the Personal Experience Inventory (PEI) developed by Winters and Henley (1988b). This comprehensive inventory measures the adolescent's involvement with drugs and alcohol; assesses the frequency, duration, and history of drug abuse; and evaluates personality characteristics and environmental circumstances of the adolescent drug abuser. Other diagnostic instruments developed recently focus primarily on psychiatric diagnoses. Such instruments include the Diagnostic Interview for Children and Adolescents (DICA), the Diagnostic Interview Schedule for Children (DISC), and the children's version of the Schedule for Affective Disorders and Schizophrenia (K-SADS).

Tarter (1990) has recently presented a procedure for systematically evaluating and treating adolescents with known or suspected substance abuse. This method uses a decision-tree approach. The Drug Use Screening Inventory (DUSI), incorporating 10 domains, can be administered in individual or group settings and can identify medical and psychopathologic disturbances as well as psychosocial maladjustments that are frequently concomitant to drug use in adolescents. The domains include:

- Substance use behavior

- Behavior patterns

- Health status

- Psychiatric disorders

- Social skills

- Family system

- School

- Work

- Peer relationships

- Leisure and recreation

Another instrument is the Substance Use Disorder Diagnostic Schedule (SUDDS) developed by Harrison and Hoffman (1985). Finally, Kaminer, Bukstein, and Tarter (1991) and Bukstein, Glancey, and Kaminer (1992) have been developing the Teen Addiction Severity Index (TASI).

Environmental Control:

At the inpatient level of treatment, it is possible to do much with environmental control, including the prevention of drug use and unsafe behaviors of other types. Treatment-resistant adolescents often act out regressively. In these cases, environmental control can provide necessary structure. It is recommended that a thorough behavior modification system be enforced on the adolescent unit.

THE CONTRACT

Following the evaluation or the initial treatment sessions, the findings and recommendations should be reviewed with the adolescent and parents. At this point in outpatient treatment or at the end of inpatient treatment, a written contract is useful. Elements of such a contract might include:

- Total abstinence from any alcohol or mind-altering drugs

- Supervised urine drug screens once or twice per week on an unannounced basis

- Attendance at outpatient treatment sessions for both the adolescent and family members unless there is an emergency

- Attendance at 12-step recovery meetings (Alcoholics Anonymous, Narcotics Anonymous, Cocaine Anonymous), with a frequency recommended by the counselor/therapist

- Specific "home" guidelines for the adolescent including curfew, choice of friends and activities, regular participation in family activities, study scheduling, and participation in household chores

- An agreement by the adolescent and parents to consider immediate intervention or increased frequency of treatment, including inpatient treatment, if any of the above conditions are not complied with or if a contaminated urine sample is obtained

CONCLUSION

This chapter has focused on multiple considerations in the evaluation of the adolescent substance abuser. The evaluation itself is a crucial part of the beginning of treatment. Therefore, the quality of treatment rests in the thoroughness of the evaluation and the recommendations that follow from it.

REFERENCES

Adlaf, E. M., & Smart, R. G. (1985). Drug use and religious affiliations, feelings, and behaviors. *British Journal of Addiction, 80*, 163-171.

American Psychiatric Association (1994). *Diagnostic and statistical manual of mental disorders* (4th ed.). Washington, DC: Author.

Amoateng, A. Y., & Bahr, S. J. (1986). Religion, family, and adolescent drug use. *Sociological Perspectives, 29*(1), 53-76.

Ayers, W. H. (1992, January 30). *Adolescent psychiatric diagnostic evaluation.* Presented at the Review Course in Adolescent Psychiatry, American Society of Adolescent Psychiatry, San Diego.

Bailey, G. W. (1992). Children, adolescents, and substance abuse. *Journal of the American Academy of Child and Adolescent Psychiatry, 31*, 1015-1018.

Bennett, L. A., Wolin, S. J., & Reiss, D. A. (1988). Cognitive, behavioral, and emotional problems among school-age children of alcoholic parents. *American Journal of Psychiatry, 145*(2), 185-190.

Bukstein, O. G., Glancy, L. J., & Kaminer, Y. (1992). Patterns of affective comorbidity in a clinical population dually diagnosed adolescent substance abusers. *Journal of the American Academy of Child and Adolescent Psychiatry, 31*, 1041-1045.

Clayton, R. R. (1992). Transitions in drug use: Risk and protective factors. In M. Glanz & R. Pickens (Eds.), *Vulnerability to drug abuse* (pp. 15-51). Washington DC: American Psychological Association.

Cloninger, C. R., Bodman, M., & Sigvardsson, S. (1981). Inheritance of alcohol abuse: Cross-fostering analysis of adopted men. *Archives of General Psychiatry, 38*, 861-867.

Crumley, F. E. (1990). Adolescent suicide attempts. *Journal of the American Medical Association, 263*, 3051-3053.

Estroff, T. W., & Gold, M. S. (1984). Psychiatric misdiagnosis. In M. S. Gold, R. B. Lydeard, & J. S. Carman (Eds.), *Advances in psychopharmacology – Predicting and improving treatment response* (pp. 34-66). Boca Raton, FL: CRC Press.

Fowler, R. C., et al. (1986). Suicide study, II: Substance abuse in young cases. *Archives of General Psychiatry, 43,* 962–965.

Gartner, J., Larson, D. B., & Allen, G. D. (1991). Religious commitment and mental health: A review of the empirical literature. *Journal of Psychology and Theology, 19,* 6-25.

Harrison, P. A, & Hoffman, N. G. (1985). *Substance use disorder diagnostic schedule manual.* St. Paul, MN: Ramsey Clinic.

Johnson, L. D., Sher, K. J., & Rolf, J. E. (1991). Models of vulnerability to psychopathology in children of alcoholics: An overview. *Alcohol, Health, and Research World, 15,* 33-42.

Kaminer, Y. (1991). Adolescent substance abuse. In R. J. Frances & S. I. Miller (Eds.), *Clinical textbook of addictive disorders* (pp. 320-346). New York: Guilford Press.

Kaminer, Y. (1992). Psychoactive substance abuse and dependence as a risk factor in adolescent-attempted and completed suicide. *American Journal of the Addictions, 1,* 21-29.

Kaminer, Y. (1994). *Adolescent substance abuse: A comprehensive guide to theory and practice.* New York: Plenum Press.

Kaminer, Y., Bukstein, O. G , & Tarter, R. E. (1991). The Teen Addiction Severity Index: Rationale and reliability. *International Journal of the Addictions, 26,* 9-46.

Kandel, D. B., Ravels, V. H., & Davis, M. (1991). Suicidal ideation in adolescence: Depression, substance use, and other risk factors. *Journal of Youth and Adolescence, 20,* 289-309.

Larson, D., & Larson, S. (1994). The forgotten factor in physical and mental health: What does the research show? *Independent Study Seminar 1994.* Rockville, MD: National Institute for Health Care Research.

Martin, C. S., Arria, A., Mezzizh, A., Bukstein, O. (1993). Patterns of polydrug use in adolescent alcohol abusers. *American Journal of Drug and Alcohol Abuse, 19*(4), 511-521.

Muffler, J., Langrod, J., & Larson, D. (1992). There is a balm in Gilead: Religion and substance abuse treatment. In J. Lowinson, P. Ruiz, & R. Millman (Eds.), *Substance abuse: A comprehensive textbook.* Baltimore: Williams & Wilkins.

Newcombe, M. D., Maddahian, E., & Bentlor, P. M. (1986). Risk factors for drug use among adolescents: Concurrent and longitudinal analyses. *American Journal of Public Health, 76,* 525-531.

Oetting, E. R., et al. (1989). Links from emotional distress to adolescent drug use: A path model. *Journal of Consulting and Clinical Psychology, 57,* 227-231.

Stowell, R.J.A. (1991). Dual diagnosis issues. *Psychiatric Annals, 21*(2), 98-104.

Stowell, R.J.A., & Estroff, T. W. (1992). Psychiatric disorders in substance-abusing adolescent inpatients: A pilot study. *Journal of the American Academy of Child and Adolescent Psychiatry, 31,* 1036-1040.

Tarter, R. E. (1990). Evaluation and treatment of adolescent substance abuse: A decision-tree method. *American Journal of Drug and Alcohol Abuse, 16,* 1-46.

Tarter, R. E., Blackson, T., Martin, C., Loeber, R., & Moss, H. B. (1993). Characteristics and correlates of child discipline practices in substance abuse and normal families. *American Journal on Addictions, 2,* 18-25.

Winters, K. C., & Henley, G. (1988a). Assessing adolescents who abuse chemicals. In *The Chemical Dependency Adolescent Assessment Project in Adolescent Drug Abuse – Analysis of treatment research* (Monograph Series 77, pp. 4-18). Kensington, MD: National Institute on Drug Abuse.

Winters, K., & Henley, G. (1988b). *Personal Experience Inventory test and manual.* Los Angeles: Western Psychological Services.

Worden, M. (1985). Adolescent treatment on the hot seat. *United States Journal of Drug and Alcohol Dependence, 9*(6), 1-15.

FOR FURTHER READING

Bukstein, O. G., Brent, D. A., & Kaminer, Y. (1989). Comorbidity of substance abuse and other psychiatric disorders in adolescents. *American Journal of Psychiatry, 146,* 1131-1141.

Grilo, G., Becker, D., Walker, M., Levy, K., Edell, W., & McGlashan, T. (1995). Psychiatric comorbidity in adolescent inpatients with substance use disorders. *Journal of American Academy Child Adolescent Psychiatry, 34,* 1085-1091.

Litt, M. D., Babor, T. F., Delboca, F. K., Kadden, R. M., & Cooney, N. L. (1992). Types of alcoholics II: Application of an empirically derived typology to treatment matching. *Archives of General Psychiatry, 49,* 609-614.

Rivinus, T. M. (1992). College age substance abuse as a developmental arrest. *Journal of College Student Psychotherapy, 6,* 141-166.

Shedler, J., & Block, J. (1990). Adolescent drug use and psychological health. *American Psychologist, 45,* 612-630.

11

Adolescent Suicide

James C. Brown, PhD

Dr. Brown is Chairman of The Academy of Clinical Mental Health Counselors and Associate Dean for Student Programs, School of Dentistry, University of Mississippi Medical Center, Jackson, MS.

KEY POINTS

- Risk factors for adolescent suicide can be categorized under psychiatric disorders, personality traits and behavioral patterns, family environment, and other sociocultural or demographic factors.

- The best predictor of the risk of suicide is prior suicide attempts, threats, ideation, or some combination thereof.

- Clinicians should understand the distinction between crisis management and therapy. Although crisis intervention is critical, the therapist should continue to focus on the suicide option and its dynamics even after the crisis has passed.

- Components of crisis management include therapist availability, contingency planning, prob-lem-solving training, formation of a supportive network, acute conflict resolution, removal of possible means of suicide, and making the client aware of community resources.

- Treatment of suicidal adolescents can incorporate cognitive-behavioral therapy, family-oriented intervention, and the identification and use of support systems.

- School-based and community approaches for suicide prevention should include early detection and referral-making skills, resource identification, suicide education for professionals working with children, parent education, primary prevention, and school-based postvention (to help reintegrate students who attempt suicide).

INTRODUCTION

Suicide is the second most common cause of death in adolescents (15–19 years of age) and young adults between the ages of 20 and 24 (Brent & Kolko, 1990a; National Center for Health Statistics, 1993). Although the suicide rates for other age groups have remained relatively stable, the rate for 15- to 24-year-olds has more than tripled over the past 30 years and has quadrupled for adolescents between the ages of 15 and 19 years during this same period (Berman & Jobes, 1991; Blumenthal & Kupfer, 1990). Given the finding that an alarming percentage of adolescents display suicidal ideation or behavior (Brent et al., 1986; Carlson & Cantwell, 1982) and that the assessment of suicidality of persons in these age groups has been the most commonly reported psychiatric emergency for a number of years (Mattsson, Seese, & Hawkins, 1969; Shafii, Whittinghill, & Healy, 1979), it should be clear that the assessment of suicide potential and appropriate preventive intervention efforts should be matters of significant interest and high priority for all mental health professionals.

EPIDEMIOLOGIC ISSUES IN ADOLESCENT SUICIDE

Epidemiology is the study of the distribution and determinants of a disease or related entity in a population. Epidemiologic data are thus important in dealing with phenomena such as suicide because the data can indicate potential causal relationships and suggest intervention and prevention strategies as well as prediction models. However, epidemiology has certain limitations and constraints, especially when considering suicide; for example, possible distortion of the formal reporting of suicide data is possible. Some increase in the listed suicide rate may result from the increased willingness of coroners and other officials to list suicide, rather than the traditional "accidental" cause, as the cause of death on death certificates. It is also possible that the official listing of suicide as the cause of death still may be conservative because of perceived associated emotional pain and stigma for survivors (Males, 1991; Smith, 1991). Despite this, the rate of suicide in adolescents has clearly increased (Brent & Kolko, 1990b), and a wide range of risk factors for suicide in adolescents drawn from epidemiologic studies has been reported. These factors can be grouped under four general headings: (a) psychiatric disorders, (b) personality traits and behavioral patterns, (c) family environment, and (d) other sociocultural or demographic factors.

Psychiatric Disorders:

A consensus exists that the majority of adolescent suicide victims have at least one diagnosable psychiatric disorder at the time of their suicide (Blumenthal & Kupfer, 1988; Brent et al., 1988; Shafii, Steltz-Lenarsky, Derrick, Beckner, & Whittinghill, 1988). It has even been suggested that psychopathology is a necessary condition for suicide in adolescents (Rich, Young, & Fowler, 1986). Runeson (1989) reported on 58 suicide completers between the ages of 15 and 29, 57 of whom had an Axis I or Axis II disorder as diagnosed with criteria from the revised third edition of the *Diagnostic and Statistical Manual of Mental Disorders* (DSM-III-R). As noted by Shafii and associates, it probably is safe to conclude that suicide in adolescents is not an impulsive act committed by emotionally healthy persons but rather "the final outcome of serious emotional disorders" (Shafii et al., 1988, p. 232).

Research has consistently found that depressive syndromes, including major depression, dysthymia, adjustment disorder with depressed mood, and bipolar disorder, frequently characterize adolescent suicide victims (Brent et al., 1988; Shafii et al., 1988). This relationship between depression and suicide, as pointed out by Carlson and Cantwell (1982), is complex. Although a majority of adolescent suicide victims have exhibited symptoms of depression, it should not be assumed that most depressed adolescents are suicidal.

Substance use disorder also has been linked to more than one third of adolescent suicides, existing with other affective disorders as well as alone (Brent et al., 1988; Shaffer & Gould, 1987). Downey (1991) suggested that increased drug use is the major factor in the upsurge in adolescent suicide. Adolescent substance users are three times more likely than controls to attempt suicide and to use more lethal suicide methods (Brent, Perper, & Allman, 1987). The substance use most commonly associated with adolescent suicide victims is alcohol (Shaffer, Garland, Gould, Fisher, & Trautman, 1988; Shafii et al., 1988).

Another major area of pathology among adolescent suicides is conduct disorder. Apter, Bleich, Plutchik, Mendelsohn, and Tyano (1988) found a greater suicide potential, as judged by scaled scores on the child and adolescent version of the Schedule for Affective Disorders and Schizophrenia (K-SADS), for adolescents with diagnosed conduct disorders than for those with major depressive disorders. A history of aggression and antisocial behavior is often associated with conduct disorders in adolescent suicides (Plutchik, van Pragg, & Conte, 1989; Shaffer et al., 1988). In fact, this may explain the frequency of borderline personality diagnosis among adolescents who attempt suicide (Friedman, Clarkin, & Corn, 1982; Gibbs, 1981; Runeson, 1989).

Personality Traits and Behavioral Patterns:

Several personality characteristics have consistently been reported in adolescent suicides. Aggression and antisocial behavior are common in adolescent suicide victims, as are related symptoms of intense rage and impulsive behavior (Berman & Jobes, 1991; Shafii, Carrigan, Whittinghill, & Derrick, 1985). This cluster of symptoms was found in approximately half the adolescent suicide cases studied by Shaffer and colleagues (1988).

Other behavioral traits are social withdrawal and alienation, loneliness, lack of a peer support system, and extreme sensitivity (Farberow, 1989; Hoberman & Garfinkel, 1988;

Shafii et al., 1985). As Berman and Jobes (1991) pointed out, this withdrawal or alienation phenomenon is possibly predictive of general emotional disturbance, particularly depression. These common emotional threads manifest with a number of other behavioral risk factors; for instance, poor academic performance, acting-out behaviors in school, runaway behavior, and various family conflicts.

Related behaviors that also help identify adolescents at high risk for suicide are perfectionist tendencies and excessive anxiety when faced with certain stressors (Blumenthal & Kupfer, 1990). Offering more specific findings, Cohen-Sandler, Berman, and King (1982) suggested that perfectionist adolescents who feel threatened by certain academic and social challenges constitute one of three major subgroups who commit suicide. The other two subgroups include adolescents with conduct disorders compounded by substance abuse and adolescents suffering from depression.

Family Environment:

One of the variables most commonly cited in the literature on adolescent suicide is the role of the family environment, especially the parental system. Clearly, given the major role of the family in the developmental process of children and adolescents, it is no surprise that this same environment is often linked to suicidal behavior.

Generally, when a significant parental conflict exists, the potential exists for negative emotional fallout in adolescent members of the family. Shafii and co-workers (1985) found significantly higher levels of family conflict, including violence and suicidal tendencies, in families of adolescent suicide victims. This finding is supported by other studies in which suicidal adolescents report family time as being less pleasant, parents are perceived more negatively (McKenry, Tishler, & Kelly, 1983), less affection is perceived (Korella, 1972), and family relationships are generally reported as weaker than those of nonsuicidal adolescents (Slap, Vorters, Chaudhuri, &

256   *The Hatherleigh Guide to Child and Adolescent Therapy*

Centor, 1989). Pfeffer (1989) described family dynamics commonly associated with adolescent suicide in two broad categories: familial stress, especially related to the parental system, and parental dysfunction (suicidality and psychopathology).

The first of Pfeffer's groupings, family parental stress, includes findings that changes (or threatened changes) in the parental system related to such factors as death, separation, and divorce are significantly tied to adolescent suicidal behavior (Cohen-Sandler et al., 1982; Garfinkel, Froese, & Hood, 1982; Kosky, 1983; Stanley & Barter, 1970). The functional link these changes have to the world of the adolescent is in real and perceived loss of parental support (Stanley & Barter, 1970).

Pfeffer's second category notes the significant negative impact of parental dysfunction and pathology. The pathologic behaviors referred to by Pfeffer that have been documented as familial risk factors for suicide include generalized mental disorders, depression, substance abuse, and aggression toward and abuse and neglect of the children in question (Cohen-Sandler et al., 1982; Deykin, Hsieh, Joshi, & McNamara, 1986; Garfinkel et al., 1982; McKenry et al., 1983; Shaffer & Gould, 1987; Tishler, McKenry & Morgan, 1981).

A recent study by Miller, King, Shain, and Naylor (1992) adds other familial data to the risk cluster. Their research compared suicidal adolescents with normal controls and found the suicidal group more likely to experience isolation in the family, especially within an inflexible family system. Exposure to the suicidal behavior of another family member is a significant risk factor for adolescent suicide (Harkavy-Friedman, Asnis, Boeck, & Difiore, 1987; Shafii et al., 1985; Smith & Crawford, 1986). Murphy and Wetzel (1982) have estimated that as many as 8% of adolescents who attempt suicide had a family member who committed suicide.

Sociocultural Factors:

Several contributing factors to the risk of suicide in adolescents do not fit easily into the previously mentioned categories. These factors are referred to as "interaction" factors between the individual and the environment. Shaffer and associates (1988) discuss the role of precipitants, noting that a significant number of adolescent suicide victims were involved in a disciplinary confrontation shortly before their death and feared the consequences. According to Blumenthal and Kupfer (1988), this precipitating event is typically humiliating, and the young person is unable to cope with the perceived guilt or shame.

The role of stressful life events also has been discussed as a risk factor; significantly increased levels of life stress have been found in suicidal adolescents compared with normal controls (Rubenstein, Heeren, Houseman, Rubin, & Stechler, 1989; Schotte & Clum, 1987). According to Rubenstein and colleagues (1989), high school students who had reported suicide attempts or for whom there were assumed attempts in the previous year had stress scores 33% higher than nonsuicidal students. The identified stress areas significantly associated with suicide were concerns of sexuality, family suicide, family and peer loss, and achievement pressure. These life stressors have been reported as being consistently greater in suicidal adolescents from early childhood through adolescence than for others (Cohen-Sandler et al., 1982).

Also relevant is a commonly reported lack of or ineffective problem-solving and coping skills by suicidal adolescents. The fact that suicide typically occurs as part of a stressful life environment would suggest such a deficit. Berman and Jobes (1991) suggested these limited or lacking cognitive abilities distort perceptions, limit alternatives, and increase feelings of hopelessness and impulsive behavior. Thus, the risk of suicide greatly increases.

Another significant sociocultural phenomenon of particular relevance to teenage suicide is the matter of suicide imitation or the "copycat" dynamic. Exposure of adolescent suicide victims to suicide within the family or social network is more common than for controls (Harkavy-Friedman et al., 1987). Given the commonly accepted adolescent behaviors of susceptibility to suggestion, imitation, and peer emulation, imitation may be a significant factor in adolescent suicide.

However, as Berman and Jobes (1991) noted, exposure to another's suicide is probably best considered an accelerating risk factor for those already predisposed. Two areas of research would suggest support for this conclusion: the well-publicized studies of media influence and so-called cluster (closely grouped) suicides. Gould and Shaffer (1986) noted that strong evidence supports the existence of imitative suicides following media coverage of actual suicides. They also suggested that fictional suicide presentations may increase suicide attempts.

The data are far from conclusive as to whether a media effect exists on subsequent cluster suicide in adolescents; however, this does not mean that suicide clusters are not a genuine occurrence. As Berman and Jobes (1991) pointed out, there is little dispute that suicide clusters exist and that suicidal adolescents within a cluster can be identified by known risk factors. The evidence is much more solid that individual cases of suicide have been influenced significantly by media presentations of nonfictional suicides.

Probably the single most predictive factor of the risk of suicide in adolescents is a history of prior suicide attempts. In a summary of the related literature, Farberow (1989) noted that prior suicide attempts, threats, ideation, or some combination of these are the most significant predictors of risk of suicide in adolescents. Specifically, he found that between 22% and 71% of adolescents who attempted suicide had documented prior attempts, threats, or ideation. More tragically, Reynolds and Eaton (1986) and Kotila and Lonnquist (1987) reported that adolescents who repeat suicide attempts after unsuccessful initial attempts are five times more likely to "succeed" than those trying for the first time.

TREATMENT OF THE IDENTIFIED SUICIDAL ADOLESCENT

Unfortunately, the mental health professional is usually not the first to observe signs that indicate suicidal risk. Those who do (i.e., family and friends) may not perceive the significance of the cues – and even if they do, they may be unsure as to what action to take. In addition, adolescents rarely seek professional help for problems linked to suicidal behavior. Most suicidal adolescents seen by mental health professionals are referred by other people (Berman & Jobes, 1991). Therefore, the vital first step for the mental health professional working with referred adolescents is to determine or verify the risk of suicide and then develop appropriate intervention.

A number of clinically and research-based indicators of suicide risk in adolescents are known. Mental health professionals must be aware of these indicators and stay abreast of new relevant findings in the professional literature. The presence of even one of the identified risk factors should be a "red flag" for considering an adolescent at risk.

Fremouw, de Perczel, and Ellis (1990) suggested that clinicians treating suicidal adolescents should consider the viable distinction between crisis management and therapy. This is in contrast to much of the material dealing with this topic, which emphasizes the crisis management or immediate prevention aspect of care. Fremouw and co-workers (1990) do not ignore the importance of crisis intervention. However, they do emphasize the need for focusing on the suicide option and its dynamics. They suggest that after the suicide crisis has passed, the typical therapeutic approach is "therapy as usual," without considering the reality that suicide is not necessarily a transient matter. Suicidal clients have specific needs and require therapy that addresses the suicide dynamics in their lives; for example, problem-solving style, cognitive deficits or distortions, and dysfunctional behavior patterns.

Crisis Management:

Once a determination of suicidal risk has been made, immediate intervention must be initiated to reduce the risk of harm or death by the client. Although little empirical research has been conducted to indicate the most effective crisis management strategies, a broad consensus exists among therapists.

The therapist's level of activity and direct involvement with the suicidal client increases significantly compared with noncrisis clients and periods. The rationale for this "therapeutic activism" (Fremouw et al., 1990) is simply that the suicidal state is not conducive to rational, effective coping and problem solving; it is up to the therapist to intervene and fill this role for the client. The following components of the therapist's active involvement are seen as necessary:

- *Availability*. The therapist's availability is of primary importance for the suicidal client. The client should be given reassurance of the counselor's availability with specific directions and information about access to the counselor.

- *Increased contact*. Backup counseling sessions with the suicidal client should be scheduled more frequently than normal and the counselor and client should stay in contact between sessions. This contact can be initiated by the counselor or the client can be directed to call between sessions.

- *Contingency plans*. The mental health professional should plan for coverage by a colleague or agency during times when he or she might not be available to the client. The client should be provided with detailed information about such contingencies, including relevant addresses and telephone numbers. It is appropriate to provide more than one backup for suicidal clients in crisis situations.

- *No-suicide contract*. Although its value has been questioned, it is prudent to ask the client to enter into a contractual agreement that suicide attempts will not be made within a specified period. The contract can also include alternatives to suicide and the agreed-on behavior of contacting the counselor or other specified professional if the client reaches a crisis point.

- *Reassurance.* The basic message of suicide's irreversibility — the fact that most crises eventually pass and that nothing is lost by postponing the consideration of suicide while the counselor works with the client to solve the relevant problems — should be stressed.

- *Problem-solving training.* Suicidal clients who feel overwhelmed and hopeless in dealing with their problems can often be helped through systematic problem-solving instruction by the counselor. The isolation of one problem at a time from among the many faced by the suicidal client and the development of problem-solving strategies to address that problem can often improve the common feelings of hopelessness and despair.

- *A support network.* To aid the client (as well as the therapist), the therapist should try to ensure that the client has access to a support network of family and friends. Although initially unacceptable by some suicidal clients, the involvement of family and friends in the crisis management stage is usually desirable.

- *Aid in acute conflict resolution.* The suicidal crisis of a young person is often initiated by acute, interpersonal conflicts, such as disagreements with parents, other authority figures, or a boyfriend or girlfriend. The therapist's direct involvement in providing understanding and solutions to these problems can help defuse the crisis situation.

- *Communication with the client's physicians.* Because of the eminent danger of prescribed medications, particularly psychotropic drugs, the counselor must work with and communicate readily with any physicians who may be treating the client.

- *Removal of possible means of committing suicide.* The therapist should inquire directly as to availability of firearms, other weapons, and potentially fatal drugs in the client's environment. If at all possible, the therapist should do whatever is necessary in working together with the client's family to remove these things from the client's immediate environment.

- *Between-session homework.* The client should be helped in systematically structuring the time between counseling sessions. Enjoyable activities, physical exercise, and other time-structuring events are diversions and reduce the time available for dwelling on crisis-induced problems.

- *Knowledge of community resources.* When dealing with a potential suicide victim via the telephone, the counselor must be able to contact the police and paramedics immediately. The mental health professional should always obtain the exact location of the client and the telephone number as soon as possible in a telephone conversation in which a suicidal risk has been determined. It is thus possible for an emergency response to be made in the event that the client actually attempts suicide.

- *Hospitalization.* When other interventions are not possible or sufficient, hospitalization of the suicidal adolescent should be seriously considered. The advantages and disadvantages of hospitalization should be weighed. These pros and cons have been discussed in the literature (Fremouw et al., 1990). At the very least, the therapist should have available the resource of hospitalization, either directly or in collaboration, for suicidal clients.

Cognitive-Behavioral Therapy:

The therapeutic treatment of an adolescent at risk for committing suicide must be based on individual dynamics and needs. An individual analysis of the intrapersonal and interpersonal variables of the suicidal behavioral pattern must be made. Based on this assessment, specific areas of intervention can be developed and therapeutic goals set. A number of therapeutic approaches can be used to achieve established goals, although cognitive-behavioral therapy frequently has been recommended as a viable therapeutic modality for suicidal adolescents, especially in cases of comorbid depression. The cognitive therapy model presented by Beck, Rush, Shaw, and Emery (1978) and the concise presentation of this model for depression by Jarrett and Rush (1992) are valuable resources for therapeutic work with suicidal adolescents. These resources should be consulted for detailed discussions of treatment of depression associated with suicidal adolescents.

Cognitive-behavioral approaches, especially using cognitive restructuring, can also be used to deal with the typical feelings of hopelessness experienced by suicidal adolescents. The client's negative expectations can be pinpointed, challenged, and modified as part of the restructuring technique. This model also calls for management of the environment to facilitate involvement in increased pleasurable activity.

Suicidal adolescents often demonstrate poor or nonexistent problem-solving skills, especially in situations involving interpersonal conflict. The cognitive-behavioral model allows this problem to be addressed directly through specific education, training, and interpersonal problem-solving skills gleaned through exercises, rehearsal, and modeling. The typical problem-solving approach teaches adolescents how to identify the specific problems involved, develop alternative solutions and anticipate obstacles and probable behavioral consequences, make decisions, and select and implement the preferred strategy or solution. Such skills training has improved problem-solving ability, decreased depression, and increased measures of self-concept and self-esteem (Kolko & Brent, 1987).

The final specific target for cognitive-behavioral treatment is anger and aggression management, another typically diagnosed symptom in this client population. Several behavioral models effectively teach management and coping with anger. Typical techniques in these models include cognitive control (i.e., understanding feelings and preparing self-statements for confronting anger cues); emotional controls using relaxation and humor; and behavioral controls using effective communication, problem solving, and assertion training (Feindler & Ecton, 1986; Lochman & Curry, 1986; Novaco, 1979).

Family Intervention:

Clearly, one of the vital treatment considerations of suicidal adolescents involves the family. The therapist's assessment must include a determination of the contribution of family members to the possible development and maintenance of suicidal behavior. Before actively involving family members in treatment, the therapist must have a clear and thorough understanding of the particular family dynamics.

If the family is seen as a potentially valuable ally, treatment of the individual client can be enhanced significantly. Family members can be taught to recognize the signs and symptoms of increased risk and respond appropriately to these symptoms, including when professionals should be contacted. Family members can also be helpful in actively removing potential hazards from the home, such as firearms and medications.

When working with suicidal adolescents who come from dysfunctional families, the family itself may become the focus of intervention. The family may be so dysfunctional that it is unable to provide the aid and support required by the adolescent. In these cases, the therapist must be prepared to intervene when it is clear that the family is maintaining potential suicidal behavior. Such intervention might include hospital-ization; placement of the adolescent with other, more functional family members; and family or individual therapy, focusing specifically on the identified dysfunction.

Support Systems:

In addition to the obvious potential support system of the family, significant others in the adolescent's environment may be included in the therapeutic process. Group therapy has been particularly effective in working with suicidal adolescents (Curan, 1987; Davis, 1983). Particularly with adolescent clients, the support and understanding from peers appear to be key factors, especially when the client mistrusts and resents adults. When drugs and alcohol are involved as part of the identified symptomatology, group therapy and available Alcoholics Anonymous (AA) and Narcotics Anonymous (NA) groups should be considered as potential support networks to augment individual therapy.

Fremouw and associates (1990) pointed out that children and adolescents often relate to a particular person in their environment. Therefore, the mental health professional should involve that person in therapy. They provide an example of a child's favorite teacher being asked to participate in treatment by involving the child in various pleasurable activities. In fact, the general school environment may provide a source of additional support for suicidal adolescents. An extensive model for prevention, intervention, and postvention of suicide within the school system has been developed by Poland (1989) and is a valuable resource for the counselor who plans to work with the school system on such programs.

Guidelines for treating suicidal clients drawn from Linehan (1981) are offered in Table 11.1.

PREVENTION

Mental health professionals are increasingly being requested

Table 11.1
GUIDELINES FOR TREATING SUICIDAL ADOLESCENTS

General procedures
- Talk about suicide openly and matter of factly.
- Avoid pejorative explanations of suicidal behavior or motives.
- Present a problem-solving theory of suicidal behavior, and maintain the stance that suicide is a maladaptive and ineffective solution.
- Involve significant others, including other therapists.
- Schedule sessions frequently enough, and maintain session discipline such that at least some therapy time is devoted to long-term treatment goals.
- Be aware of the multitude of variables impinging on clients, and avoid omnipotent taking or accepting of responsibility for client's suicidal behaviors.
- Maintain professional consultation with a colleague.
- Maintain occasional contact with persons who reject therapy.

Precrisis planning procedures
- Anticipate and plan for crisis situations.
- Continually assess the risk of suicide and "parasuicide" (i.e., all forms of self-harming behavior, even when the intent does not appear to be lethal).
- Be accessible.
- Use local emergency/crisis/suicide services.
- Give the client a crisis card that includes the telephone numbers of therapists, police, emergency services, hospital, and significant others.
- Keep telephone numbers and addresses of clients and their significant others with you.
- Make a short-term antisuicide contract and keep it up to date.
- Contact the client's physician regarding the risks of overprescribing medications.

Therapeutic maintenance procedures
- Do not force the client to resort to suicidal talk or ideation to get your attention.
- Be empathic; provide noncontingent warmth and attention.
- Clarify and reinforce nonsuicidal responses to problems.
- Identify to the client your likely responses to suicidal behaviors (e.g., if the client dies, you will be sad but will continue on with life).
- Ensure that the client has realistic expectations about the responses of others to future suicidal behaviors.

to become actively involved in community suicide prevention programs, especially those of the schools. Although significant research indicating effectiveness of these prevention efforts is lacking (Eddy, Wolpert, & Rosenberg, 1989; Shaffer et al., 1988), this has not deterred the growing interest and progress in developing such programs.

Various specific and general prevention programs have been proposed and developed. Among these are a number of consensus components, such as improving effectiveness of community crisis clinics and telephone hot lines, restricting access to lethal means (e.g., firearms), and developing prevention programs in the schools. Berman and Jobes (1991) reviewed a number of these proposed models and suggested that priority be given to the following seven school-based and community-based approaches:

- *Early detection and referral-making skills.* Within the school setting, faculty and students should be taught to recognize suicide risk symptoms and why and how to refer a student at risk to the appropriate professionals.

- *Resource identification.* Berman and Jobes (1991) suggested that professionals and agencies to whom references could be made should not only be identified but evaluated for competency as well.

- *Help-seeking behavior.* The encouragement and reinforcement of the notion of seeking and receiving help should be emphasized within the community.

- *Professional education.* The training of professionals who deal with adolescent suicide must be upgraded and evaluated by schools and agencies concerned with prevention.

- *Parent education.* Parents must be educated concerning the recognition of risk factors, appropriate referrals, and proactive involvement in eliminating or reducing potential means of suicide in the home.

• *Primary prevention.* The teaching of behavior and coping skills, such as problem solving, anxiety management, assertiveness training, and self-esteem training, is probably the most effective preventive strategy possible. These adaptive skills should be taught beginning in the elementary grades and followed up throughout the remaining grades.

• *School-based postvention.* Interventions that follow suicidal behavior often have a preventive effect. Students who attempt suicide need a positive reintegration effort after hospitalization. The reintegration plan, if successful, can reduce or eliminate the chance of a repeated attempt. The tragic matter of working with survivors of a completed suicide within the school setting also has a potential positive preventive impact.

CONCLUSION

Through the Centers for Disease Control and Prevention, the federal government has assumed an active role in the development of suicide prevention programs for adolescents, typically in conjunction with public school interest and efforts. Mental health professionals will continue to play a major role in prevention through direct intervention, consultation services to schools and agencies, and as researcher-evaluators of prevention efforts (Berman & Jobes, 1991). Therefore, mental health professionals must increase their skills and expertise required to assess suicidal risk in adolescents and to intervene effectively as clinicians and consultants.

REFERENCES

Apter, A., Bleich, A., Plutchik, R., Mendelsohn, S., & Tyano, S. (1988). Suicidal behavior, depression, and conduct disorder in hospitalized adolescents. *Journal of the American Academy of Child and Adolescent Psychiatry, 27,* 696-699.

Beck, A. T., Rush, A. J., Shaw, B. F., & Emery, G. (1978). *Cognitive therapy of depression: A treatment manual.* New York: Guilford Press.

Berman, A. L., & Jobes, P. A. (1991). *Adolescent suicide: Assessment and intervention.* Washington, DC: American Psychological Association.

Blumenthal, S. J., & Kupfer, D. J. (1988). Overview of early detection and treatment strategies for suicidal behavior in young people. *Journal of Adolescent and Adolescence, 17,* 1-24.

Blumenthal, S. J., & Kupfer, D. J. (Eds.). (1990). *Suicide over the life cycle.* Washington, DC: American Psychiatric Press.

Brent, D. A., Kalas, R., Edelbrock, C., Costello, A. J., Dulcan, M., & Conover, N. (1986). Psychopathology and its relationship to suicidal ideation in childhood and adolescence. *Journal of the American Academy of Child Psychiatry, 35,* 666-673.

Brent, D. A., & Kolko, D. J. (1990a). Suicide and suicidal behavior in children and adolescents. In B. D. Garfinkel, G. A. Carlson, & E. B. Weller (Eds.), *Psychiatric disorders in children and adolescents* (pp. 372-391). Philadelphia: Saunders.

Brent, D. A., & Kolko, D. J. (1990b). The assessment and treatment of children and adolescents at risk for suicide. In S. J. Blumenthal & D. J. Kupfer (Eds.), *Suicide over the life cycle* (pp. 253-302). Washington, DC: American Psychiatric Press.

Brent, D. A., Perper, J. A., & Allman, C. J. (1987). Alcohol, firearms, and suicide among adolescents: Temporal trends in Allegheny County, Pennsylvania, 1960-1983. *Journal of the American Medical Association, 257,* 3369-3372.

Brent, D. A., Perper, J. A., Goldstein, C., Kolko, D., Allan, M., Allman, C., & Zelenak, J. (1988). Risk factors for adolescent suicide: A comparison of adolescent suicide victims with suicidal inpatients. *Archives of General Psychiatry, 45,* 581–588.

Carlson, G. A., & Cantwell, D. P. (1982). Suicidal behavior and depression in children and adolescents. *Journal of the American Academy of Child Psychiatry, 21,* 361–368.

Cohen-Sandler, R., Berman, A. L., & King, R. (1982). Life stress and symptomatology: Determinants of suicidal behavior in children. *Journal of the American Academy of Child Psychiatry, 21,* 178–186.

Curan, D. K. (1987). *Adolescent suicidal behavior.* New York: Hemisphere Publishing Corp.

Davis, P. A. (1983). *Suicidal adolescents.* Springfield, IL: Charles C. Thomas.

Deykin, E. Y., Hsieh, C. C., Joshi, N., & McNamara, J. J. (1986). Adolescent suicidal and self-destructive behavior: Results of an intervention study. *Journal of Adolescent Health Care, 7,* 88–95.

Downey, A. M. (1991). The impact of drug abuse upon adolescent suicide. *Omega: Journal of Death and Dying, 22,* 261–275.

Eddy, D. M., Wolpert, R. L., & Rosenberg, M. L. (1989). Estimating the effectiveness of interventions to prevent adolescent suicides: A report to the Secretary's Task Force on Adolescent Suicide. In *Report of the Secretary's Task Force on Youth Suicide* (pp. 37–81). (DHHS Publication No. ADM 89-1624). Washington, DC: U.S. Government Printing Office.

Farberow, N. L. (1989). Preparatory and prior suicidal behavior factors. In *Alcohol, drug abuse, and mental health administration: Report of the Secretary's Task Force on Adolescent Suicide: Volume 2. Risk factors for adolescent suicide* (pp. 34–55). (DHHS Publication No. ADM 89-1622). Washington, DC: U.S. Government Printing Office.

Feindler, E. L., & Ecton, R. B. (1986). *Adolescent anger control: Cognitive-behavioral techniques.* New York: Pergamon Press.

Fremouw, W. J., de Perczel, M., & Ellis, T. W. (1990). *Suicide risk: Assessment and response guidelines.* New York: Pergamon Press.

Friedman, R. C., Clarkin, J. F., & Corn, R. (1982). DSM-III and affective pathology in hospitalized adolescents. *Journal of Nervous and Mental Disease, 170,* 511–521.

Garfinkel, B. D., Froese, A., & Hood, J. (1982). Suicide attempts in children and adolescents. *American Journal of Psychiatry, 139,* 1257–1261.

Gibbs, J. T. (1981). Depression and suicidal behavior among delinquent females. *Journal of Adolescence, 10,* 159–167.

Gould, M. S., & Shaffer, D. (1986). The impact of suicide in television movies: Evidence of imitation. *New England Journal of Medicine, 315,* 690–694.

Harkavy-Friedman, J., Asnis, G., Boeck, M., & Difiore, J. (1987). Prevalence of specific suicidal behaviors in a high school sample. *American Journal of Psychiatry, 144,* 1203–1206.

Hoberman, H. M., & Garfinkel, B. D. (1988). Completed suicide in children and adolescents. *Journal of the American Academy of Child and Adolescent Psychiatry, 27,* 689–695.

Jarrett, R. B., & Rush, A. J. (1992). Cognitive therapy for depression. *Directions in Mental Health Counseling, 2*(2), 4–20.

Kolko, D. J., & Brent, D. A. (1987). *Cognitive-behavioral interventions for suicidal adolescents.* Presented at the annual meeting of the American Association of Suicidology, San Francisco.

Korella, K. (1972). Teenage suicide gestures: A study of suicidal behavior among high school students. *Dissertation Abstracts International, 32,* 5039A.

Kosky, R. (1983). Childhood suicidal behavior. *Journal of Child Psychology and Psychiatry, 24,* 457–468.

Kotila, L., & Lonnquist, J. (1987). Adolescents who make suicide attempts repeatedly. *Acta Psychiatrica Scandinavica, 76,* 386–393.

Linehan, M. (1981). A social-behavioral analysis of suicide and parasuicide: Implications for clinical assessment and treatment. In H. Glazer & J. Clarkin (Eds.), *Depression: Behavioral and directive intervention strategies* (pp. 229–294). New York: Garland.

Lochman, J. E., & Curry, J. F. (1986). Effects of social problem-solving training and self-instruction training with aggressive boys. *Journal of Clinical Psychology, 15*, 159–164.

Males, M. (1991). Teen suicide and changing cause-of-death certification, 1953–1987. *Suicide and Life-Threatening Behavior, 21*, 245–249.

Mattsson, A., Seese, L. R., & Hawkins, J. W. (1969). Suicidal behavior as a child psychiatric emergency. *Archives of General Psychiatry, 20*, 100–109.

McKenry, P. C., Tishler, C. L., & Kelly, C. (1983). The role of drugs in adolescent suicide attempts. *Suicide and Life-Threatening Behavior, 13*, 166–175.

Miller, K. E., King, C. A., Shain, B. N., & Naylor, M. W. (1992). Suicidal adolescents' perceptions of their family environment. *Suicide and Life Threatening Behavior, 22*, 226–239.

Murphy, G., & Wetzel, R. (1982). Family history of suicidal behavior among suicide attempters. *Journal of Nervous and Mental Disease, 170*, 86–90.

National Center for Health Statistics (1993). *Monthly vital statistics report* (Vol. 41, No. 7). Hyattsville, MD: U.S. Public Health Service.

Novaco, R. (1979). The cognitive-behavioral regulation of anger. In P. C. Kendall & S. D. Hollon (Eds.), *Cognitive-behavioral interventions: Therapy, research, and procedures* (pp. 241–286). New York: Academic Press.

Pfeffer, C. R. (1989). Family characteristics and support systems as risk factors for adolescent suicide. In *Alcohol, drug abuse, and mental health administration, Report of the Secretary's Task Force on Adolescent Suicide, Volume 2: Risk factors for adolescent suicide* (pp. 71–81). (DHHS Publication No. ADM 89-1622). Washington, DC: U.S. Government Printing Office.

Plutchik, R., van Pragg, H. M., & Conte, H. R. (1989). Correlates of suicide and violence risk, III: A two-stage model of countervailing forces. *Psychiatric Research, 28*, 215–225.

Poland, S. (1989). *Suicide intervention in the schools.* New York: Guilford Press.

Reynolds, P., & Eaton, P. (1986). Multiple attempters of suicide presenting at an emergency department. *Canadian Journal of Psychiatry, 31,* 328–330.

Rich, C. L., Young, D., & Fowler, R. C. (1986). San Diego Suicide Study, I: Young vs. old subjects. *Archives of General Psychiatry, 31,* 328–330.

Rubenstein, J. L., Heeren, T., Houseman, D., Rubin, C., & Stechler, G. (1989). Suicidal behavior in 'normal' adolescents: Risk and protective factors. *American Journal of Orthopsychiatry, 59,* 59–71.

Runeson, B. (1989). Mental disorder in adolescent suicide. *Acta Psychiatrica Scandinavica, 79,* 490–497.

Schotte, D., & Clum, G. (1987). Problem-solving skills in suicidal psychiatric patients. *Journal of Counseling and Clinical Psychology, 55,* 49–54.

Shaffer, D., Garland, A., Gould, M., Fisher, P., & Trautman, P. (1988). Preventing teenage suicide: A critical review. *Journal of the American Academy of Child and Adolescent Psychiatry, 27,* 675–687.

Shaffer, D., & Gould, M. (1987). *A study of completed and attempted suicide in adolescents* (Grant no. MH 38198): Progress report. Rockville, MD: National Institute of Mental Health.

Shafii, M., Carrigan, S., Whittinghill, J. R., & Derrick, A. M. (1985). Psychological autopsy of completed suicide in children and adolescents. *American Journal of Psychiatry, 142,* 1061–1064.

Shafii, M., Steltz-Lenarsky, J., Derrick, A. M., Beckner, C., & Whittinghill, J. R. (1988). Comorbidity of mental disorders in the postmortem diagnosis of completed suicide in children and adolescents. *Journal of Affective Disorders, 15,* 227–233.

Shafii, M., Whittinghill, J. R., & Healy, M. H. (1979). The pediatric-psychiatric model for emergencies in child psychiatry: A study of 994 cases. *American Journal of Psychiatry, 136,* 1600–1601.

Slap, G. B., Vorters, D. F., Chaudhuri, S., & Centor, R. M. (1989). Risk factors for attempted suicide during adolescence. *Pediatrics, 84,* 762–772.

Smith, K. (1991). Comments on 'teen suicide and changing cause-of-death certification, 1953–1987.' *Suicide and Life-Threatening Behavior, 21*, 260–262.

Smith, K., & Crawford, S. (1986). Suicidal behaviors among normal high school students. *Suicide and Life-Threatening Behavior, 16*, 313–325.

Stanley, E. J., & Barter, J. T. (1970). Adolescent suicide behavior. *American Journal of Orthopsychiatry, 40*, 87–96.

Tishler, C. L., McKenry, P. C., & Morgan, K. C. (1981). Adolescent suicide attempts: Some significant factors. *Suicide and Life-Threatening Behavior, 11*, 86–92.

12

Protecting the Confidentiality of Children and Adolescents

Edward E. Bartlett, PhD

Dr. Bartlett is Associate Adjunct Professor, George Washington University School of Medicine, Washington, DC.

KEY POINTS

- A client's right of confidentiality ensures that what he or she expresses in confidence will not be disclosed to outside parties without implied or expressed authorization. Failure to observe confidentiality measures may impede achievement of therapeutic goals, compromise the client's trust, and result in a professional liability lawsuit.

- For young minors, the parent or guardian is the legal decision maker, and can legally obtain information about diagnosis, prognosis, and course of therapy. Only a custodial parent can authorize treatment or release of confidential information.

- Threats to client confidentiality arise from actions of therapists, staff members, clients, parents, and other sources.

- Laws in most states authorize or mandate the release of certain types of information, such as gunshot wounds, child abuse, venereal disease, the need to institute civil commitment, and existence of potential harm to an identifiable victim. Problems can arise when the right of client confidentiality conflicts with the "public's right to know."

- Clinics and individual practitioners should develop specific procedures to protect confidentiality, outline these procedures in client information brochures, and reinforce them verbally with clients and staff members.

INTRODUCTION

Some would argue that the tenet of confidentiality has become so riddled with exceptions and compromises as to render it chimerical. Yet the fact that the concept is under siege constitutes the strongest argument that it needs to be staunchly defended. Threats to client confidentiality arise from actions of therapists, staff, clients, parents, and other sources. Some examples of such actions are highlighted below.

Therapists and Support Staff:

- Mental health professionals who discuss details of the client's case while in a cafeteria, elevator, or cocktail party

- The counselor who informs a collection agency of the client's diagnosis or even the fact the client is being seen for a mental health problem

- A physician who treats the patient for a condition unrelated to the psychological disturbance and who requests gratuitous information

- The physician who receives psychological information on the patient's specific authorization, who later releases that information to a subsequent physician with only a general patient authorization for release of records

- The therapist who publishes sensitive information after the client's death

- The psychologist who complies with a subpoena that is not ordered by the court

- The therapist who holds counseling sessions at home and lives with others

- The home telephone answering machine of a therapist who lives with others

- The receptionist who stacks clients' charts on a desk with their names in full view of incoming clients

- Receptionists, filing clerks, and housekeeping personnel who are "curious" to learn private information about an acquaintance or prominent member of the community

Clients:

- Participants in group therapy who discuss the participants' comments outside the group

- Clients who sign a standard release authorization for their medical records, not realizing these records contain sensitive psychological information

Parents and Friends:

- Parents who request information about the progress of their child

- Friends who inquire of the parents or child about the treatment

- The family member who imparts a "secret" to the therapist

Other Sources:

- Managed care organizations and insurance companies that request a copy of the entire record for utilization review purposes

- Insurance companies that sell mailing lists of persons culled from their billing records

- The judge who orders or allows confidential psychological information about a child to be disclosed in open custody hearings

- Information released to a third party, which is used for purposes other than for what it was intended

- The proliferation of computerized client/patient records and computer networks

- Reception areas of mental health clinics where a client may encounter an acquaintance awaiting therapy

- Outside transcription agencies

As these lists reveal, the threats to client confidentiality are multiple and insidious, and pose particular challenges to the mental health professional working in a group practice or medical clinic setting. In addition, the recent advent of utilization review and case management has strained the integrity of client confidentiality. This chapter summarizes current perspectives on confidentiality, explains its applications to psychological counseling of children and adolescents, and provides recommendations for improving confidentiality protections.

WHAT IS CONFIDENTIALITY?

Confidentiality refers to the client's right to have communications expressed in confidence not be disclosed to outside parties without implied or expressed authorization. Hippocrates (1923) laid the foundation for the modern-day concept of confidentiality: "Whatsoever things I see or hear concerning the life of man, in any attendance on the sick or even apart therefrom, which ought not to be voiced about, I will keep silent thereupon." The rationale for confidentiality derives from the fact that the therapist must elicit private information about the client's experiences, fears, desires, and actions, and that the client is unlikely to divulge such information if it will be made public.

The legal basis for confidentiality derives from four sources: (a) the constitutional right of privacy, (b) confidentiality provisions in state laws, (c) common law that has evolved from court decisions, and (d) the ethical canons of mental health professionals. The ethical foundation of confidentiality springs from the canon of autonomy.

The American Psychological Association, the American Counseling Association, the American Personnel and Guidance Association, the American Psychiatric Association, and the American Academy of Child and Adolescent Psychiatry all have developed guidelines on ethics and confidentiality.

A related concept is that of privilege, which refers to the fact that a professional, under certain prescribed conditions, is not subject to arrest or prosecution for withholding information needed by the court to settle litigation. Persons' communications with their attorney, clergy, or physician are confidential *and* privileged (with a number of exceptions, as discussed below). In general, clients' communications to their therapist are deemed confidential *but not privileged*. As a result, psychologists, counselors, and social workers are working in a number of states to strengthen pertinent confidentiality statutes.

EXCEPTIONS TO CONFIDENTIALITY

The duty to protect the client's confidentiality is implicit in the establishment of the therapist-client relationship. However, confidentiality is not an absolute mandate and the issues become murkier in the context of treating children and adolescents. Most states distinguish between young minors and mature minors. For young minors, children generally under 14 years of age, the parent or guardian is the legal decision-maker and can legally obtain information about the diagnosis, prognosis, therapy, and so on. An emancipated minor is an adolescent over age 14 to 15 who lives away from parents, is self-supporting, or is married. A mature minor is judged to be capable to give consent for treatment and to authorize disclosure of sensitive health information (Morrissey, Hofman, & Thrope, 1986).

Laws in most states authorize or require the release of sensitive psychological information, such as gunshot wounds, venereal disease, child abuse, need to institute civil commitment, and potential harm to an identifiable victim. When the therapist is acting as an agent of the court, insurance company, or other organization, confidentiality strictures are relaxed. In such an instance, the therapist should explicitly advise the client that the information gained will be used to reach an assessment or recommendation for the other organization.

The existence (or likelihood) of a noncustodial parent further complicates the picture. Only a custodial parent can authorize treatment or release of confidential information. This poses numerous potential difficulties:

- The child begins therapy. The parents divorce. The parent with whom the therapist has established the most rapport becomes the noncustodial parent.

- The parents are recently separated and custody of the child has not been established.

- Information the child reveals to the therapist could determine the outcome of a child custody battle.

- Information the child reveals to the therapist would assist the judge, but would be highly embarrassing and traumatic to the child.

- The custodial parent gives a one-sided explanation of the child's problems, thus biasing the therapist's assessment.

- The noncustodial parent begins the child in therapy to extract information to challenge the custody award.

- The noncustodial parent is paying for the therapy and feels entitled to information about the progress of treatment.

- The therapist believes that family therapy is warranted, but one parent is reluctant to participate.

If the adolescent exhibits homicidal or suicidal tendencies, and identifies a specific potential victim, the therapist is obligated under the *Tarasoff*-driven notion of "duty to warn" to compromise strict confidentiality guidelines (*Tarasoff v. Board of Regents of the University of California,* 1976). Indicated actions include warning the named person, advising the parents and local police of the danger, and, in some cases, hospitalizing the client.

Thus, confidentiality cannot be considered an absolute mandate. Rather, it must be viewed as an ideal that is applied in varying degrees, depending on the sensitivity of the information, client's age and intellectual capacity, agency of the therapist, pertinent state laws, and concurrent litigation.

COMPUTER ISSUES

The growth of the use of computers in health care settings imposes a new set of risks to client confidentiality. This is particularly true of the therapist who works for a health maintenance organization. The computer-based patient record is expected to become the standard in health care settings (inpatient and outpatient) by the end of the century.

The existence of the computer-based patient records with sensitive psychological information can exaggerate many of the problems listed at the beginning of this chapter. In addition, new confidentiality problems arise:

- Health professionals who gain access to psychological information that is not pertinent to the condition they are treating

- Breaches of the computer security system by outside persons

- Employees who disclose their security password to others

The following case illustrates the type of abuse that can occur:

A banker who served on a statewide health information commission that had access to hospital tumor records managed to obtain the names of all persons recently diagnosed with cancer. These names were compared with a list of loan recipients from the bank. Shortly thereafter, the bank recalled their loans.

Many health care facilities are taking special measures to provide protection. These measures include:

- Establishing three access levels for data elements: nonprivileged (demographic information); privileged (illness-related information); and deniable (mental health, drug and alcohol use, and human immunodeficiency virus [HIV] information)

- Controlling access to these three levels of information by use of access codes

- Developing organizational policy regarding confidentiality

- Incorporating confidentiality provisions into job descriptions

- Providing regular training to employees on confidentiality procedures

- Ensuring that the computer can track when different data elements were accessed and by whom

- Ensuring that insurance companies and other third parties protect confidentiality of data

---

Table 12.1
SAMPLE CONFIDENTIALITY STATEMENT
(SIGNED BY CLINIC EMPLOYEES)

I understand that information about clients, their illnesses, and their personal lives must be kept confidential. When talking with a client about any matter, I will do it in such a way that other clients will not overhear. I will not give advice on personal matters to clients, even if they ask. It is improper for me to reveal information on a client even to another member of the client's family. If clients ask questions about their own case or about another member of their family, I will refer them to their mental health care provider.

Any breach of confidentiality on my part will be grounds for termination without notice. This also applies to unauthorized release of business information.

_____
Employee

                       _____
                       Date

_____
Witness

- Having employees sign a security statement (Table 12.1)

Table 12.2
SAMPLE INFORMATION FOR PATIENT
INFORMATION BROCHURE (PROVIDED TO MATURE MINORS)

Confidentiality is an important part of treatment. As a general rule, I cannot reveal information about you to others, including family members and insurance companies, without your permission. Some exceptions to this include emergencies, child abuse, and some legal situations. If you are living with your parents and they are paying for the therapy, they may ask me general information about your progress. I will not tell them detailed or private information that you do not want shared with them.

It is not a good idea for friends or others to ask you details about your individual therapy sessions. If others wish to inform me about you, I prefer they do so in your presence. Occasional meetings with family members may be helpful for this and other reasons. Such sessions will take place with your permission. I will be glad to answer your questions about this.

In the acute inpatient setting, it is possible for up to 70 to 80 caregivers to access the patient's chart. This large number represents an inherent risk of confidentiality breaches. Thus, implementing the security measures listed above may enhance the confidentiality of patient records.

MEASURES TO PROTECT CLIENT CONFIDENTIALITY

The first step in protecting client confidentiality is gaining an appreciation of the many ways that confidentiality can be compromised, even by well-intentioned persons. All persons associated with the care of clients with psychological concerns should enshrine the axiom that communications given in confidence should not be disclosed to outside parties without implied or express authorization. Clients should be made aware of certain exceptions to confidentiality guidelines.

Develop specific procedures to protect confidentiality. Outline these in the client information brochure as well as verbally to the client. An example of information to include in the client information brochure is shown in Table 12.2. Advise the client that you may wish to discuss his or her problem with other mental health professionals to provide the best care (with the client's verbal consent). Many therapists do this routinely during the first visit; some wait for the second visit when more rapport is established. If you are acting as an agent of the court or another third party, provide the adolescent client with a Miranda-type warning to the effect that information may be shared with a given third party.

GENERAL GUIDELINES REGARDING RELEASE OF INFORMATION

Table 12.3 presents general recommendations regarding release of confidential information. The matrix presents the recipient of information in the left column and the client's age across the top row. To locate the pertinent recommendation, identify the appropriate recipient and client age. For example, if the custodial parent requests information about the diagnosis of a young minor, advise the client you are doing so, but formal consent is not necessary. If the custodial parent requests detailed information about an adolescent's problems, this should not be disclosed. If you are reporting child abuse, the client's permission is not necessary, but therapeutic considerations dictate that you advise the client in advance. A sample authorization for the release of confidential information is shown in Table 12.4.

Table 12.3
GUIDELINES FOR RELEASE OF CONFIDENTIAL
INFORMATION

This chart summarizes general confidentiality guidelines. It represents a synthesis of legal and therapeutic perspectives. These guidelines do not apply in case of an emergency. Note that state laws vary, especially pertaining to adolescents.

RECIPIENT OF INFORMATION		Client's Age			
		Preschool	*Young Minors*	*Adolescents*	*Adults and Emancipated Minors*
PARENTS	Diagnosis, treatment, and prognosis	Not applicable	Advise client in advance, but consent not needed	Advise client in advance, but consent not needed	Obtain consent from client
	Detailed clinical information	Not applicable	Use high level of discretion	Generally, do not disclose	
	High potential for violence	Not applicable	Advise client in advance, but consent not needed	Advise client in advance, but consent not needed	
CUSTODY PROCEEDINGS		Not applicable	Advise client in advance	Discuss and negotiate with client in advance	Not applicable
		Encourage parents to obtain settlement or mediation. Early on, obtain from parents a waiver of right to subpoena or negotiate with judge to provide only limited information regarding the diagnosis, treatment, and prognosis.			
NONCUSTODIAL PARENT		Obtain consent from custodial parent	Obtain consent from custodial parent	Obtain consent from custodial parent; advise client of disclosure	Obtain consent from client
SUBSEQUENT MENTAL HEALTH PROFESSIONALS OR PHYSICIANS		Obtain consent from parent	Obtain consent from parent	If client is a minor at time of request, obtain consent from parent. If client is an adult, obtain consent from client.	Obtain consent from client

RECIPIENT OF INFORMATION	Client's Age			
	Preschool	*Young Minors*	*Adolescents*	*Adults and Emancipated Minors*
OTHER CONCERNED ADULTS (REFERRING PHYSICIAN, CONSULTING PHYSICIAN, TEACHER, CLERGY, ETC.)	Obtain consent from parent in advance	Obtain consent from parent in advance	Obtain consent from client and parent in advance	Obtain consent from client in advance
IDENTIFIED POTENTIAL VICTIM OF VIOLENCE	Not applicable	Warn potential victim; advise client in advance	Warn potential victim; advise client in advance	Warn potential victim; advise client in advance
INSURANCE COMPANY (PROVIDE ONLY A CLINICAL SUMMARY, IF POSSIBLE)	Obtain consent from parent	Obtain consent from parent	Obtain consent from parent	Obtain consent from client
INFORMATION REPORTABLE BY STATE LAW (CHILD ABUSE, GUNSHOT WOUNDS, ETC.)	Consent not needed	Consent not needed	Consent not needed, but advise client in advance	Consent not needed, but advise client in advance
COLLECTION AGENCY	Provide only client's name and amount owed; do not indicate client is being treated for a mental health problem.			

Some therapists maintain a separate set of informal notes, recording the client's fantasies and the counselor's speculations and impressions. The legal status of such notes is unclear and is protected only in a limited number of jurisdictions.

CUSTODY CONFLICTS

To protect the client's confidentiality in the course of a custody battle, the therapist must resolve several issues. First, you must negotiate and clarify your role with the child and his or her parents. Who is the real client? Is your role to provide

Table 12.4
SAMPLE AUTHORIZATION FOR RELEASE OF
CONFIDENTIAL INFORMATION

Client's name _____

Date of birth _____

I hereby request and authorize _____

to release to _____

(Address) _____

The following confidential information:

____ Admission history   ____ HIV/AIDS

____ Drug/alcohol use   ____ Lab/x-ray

____ Medical history   ____ Discharge summary

____ Psychological testing   ____ Other (Specify)

____ Mental health history

I understand that this authorization to release information is subject to revocation at any time, provided that I notify the above-named in writing. This authorization will expire 90 days from the date signed.

_____   _____
Signature of Client   Date

_____   _____
Signature of Parent or Guardian   Date

PROHIBITION OF REDISCLOSURE: This information has been disclosed to you, whose confidentiality is protected by state and federal regulations. Any further disclosure of this information is strictly prohibited without the specific written consent of the person to whom it pertains. A general authorization for the release of medical and other information is *not* sufficient for this purpose.

treatment, evaluation, or parental mediation? If the parent disagrees with previous psychological evaluations, should you refuse to accept this referral? If one parent requests counseling about custody problems, will you request to see the other parent?

Next, direct parents to focus on the *child's* welfare. Indicate you will communicate with both parents as part of the evaluation, including the noncustodial parent. Warn that in case of parental conflicts, you will not take sides, but you may ask both parents to come in to discuss the problem. Emphasize to both parents the fact that the child's needs are paramount and that parents should not trap the child in their conflicts.

Set clear ground rules from the beginning. Before your initial evaluation, set objectives and agree on the number of visits. Set clear rules regarding keeping appointments, telephone communications, and the like. Discuss the writing of the evaluation report and to whom it will be sent. Some state statutes permit you to request the parents to sign a waiver of right to subpoena.

Once you have established the ground rules and have communicated your role as an advocate for the child and disinterested party in the custody conflict, explain your confidentiality procedures to the client and parents. Provide a written handout summarizing these procedures.

If the custody issue becomes heated and you receive a subpoena for your records, comply only if a judge has approved it. If in doubt, check with your attorney first. Even for a court-ordered subpoena, the therapist may be able to negotiate with the judge regarding what information you will release and how it will be used in the legal proceedings.

CONCLUSION

Managed care is currently revamping the provision of mental health services, which imposes new threats to traditional confidentiality tenets. Protecting the client's confidentiality is a duty of the therapist, and ethical practice requires constant attention to the issue. The most troublesome situations arise when the right to client confidentiality conflicts with the public's right to know. Resolving these conflicts requires the therapist to become familiar with general confidentiality principles and pertinent state law and to obtain legal counsel when needed.

Failure to observe confidentiality measures may embarrass the client and family, impede achievement of therapeutic goals, compromise the client's trust in the therapist, and even result in a professional liability lawsuit. The therapist must become aware of the myriad threats to client confidentiality and implement appropriate safeguards.

REFERENCES

Hippocrates (1923). *On decorum and the physician* (Vol. 2, E.H.S. Jones, Trans.). London: William Heinemann.

Morrissey, J. M., Hofman, A. D., & Thrope, J. C. (1986). *Consent and confidentiality in the health care of children and adolescents.* New York: The Free Press.

Tarasoff v. Board of Regents of Univ. of Cal., 17 Cal. 3d 425, 551 P. 2d 334, 345, 131 Cal. Rptr. 14 (1976).

Name Index

A

Abramowitz, A. J., 59, 71
Achenbach, T., 35, 36
Achenbach, T. M., 53, 71
Ackerman, P. T., 49, 71
Addalli, K. A., 76
Adlaf, E. M., 238, 246
Adler, R., 12, 16
Akiskal, H.S., 80, 98
Alessi, N. E., 15, 16
Alexander, R., 225
Allan, M., 270
Allan, M. J., 159, 169
Allen, G. D., 238, 247
Allman, C., 270
Allman, C. J., 254, 269
Alman, P., 36
Aluwahlia, S., 38
Ambrosini, P., 38, 172
Ambrosini, P. J., 11, 14, 16, 165, 169
Amoateng, A. Y., 238, 246
Anderson, D., 226
Anderson, J. C., 4, 174
Andrews, J., 166, 171
Angold, A., 156, 158, 169
Aponte, J. F., 104, 122
Appell, J., 205, 224
Apter, A., 254, 269
Arbuthnot, J., 219, 223
Aronson, Seth, 177, 189
Arria, A., 228, 247
Asnis, G., 256, 271
Atkins, M., 24, 38
Austin, G. W., 205, 224
Axline, V., 135, 149
Ayers, W. H., 230, 246

B

Babor, T. F., 249
Bagnato, S. J., 7, 20
Bahr, S. J., 238, 246
Bailey, G. W., 228, 246
Baker, L., 46, 47, 71, 72
Balthazor, M. J., 56, 71

Bandura, A., 135, 149, 225
Barcai, A., 12, 17
Barkley, R. A., 42, 43, 47, 48, 49, 52,
    53, 55, 57, 58, 59, 71, 72, 74
Barr, R. G., 56, 73
Barter, J. T., 256, 274
Bartholet, E., 104, 120
Bassuk, E., 80, 82, 83, 98
Beardslee, W. R., 18, 164, 169
Beaty, A., 82, 98
Beck, A. T., 130, 131, 132, 133, 149,
    263, 269
Beck, N., 170
Beck, S., 81, 98
Becker, D., 249
Beckner, C., 253, 273
Bedrosian, R., 142, 150
Beidel, D., 5, 21
Beitchman, J., 24, 36
Beland, K., 36
Bell, R., 35, 38
Bemporad, J. R., 164, 167, 169
Bender, M.E.S., 48, 77
Bennett, L. A., 236, 246
Bentlor, P. M., 238, 248
Berkovitz, I., 180, 188
Berman, A. L., 252, 254, 255, 257, 258,
    259, 267, 268, 269, 270
Berman, J. S., 93, 98
Bernfeld, G., 48, 72
Bernstein, G. A., 3, 4, 5, 8, 10, 12, 17
Berry, C. A., 50, 72
Bianchi, M. D., 11, 16, 165, 169
Biederman, J., 6, 17, 21, 49, 72
Bierman, K. L., 130, 149
Bird, H., 38
Blackson, T., 230, 248
Blakely, C. H., 225
Bleich, A., 254, 269
Blick, L. C., 35, 36
Block, J., 249
Bloomquist, M. L., 69, 72
Blos, P., 184, 188
Blum, G. S., 116, 120

D

DaCosta, G., 36
Damon, J., 35, 38
Damon, L., 35, 37
Davidson, III, W.S., 225
Davies, M., 100, 172, 173
Davine, M., 46, 73
Davis, F., 182, 188
Davis, M., 241, 247
Davis, P. A., 265, 270
Davison, G. C., 149
de Misquita, P. B., 4, 18
de Perczel, M., 259, 270
Dean, J., 84, 100
Deblinger, E., 24, 37, 38
Delboca, F. K., 249
Derrick, A. M., 253, 254, 273
Dewald, P. A., 149
Deykin, E. Y., 158, 159, 171, 256, 270
Diamond, R., 165, 172
Dies, K., 187, 188
Difiore, J., 256, 271
Dilsaver, S. C., 15, 16
Dinicola, V. F., 164, 172
Dolinski, A., 173
Dorner, P., 104, 121
Dotemoto, S., 48, 78
Douglas, V. I., 43, 47, 56, 73
Downey, A. M., 254, 270
Driscoll, M. S., 43, 73
Dubois, C., 171
Dulcan, M., 269
DuPaul, G. J., 53, 54, 57, 74
Duprau, J., 117
Dykman, R. A., 49, 71

E

Easson, W. M., 104, 112, 121
Eaton, P., 258, 273
Ecton, R. B., 264, 270
Eddy, D. M., 267, 270
Edelbrock, C., 35, 36, 269
Edelbrock, C. S., 48, 53, 54, 71, 72, 74
Edell, W., 249
Edelsohn, G. A., 34, 37
Egan, G., 149
Eiduson, B. N., 111, 112, 121
Elia, J., 11, 16, 58, 74, 165, 169
Ellis, A., 130, 150
Ellis, J., 50, 75
Ellis, T. W., 259, 270
Emery, G., 130, 131, 132, 133, 142, 144,

149, 150, 263, 269
Endman, M. W., 48, 72
Erikson, Erik, 184, 188
Eshleman, S., 18
Estroff, T. W., 229, 230, 246, 248
Everson, M. D., 34, 35, 37

F

Fad-mina, J., 149
Faherty, S., 35, 38
Fallahi, C., 170
Farberow, N. L., 254, 258, 270
Farone, S. V., 17
Farrington, D. P., 206, 223
Feehan, M., 20, 171
Fehrenbach, P. A., 225
Feigelman, W., 104, 121
Feinberg, T. L., 170
Feindler, E. L., 218, 219, 223, 264, 270
Felsenfeld, N., 182, 189
Fendrich, M., 159, 173
Ferguson, H. B., 164, 171, 172
Fine, S., 166, 170
Finkelhor, D., 24, 28, 37
Finkelstein, R., 4, 19, 170
Fischer, B., 117
Fischer, M., 48, 72
Fishbein, M., 13, 14, 18
Fisher, P., 38, 254, 273
Fixsen, D. L., 142, 150
Fleming, J. E., 159, 160, 170
Flynn, J. M., 226
Foa, E., 24, 38
Fodor, I., 82, 99
Folkman, S., 89, 99
Fonagy, P., 63, 70, 74
Forth, A., 166, 170
Fowler, R. C., 241, 247, 253, 273
Francis, G., 8, 12, 19
Frank, J. D., 149
Freeman, R., 164, 165, 172
Fremouw, W. J., 259, 260, 263, 265, 270
Freud, Anna, 184, 188
Fried, J., 172
Friedman, R. C., 254, 271
Friedrich, W. N., 24, 38
Fristad, M. A., 85, 88, 99
Fritz, G. K., 158, 169
Froese, A., 256, 271
Fudge, H., 160, 170
Fuller, D., 209, 224
Fyer, A. J., 6, 18, 19

G

Gabrielli, W. F., 104, 122
Garber, J., 142, 150, 154, 169
Garcia-Coll, C., 18
Gardner, R., 179, 188
Gardner, R. A., 116, 121
Garfinkel, B., 158, 173
Garfinkel, B. D., 5, 12, 17, 158, 170,
    254, 256, 271
Garland, A., 254, 273
Garland, J., 183, 188
Garmezy, N., 89, 99
Gartner, J., 238, 247
Gatsonis, C., 4, 19
Gelder, M. G., 20
Gelernter, C. S., 14, 18
Geller, B., 164, 170
Gendlin, G. T., 132, 151
Genshaft, J. L., 86, 102
Gentile, C., 35, 39
Gershaw, N. J., 67, 74, 76, 205, 223
Gerwirtzman, R., 82, 99
Giampino, T. L., 76
Gibbs, J. C., 209, 223, 224
Gibbs, J. T., 254, 271
Gilbert, M., 166, 170
Gilbert, P., 14, 21
Gill, M. M., 149
Gilliam, W. S., 4, 18
Gittleman, R., 10, 11, 18, 81, 100
Glancy, L. J., 244, 246
Glatzer, H. T., 115, 121
Glick, Barry, 196, 197, 205, 209, 210,
    217, 219, 223
Glow, P. H., 48, 74
Glow, R. S., 48, 74
Goetz, D., 100
Gold, E., 24, 38
Gold, M. S., 229, 246
Goldstein, A. P., 67, 74, 76, 196, 197,
    205, 209, 210, 217, 219, 223, 225
Goldstein, C., 270
Goldstein, M., 43, 46, 47, 48, 50, 51,
    53, 55, 57, 58, 59, 67, 74
Goldstein, Sam, 43, 46, 47, 48, 50, 51,
    53, 55, 57, 58, 59, 67, 74, 75
Gomez-Schwartz, B., 24, 34, 38
Gordon, D. A., 219, 223
Gordon, M., 55, 75
Gorman, J. M., 6, 15, 18
Gould, M., 38, 254, 273
Gould, M. S., 258, 271
Graham, D. L., 164, 170
Graham, P., 104, 121, 157, 172

Gravelle, K., 117
Greenberg, L., 55, 75
Greenhill, L. L., 57, 75
Grilo, G., 249
Grimley, L. K., 42, 75
Guevremont, D. C., 53, 66, 74, 75

H

Haenlein, M., 72, 75
Haizlip, T., 183, 188
Haley, G., 166, 170
Hall, J., 99
Hamilton, S. B., 225
Hanna, G., 58, 77
Harkavy-Friedman, J., 256, 257, 271
Harrington, R., 160, 170
Harrison, P. A., 244, 247
Hart, B., 142, 151
Hauser, P., 51, 52, 75
Hawkins, J. W., 252, 272
Hazzard, Ann, 29, 34, 35, 37, 38, 39
Healy, M. H., 252, 273
Hechtman, L., 48, 49, 77, 78
Heeren, T., 257, 273
Helsel, W., 81, 99
Helsel, W. J., 9, 20
Helwig, C., 46, 73
Henig, R. M., 109, 119, 121
Henker, B., 48, 56, 78
Henley, G., 230, 243, 248
Henry, D., 24, 37
Hern, K. L., 51, 75
Herrnstein, R. J., 104, 121
Hersen, M., 4, 8, 11, 12, 19, 21
Herzov, L., 10, 18
Higgitt, A., 63, 74
Hill, J., 160, 170
Hindman, J., 33, 38
Hippocrates, 278, 290
Hirshfeld, D. R., 6, 21
Hobbs, T. R., 225
Hoberman, H. M., 158, 170, 254, 271
Hoeper, E. W., 170
Hoffman, I., 149
Hoffman, N. G., 244, 247
Hofman, A, D., 280, 290
Holt, M. M., 225
Hong, G. K., 157, 170
Hood, J., 15, 17, 36, 256, 271
Hoppe, C. M., 48, 77
Hops, H., 166, 171
Horowitz, J., 24, 38
Hoshman, L. T., 205, 224
Houseman, D., 257, 273

Rosenberg, R., 81, 98
Rosenberg, T., 170
Rosenthal, L., 182, 189
Rosenthal, M. K., 12, 17
Ross, D. C., 10, 21
Ross, D. M., 42, 50, 77
Ross, S. A., 42, 50, 77
Roth, D., 84, 85, 100
Roth, J., 18
Rothlind, J., 43, 77
Rotter, J. B., 149
Rubama, I., 197, 205, 223
Rubenstein, J. L., 257, 273
Rubert, M. P., 20
Rubin, C., 257, 273
Rubin, L., 80, 82, 83, 98
Rule, B. G., 226
Runeson, B., 253, 254, 273
Runtz, M., 24, 36
Runyon, D. K., 34, 37
Rush, A. J., 130, 149, 263, 269, 271
Rutter, M., 2, 21, 89, 100, 157, 160,
　　170, 172
Ryan, N., 159, 164, 172

S

Sabalis, R. F., 104, 122
Sachs, G. S., 15, 20
Samoilov, A., 171
Sas, L., 35, 39
Satterfield, J. H., 48, 77
Saveanu, T., 84, 100
Schaughency, E. A., 43, 77
Schecter, M. D., 104, 109, 111, 119,
　　121, 123
Scheidlinger, Saul, 176, 177, 180, 186,
　　189
Schell, A. M., 48, 77
Schloredt, K., 171
Schmidt, S., 159, 165, 172
Schmitz, Catherine L., 83, 84, 86, 101
Schneier, F. R., 14, 21
Schotte, D., 257, 273
Schuerman, J. R., 34, 37
Schwarts, C. E., 18
Seeley, J. R., 158, 159, 171, 172
Seese, L. R., 252, 272
Senturia, A. G., 111, 123
Shaffer, D., 35, 38, 173, 254, 257, 258,
　　267, 271, 273
Shafii, M., 252, 253, 254, 256, 273
Shain, B. N., 256, 272
Share, D. L., 42, 47, 76
Shaw, B. F., 130, 149, 263, 269

Shaw, K., 10, 12, 17
Shaywitz, B. A., 50, 72
Shaywitz, S. E., 50, 72
Shedler, J., 249
Sher, K. J., 230, 247
Sheridan, S., 67, 77
Siepker, B., 183, 189
Sigvardsson, S., 230, 246
Silber, K., 104, 121
Silva, P. A., 4, 17, 20, 50, 76, 171
Silver, L. B., 2, 21
Simeon, J., 171
Simeon, J. G., 164, 172
Simmons, III, J.Q., 104, 123
Simmons, M., 29, 37
Simon, N. M., 111, 123
Slap, G. B., 255, 273
Slavson, S., 179, 189
Sleator, E. K., 54, 77
Smallish, L., 48, 72
Smart, R. G., 246
Smith, K., 253, 256, 274
Snidman, N., 18
Snigel, J., 225
Spielberger, S., 7, 21
Spinal-Robinson, P., 35, 39
Spirito, A., 158, 169
Sprafkin, R. P., 67, 74, 76, 205, 223
Sprague, R. L., 54, 77
Stanfield, James, 33, 38
Stanley, E. J., 256, 274
Stark, K., 81, 101
Stechler, G., 257, 273
Steele, H., 63, 74
Steele, M., 63, 74
Stein, N., 225
Steltz-Lenarsky, J., 253, 273
Stevenson, J., 104, 121
Stewart, M. A., 47, 51, 76
Stott, D. H., 47, 77
Stowell, R. Jeremy A., 230, 248
Strauss, C. C., 4, 8, 9, 19, 21
Strober, M., 156, 159, 160, 164, 165,
　　172, 173
Strupp, H. H., 149
Stumphauzer, J., 226
Sulik, L., 158, 173
Sullivan, S., 46, 73
Swanson, J. M., 58, 77
Sylvester, C. E., 4, 16, 20
Szalai, J., 171

T

Takacs, D., 83, 98

Subject Index

A

violence in, 228
Family history, 7
Family size, small, as risk factor for
	separation anxiety disorder, 10
Family therapy
	for adolescent depression, 166
	contraindicated in adopted child
		syndrome, 117
	for homelessness, 90
	for suicidal adolescents, 265
Fantasies, of adopted child, 108
Fears, 2, 3, 6
	See also Phobia
	normative, 13
	of public speaking, 13
	of separation, 2, 7
Feeling Yes, Feeling No (National Film
	Board of Canada), 36
Finkelhor's model, of childhood
	sexual abuse, 28-34
Firearms, 267
Firesetting, 106
Flip-Flops, Cartwheels, and High-Tops
	(Spinal-Robinson and
	Wickham), 35
Fluoxetine (Prozac), 14, 57, 164
Food, fear of, 13
Frequency of Rearrest by Condition
	(*table*), 204

G

GABA
	See Gamma-aminobutyric acid
GAD
	See Generalized anxiety disorder
Gamma-aminobutyric acid, 6
Gangs, 204-207
	Baby Wolfpack, 207
	Lo Lives, 207
Gardner Adoption Story Cards
	(Gardner), 116
Generalization, as part of therapy, 147
Generalized anxiety disorder (GAD),
	5, 11-12
	statistics, 11
	symptoms, 11
Girls
	and ADHD, 49, 50
	aggravated assault most violent
		crime committed by, 193
	anxiety disordered, 4
	in gangs, 204
	more mature during early
		adolescence than boys, 181

more suicide attempts among, 158
	specific phobia more common in,
		13
Goals, orienting treatment toward,
	135
Grief
	felt by adopted child, 109, 110
	and homelessness, 89
Group therapy
	for adolescent depression, 166
	for adolescents, 175-187
	combined with individual
		therapy, 180
	for depression due to homeless-
		ness, 90
	four structure types
		group psychotherapy, 177
		human development and
			training groups, 177-178
		self-help and mutual help, 178
		therapeutic groups, 177
	moral education (ME) groups,
		219-221
	phases of group development
		termination, 184
		working phase, 183-184
	problem behaviors during, 185-
		187
	purpose, 178
	selecting members, 179-180
	for sexually abused children, 35
	for suicidal patients, 265
Guidelines for Release of Confiden-
	tial Information (*table*), 286,
	287
Guidelines for Treating Suicidal
	Adolescents (*table*), 266
Guilt, 29, 30, 31, 257
	low levels of in aggressive youth,
		195

H

Hallucinations, 232, 240
Hallucinogens, 232
Hansel and Gretel, 116
Headache, 11
Health care professionals, must assess
	child's potential for self-
	destruction, 89
Hepatitis B profile, 239
HIV, 239, 282
Homeless Children Interview
	Schedule, 85
Homeless Children Interview

Contributors

Seth Aronson, PsyD
Assistant Director, Child/Adolescent Psychiatry, Bronx Municipal
Hospital Center/Albert Einstein College of Medicine, Bronx, NY.

Edward E. Bartlett, PhD
Associate Adjunct Professor, George Washington University School of
Medicine, Washington, DC.

James C. Brown, PhD
Chairman, The Academy of Clinical Mental Health Counselors; and
Associate Dean for Student Programs, School of Dentistry, University of
Mississippi Medical Center, Jackson, MS.

Barry Glick, PhD, NCC
Consultant, G & G Associates, Scotia, NY.

Sam Goldstein, PhD
Clinical Director, Neurology Learning and Behavior Center, Salt Lake
City, UT; Clinical Instructor, Department of Psychiatry, and Adjunct
Professor, Department of Educational Psychology, University of Utah
School of Medicine, Salt Lake City, UT.

Ann Hazzard, PhD
Associate Professor of Pediatrics and Assistant Professor of Psychiatry at
Emory University School of Medicine, Atlanta, GA.

David Kirschner, PhD
In private practice in Merrick, NY, and Woodbury, NY.

Susan M. Knell, PhD
Adjunct Assistant Professor, Cleveland State University; and Lecturer,
Case Western Reserve University, Cleveland, OH.

Edna Menke, PhD, RN
Associate Professor, The Ohio State University College of Nursing,
Department of Family and Community Medicine, Columbus, OH.

318 *The Hatherleigh Guide to Child and Adolescent Therapy*

Barry Sarvet, MD
Director of Training at the Division of Child and Adolescent Psychiatry, University of New Mexico School of Medicine, Albuquerque, NM.

Saul Scheidlinger, PhD
Professor Emeritus of Psychiatry (Child Psychology), Albert Einstein College of Medicine, Bronx, NY.

Cathryne L. Schmitz, PhD, ACSW,
Assistant Professor, Saint Louis University School of Social Service, St. Louis, MO.

R. Jeremy A. Stowell, MD, FAPA
Former Director of Adolescent Programs, Virginia Beach Psychiatric Center; currently Medical Director, the Division of Substance Abuse, Norfolk Community Services Board; and in private practice in Virginia Beach, VA.

Janet Wagner, PhD, RN
Dean, Health and Human Services Division, Columbus State Community College, Columbus, OH.

Alayne Yates, MD
Professor of Psychiatry, the University of Hawaii, Honolulu, HI.

For information on other books in
The Hatherleigh Guides series, call the
Marketing Department at Hatherleigh
Press, 1-800-367-2550, or write:
Hatherleigh Press
Marketing Department
420 E. 51st St.
New York, NY 10022